Introduction to Phenomenological Research

Studies in Continental Thought

Martin Heidegger

Introduction to Phenomenological Research

Translated by
Daniel O. Dahlstrom

Indiana University Press
Bloomington and Indianapolis

This book is a publication of

Indiana University Press
601 North Morton Street
Bloomington, IN 47404-3797 USA

http://iupress.indiana.edu

Telephone orders   800-842-6796
Fax orders   812-855-7931
Orders by e-mail   iuporder@indiana.edu

Published in German as Martin Heidegger, *Gesamtausgabe*, volume 17: *Einführung in die phänomenologische Forschung*, edited by Friedrich-Wilhelm von Herrmann

The paper used in this publication meets the minimum requirements of American National Standard for Information Sciences—Permanence of Paper for Printed Library Materials, ANSI Z39.48–1984.

Manufactured in the United States of America

Library of Congress Cataloging-in-Publication Data

Heidegger, Martin, 1889–1976.
[Einführung in die phänomenologische Forschung. English]
Introduction to phenomenological research / Martin Heidegger ;
translated by Daniel O. Dahlstrom.
p. cm.—(Studies in Continental thought)
Includes bibliographical references.
ISBN 0-253-34570–7 (cloth : alk. paper)
1. Phenomenology. I. Dahlstrom, Daniel O. II. Title. III. Series.
B3279.H48E3613 2005
142'.7—dc22
2004022162

1   2   3   4   5   10   09   08   07   06   05

Contents

PRELIMINARY REMARK
The task of the lectures and the passion for questioning genuinely and rightly

PART ONE
ΦΑΙΝΟΜΕΝΟΝ AND ΛΟΓΟΣ IN ARISTOTLE
AND
HUSSERL'S SELF-INTERPRETATION OF PHENOMENOLOGY

Chapter One
Elucidation of the expression "phenomenology" by going back to Aristotle

Chapter Two
Present-day phenomenology in Husserl's self-interpretation

Chapter Four
Going back to Scholastic ontology: the verum esse in Thomas Aquinas

Chapter Five
The care of knowledge in Descartes

Chapter Six
The character of being of the res cogitans, of consciousness

PART THREE
DEMONSTRATING THE NEGLECT OF THE QUESTION OF BEING
AS A WAY OF POINTING TO EXISTENCE

Chapter One
Misplacing the question of the res cogitans' specific being
through care about certainty

Chapter Two
Descartes' inquiry into res cogitans' being-certain and the lack
of specification of the character of being of consciousness
as the thematic field of Husserl's phenomenology

Chapter Three
Husserl's more primordial neglect of the question of being, opposite the thematic field of phenomenology, and the task of seeing and explicating existence in its being

APPENDIX

Supplements to the lectures from the lecture notes of Helene Weiß and Herbert Marcuse

***

Translator's Foreword

Square brackets are used to indicate interpolations of original German words, of supplementary words or phrases, of alternative translations, and of an English translation of Greek and Latin texts not translated by Heidegger. Only those texts cited by Heidegger, for which he does not provide a translation or a sufficiently close paraphrase, are translated. Hence, if the text immediately following a Greek or Latin passage is not in square brackets, that text contains Heidegger's translation or paraphrase of the Greek or Latin passage. All other translations are my own. I have tried to follow the original German edition in italicizing some Latin words and not others. However, where the meaning of a Latin word or phrase is not clear from the text, a translation follows in square brackets. For example, in the following sentence from Part Two, Chapter Three, the Latin words *subjectum* and *apprehensum* are not italicized but only the latter term is translated and the translation placed in square brackets: "In affirming, willing, denying, rejecting, I have cogitationes but in the cogitationes there is something there, a subjectum that lies there from the outset as apprehensum [apprehended]."

For the most part I have tried to translate German words regularly with one English word or, if necessary, with one or more alternates. This policy applies in particular to the central term *Dasein* which is translated as "existence" or "existing" except in cases where Heidegger explicitly relates it to *Existenz* or calls attention to the *Da* in *Dasein*. In the latter, infrequent cases *Dasein* is translated "being-here" and *Existenz* is translated "existence." See, for example, the following text and translation (taken from Part Two, Chapter Five, § 34): "Es muß nun herausgestellt werden, *was Dasein selbst besagt*, was ein Grundcharakter des Daseins ist, der sich in dem *Da* ausdrückt": "It must now be established *what existence itself means*, what a basic character of existence or being-here is that expresses itself in the *here* [of being-here: *Dasein*]." This passage is instructive because in it Heidegger approaches his use of *Dasein* in *Sein und Zeit* where it applies to something equivalent (albeit not identical) to human existence. Just as frequently in the present lectures, however, he uses *Dasein* in the more generic and traditional sense that is not so restricted.

Like *Dasein*, *Angst* is used by Heidegger both in a way that prefigures the technical usage in *Sein und Zeit* and in a way that does not. Accordingly, *Angst vor Dasein* is translated "anxiety in the face of existence" in Part One, Chapter Two, § 14, but *Angst vor dem Scheiterhaufen* in Part Three, Chapter Two, § 46 is translated "fear of the stake." Among the other terms for which this latitude in using variants seemed appropriate, two others deserve mention. *Satz* is translated "sentence" when it clearly refers to a concrete linguistic entity as, for example, typically seems to be the case in the opening chapter's

interpretation of Aristotle. But it is translated "proposition," to correspond to
the Latin *propositio* and to the Platonized sense of Descartes' *cogito sum* and
search for principles which can be expressed in different sentences. *Grund-*
sätzlich is usually translated "principal" or "basic" and, only infrequently,
"fundamental." Whenever *grundsätzlich* is translated "fundamental," it is
placed in square brackets, following the translation. The German word *fun-*
damental—one of the most frequently used words in the text—is simply translated "fundamental."

The numbers in square brackets in the runningheads of the odd-numbered
pages refer to the corresponding pages of the German original. In the footnotes, all numbers, unless otherwise indicated, stand for page numbers. For
example, "op. cit., § 7, S. 10" stands for "op. cit., paragraph or section 7,
page 10" whereas "op. cit., 15" stands for "op. cit., page 15." On those rare
instances when I insert a footnote, it is placed in square brackets and indicated
by the letters "D.D." following a dash. As an aid to the reader, the volume
and page numbers of the standard twelve-volume edition of Descartes' works
by Adam and Tannery (cited as *AT*) are given in square brackets following
every footnote in the original German which includes a reference to a work
of Descartes. This standard edition is *Oeuvres de Descartes*, edited by Ch.
Adam and P. Tannery (revised edition, Paris: Vrin/C.N.R.S., 1964–76). It is
cited in the margins of the English edition, *The Philosophical Writings of*
Descartes, translated by John Cottingham, Robert Stoothoff, and Dugald Mur-
doch, volumes 1–3 (Cambridge/New York: Cambridge University Press,
1985).

Finally, I would like to thank John Sallis for proposing and encouraging
the translation and Hermann Heidegger, Hartmut Tietjen, and Friedrich-
Wilhelm von Herrmann for the warm reception they gave me and their willing
support of the project. For invaluable criticisms and suggestions, I would also
like to express my deep gratitude to Klaus Brinkmann, Omar Bozeman, Eu-
genie Schleberger Dahlstrom, Bret J. Doyle, Aaron Garrett, Al Miller, Maria
Miller, David Roochnik, Robert Scharff, Steven Scully, Claudius Strube,
Ingvild Torsen, Nicolas de Warren, and Kevin White.

I would also like to thank Indiana University Press's copy editor, David L.
Dusenbury, and managing editor, Jane Lyle, for their expert assistance in preparing the manuscript for publication.

Introduction to Phenomenological Research

Preliminary Remark

The task of the lectures and the passion for questioning
genuinely and rightly

The lectures have a twofold task: 1. Establishing and opening up the horizon within which specific *facts of the matter* are to be expected. Provisional orientation of the perspective, stripping away mistaken expectations. 2. Concretely working out the facts of the matter that have, step-by-step, been made more accessible; familiarity with the objects and with the way of dealing with them theoretically.

Before anything else, the following misguided expectations need to be stripped away: 1. No journalistic information about phenomenology, no divulging of some trick for perceiving essences. 2. More dangerous, because more entrenched: no foundation, no program or system, is given here; not even philosophy should be expected. It is my conviction that philosophy is at an end. We stand before completely new tasks that have nothing to do with traditional philosophy. This view is, however, only a clue. Only facts of the matter are of significance. Definition, classification, explication, and disputation are of secondary importance.

The task of the following considerations is threefold: 1. Elucidation of the *expression* "phenomenology"; 2. representation of the *breakthrough* of phenomenological research in Husserl's *Logical Investigations*. 3. Representation of the *development* of phenomenology from this point on, to what extent it is maintained, to what extent it has taken a turn or in the end has been given up, as far as its decisive meaning is concerned.

History of the words: φαινόμενον and λόγος—two original words of Greek philosophy; from the transformation of their meanings, it becomes possible to understand how the specific meaning of phenomenology arose. Insofar as these words enunciate "existence," we move, with their clarification, within the history of Western humanity's existence and the history of its self-interpretation. From Husserl's self-interpretation of "phenomenology" immediately after the *Logical Investigations*, it becomes understandable how he conceives and further shapes the task of phenomenological research. As a way of showing what we are up to, we will fix on existence as our main theme; that is to say, world, dealings in it, temporality, language, one's own interpretation of existence, possibilities of interpreting existence.

No acquaintance with philosophical notions is presupposed. To the contrary, [there are only] three presuppositions: a passion for *questioning* genuinely and rightly. The passion does not happen at will; it has its time and its tempo. A readiness must be there, the readiness that consists in: 1. concern for an instinctively certain mastery in regard to prejudice; 2. care about the process of becoming at home in a specific science; 3. being prepared for the fact that, when it comes to questioning in order to know, life would sooner help in questioning everything else than be of any help in questioning the soul's own inertia, the so-called theoretical consideration.

Ad 1. Not absence of prejudice, which is a utopia. The idea of having no prejudice is itself the greatest prejudice. Mastery in the face of each possibility of something establishing itself as prejudice. Not free from prejudices but free for the possibility of giving up a prejudice at the decisive moment on the basis of a critical encounter with the subject matter. That is the form of existence of a scientific human.

Ad 2. Lethargy towards knowledge is the consequence of science conceived as a collection of material that has already been worked over. This lethargy is characteristic of today's educated consciousness. One has to see that precisely this aspect is fatal. One no longer understands what is actually going on. This cowardice when it comes to questioning often adorns itself as religiosity. Ultimate questioning, questioning that confronts itself, appears as temerity to this religiosity. One flees in the face of a fundamental possibility of existence, a possibility that seems today, alas, to have lost its way. The *sciences* are one possibility of existence and of existence's critical confrontation with itself. If each person, in his place opposite his science, experienced in specific questions that he critically confronts himself and his world here, then he has understood what science means.

Ad 3. The readiness for the questioning consists in a certain *maturity of existence*: it has not lapsed into surrogates; it is also not a matter of finishing as soon as possible, but instead of holding out for years in uncertainty, of maturing from that uncertainty for the critical confrontation with the matters under investigation, of being free to reject every hasty answer. For this it is necessary to free oneself from a tradition which in Greek philosophy was genuine: scientific behavior as theory. You need not think that you have to think what is thought here.

PART ONE

ΦΑΙΝΟΜΕΝΟΝ and ΛΟΓΟΣ in Aristotle
and
Husserl's Self-Interpretation of Phenomenology

Chapter One

Elucidation of the expression "phenomenology"
by going back to Aristotle

The expression "phenomenology" first appears in the eighteenth century in
Christian Wolff's School, in Lambert's *Neues Organon*,[1] in connection with
analogous developments popular at the time, like dianoiology and alethiology,
and means a theory of illusion, a doctrine for avoiding illusion. A related
concept is found in Kant. In a letter to Johann Heinrich Lambert, he writes:
"It appears that a quite particular, although merely negative science (*phae-
nomenologia generalis*) must precede metaphysics, in which the validity and
limits of the principia of sensibility are determined."[2] Later "Phenomenology"
is the title for Hegel's major work.[3] In the Protestant theology of the nineteenth
century, phenomenology of religions is conceived as a doctrine concerning
the various manners of appearance of religions.[4] "Phenomenology" also appears in Franz Brentano's lectures on metaphysics (based upon oral communication from Husserl). Why did Husserl choose this expression? Why is the
doctrine about the avoidance of illusion named "phenomenology" in the eight-

1. Johann Heinrich Lambert, *Neues Organon oder Gedanken über die Erforschung und Bezeichnung des Wahren und dessen Unterscheidung vom Irrthum und Schein.* 2 Bände (Leipzig
1764). *Erster Band*: Dianoiologie oder Lehre von den Gesetzen des Denkens; Alethiologie oder
Lehre von der Wahrheit. *Zweiter Band*: Semiotik oder Lehre von der Bezeichnung der Gedanken
und Dinge; Phänomenologie oder Lehre von dem Schein. [New Organon or Thoughts on the
Investigation and Designation of the True and its Distinction from Error and Illusion, 2 volumes
(Leipzig, 1764). First volume: Dianoiology or doctrine of the laws of thinking; alethiology or
doctrine of truth. Second volume: Semiotics or doctrine of the designation of thoughts and
things; Phenomenology or doctrine of illusion.]
2. *Briefe von und an Kant* [Letters from and to Kant]. Erster Teil: 1749–1789. In: *Immanuel
Kants Werke*. Hrsg. v. E. Cassirer. Bd IX (Berlin 1918), S. 75. Kant mistakenly writes "*phae-
nomologia.*"
3. Georg Wilhelm Friedrich Hegel, *Phänomenologie des Geistes* [Phenomenology of Spirit].
In: *Georg Wilhelm Friedrich Hegels Werke*. Vollständige Ausgabe durch einen Verein von Freun-
den des Verewigten. Zweiter Band (Berlin 1832).
4. Pierre Daniel Chantepie de la Saussaye, *Lehrbuch der Religionsgeschichte* [Textbook of
the History of Religion]. Erster Band (Freiburg in Breisgau 1887). Vorwort, S. V; Phänomen-
ologischer Theil, S. 48–170.

eenth century, and how does φαινόμενον [phenomenon] come to have the meaning of "illusion"? Is there, then, in the expression φαινόμενον some motivation for using it to designate illusion? The term "appearance" must be left out of play since, as a purported translation of the Greek words, it creates confusion. Even Περὶ ψυχῆς, "On the soul," is misunderstood if one hangs on to the terms under discussion here. For Aristotle, perception, thinking, wanting are not experiences. Περὶ ψυχῆς is no psychology in the modern sense, but instead deals with the being of a human being (or of living beings in general) in the world.[5]

§ 1. Clarification of φαινόμενον on the basis of the Aristotelian analysis of perceiving the world by way of seeing

a) Φαινόμενον as a distinctive manner of an entity's presence: existence during the day

Phenomenology is put together from λόγος and φαινόμενον. Φαινόμενον means: something that shows itself. Φαίνομαι is the same as "to show itself," φαίνω the same as "to bring something to the light of day." The stem is φα; this is connected with φῶς which is the same as light, daylightness. In a concrete text of scientific investigations it is necessary to establish what facts of the matter are meant by the words. We shall consider the fact of the matter apart from the word and then, on the basis of the text, establish the sense in which that fact of the matter is meant by the word. For this purpose we choose Aristotle's *De anima*, B (II), chapter 7 that deals with perceiving the world by way of *seeing*.[6] It is necessary to keep every bit of knowledge from physics, physiology at bay since they lack Aristotle's focus. No explication with this sort of concreteness has ever been attempted again.

What is seeing, what is it that is perceived as such in seeing, how is what is accessible in seeing characterized with respect to its content and its perceptibility? Οὗ μὲν οὖν ἐστιν ἡ ὄψις, τοῦτ' ἐστὶν ὁρατόν.[7] "What is perceivable in seeing is the visible"; something of this sort is characterized as color.[8] Color is what is spread over something visible in itself.[9] The respective coloring of an entity is perceived each time ἐν φωτί,[10] in light, more precisely, in daylight [*im Hellen*].

5. See the Appendix, Supplement 1 (p. 223).
6. Aristotelis de anima libri III. Recognovit G. Biehl. Editio altera curavit O. Apelt. In aedibus B. G. Teubneri (Lipsiae 1911). [*The three books of Aristotle's "On the Soul,"* edited by G. Biehl, second edition by O. Apelt (Leipzig: Teubner, 1911).]
7. Op. cit., Beta 7, 418a26.
8. Op. cit., Beta 7, 418a27.
9. Op. cit., Beta 7, 418a29f.
10. Op. cit., Beta 7, 418b3.

Thus, the first thing to be made out is what *daylight* is. Daylight is apparently something that lets something else be seen through it, διαφανές [transparent].[11] This daylight is not of itself visible, but only by means of a color, alien to it.[12] Daylight is what allows something to be seen, namely, the actual color (οἰκεῖον χρῶμα[13]) of the things that I have in daylight.[14] Aristotle discovered that daylightness is not a body

(τί μὲν οὖν τὸ διαφανὲς καὶ τί τὸ φῶς, εἴρηται, ὅτι οὔτε πῦρ οὔθ᾽ ὅλως σῶμα οὐδ᾽ ἀπορροὴ σώματος οὐδενός . . . ,ἀλλὰ πυρὸς ἢ τοιούτου τινὸς παρουσία ἐν τῷ διαφανεῖ),[15]

[As for what the transparent [[*Helle*]] is and what light is, it has been explained that it is neither fire nor a body at all nor even the outflow of a body . . . but presence of fire or some such thing in the transparent,]

that it does not move,[16] but is instead the heaven's actual manner of existing,[17] allowing things to be seen, the day's being. Daylight is a *manner of presence* of [something] (παρουσία,[18] ἐντελέχεια[19]). Empedocles taught that light moves; καὶ οὐκ ὀρθῶς Ἐμπεδοκλῆς [but Empedocles was not right].[20] Trendelenburg saw in the Aristotelian doctrine a relapse; but this judgment shows that he did not understand Aristotle at all.[21]

Αἴσθησις [perception] is the manner of existing of something living in its world. The manners of perceiving things are characterized by Aristotle by means of the *sort of thing perceived*, what is accessible in the perceiving. There are *three sorts*[22] of αἰσθητά: 1. ἴδια, 2. κοινά, 3. συμβεβηκότα [things perceived: 1. special, 2. common, 3. incidentally at hand].

[1.] An ἴδιον[23] is something accessible through one specific manner of perceiving and *only through that manner of perceiving*. It has the character of being ἀεὶ ἀληθές [always true].[24] Seeing, insofar as it exists, always uncovers

11. Op. cit., Beta 7, 418b4.
12. Op. cit., Beta 7, 418b4ff.
13. Op. cit., Beta 7, 419a2.
14. Op. cit., Beta 7, 418b2f.
15. Op. cit., Beta 7, 418b13–17.
16. Op. cit., Beta 7, 418b21f.
17. Op. cit., Beta 7, 418b9.
18. Op. cit., Beta 7, 418b16.
19. Op. cit., Beta 7, 418b12, 418b30.
20. Op. cit., Beta 7, 418b20f.
21. Aristotelis de anima libri tres. Ad interpretum Graecorum auctoritatem et codicum fidem recognovit commentariis illustravit F. A. Trendelenburg. Editio altera emendata et aucta. [*The three books of Aristotle's "On the soul,"* with F. A. Trendelenburg's inspection of the authority of the Greek interpreters and the faithfulness of the codices and his illustration with commentaries; second, improved and enlarged edition.] (Berlin 1877), 306: "Itaque Empedoclis sententia vero, quod recentior aetas invenit, proprior, quam Aristoteles" [Thus, in truth, the opinion of Empedocles is more proper, as the age recently discovered, than that of Aristotle].
22. Aristotle, *De anima* (Biehl, Apelt), Beta 6, 418a8.
23. Op. cit., Beta 6, 418a11.
24. Op. cit., Gamma 3, 427b12.

only color, hearing always uncovers only sound. 2. κοινόν.²⁵ There are characteristic ways of being that are not fitted to one specific manner of perceiving, e.g., κίνησις [change]. 3. συμβεβηκός is what is regularly perceived (κατὰ συμβεβηκὸς δὲ λέγεται αἰσθητόν, οἷον εἰ τὸ λευκὸν εἴη Διάρους υἱός [something perceptible is said to be incidentally at hand, for instance, if the white thing were Diaeres' son]²⁶). For, as a rule, I do not see color, I do not hear sounds, but instead the singer's song, something that is encountered along with the immediate perceiving [*das im nächsten Vernehmen Mitbegegnende*]. When it comes to the perceptibility of something κατὰ συμβεβηκός deception is possible and even the rule.

Aristotle determined color, among other things, to be an ἴδιον.²⁷ Daylight is the presence of fire.²⁸ Daylight does not move. Only the sun moves, the presence of which is the daylight. Whoever says that daylight moves is speaking παρὰ τὰ φαινόμενα,²⁹ he is speaking past what shows itself. Φαινόμενον is what shows itself of itself to be of a certain sort and is immediately here as such. Speaking in a Kantian fashion, daylight is the condition of the possibility of the perceptibility of color. Precisely in this Kantian use of language, one can recognize the difference between what, in both cases, is understood by "condition." This is not to say, however, that Aristotle and Kant should be contrasted with one another as realists and idealists (there is no such contrast in Greek philosophy). What does "condition of the possibility of the perceptibility of color" mean, what does "being a condition" mean for Aristotle? Color is seen in daylight. The thing seen must be at daytime. Daylight is something that is part of the being of the world itself. Daylight is the sun's presence. The character of being for this manner of being-present is to let things be seen through it. Letting something be seen is the sun's manner of being. The perceptibility of things is subject to a condition, that of a specific manner of being of this world itself. "Being a condition" applies to a manner of being of the world itself. The sun's being on hand, precisely *what* we mean when we determine: *it is daytime*, is part of the existence in the world. By this means we speak of a fact of the matter that is part of the being of the world itself. The result of this is that φαινόμενον initially means nothing other than a *distinctive manner of an entity's presence*.

25. Op. cit., Beta 6, 418a17ff.
26. Op. cit., Beta 6, 418a20f.
27. On this matter, see the Appendix, Supplement 2 (p. 223).
28. Aristotle, *De anima*, B 7, 418b16.
29. Op. cit., Beta 7, 418b24.

b) Φαινόμενον as anything that of itself shows itself in daylight or darkness

The concept φαινόμενον is not limited solely to the presence of things during the day. It is broader and designates anything showing itself of itself, whether it does so *in daylight* or *in darkness*.

What, now, is darkness? For someone arguing in an empty-headed way, it is obviously not difficult to determine what it is. Daylight is διαφανές,[30] something that lets things be seen, darkness is an ἀδιαφανές, something that does not. But darkness also lets something be seen. There are visible things that are visible *only in the dark*:

οὐ πάντα δὲ ὁρατὰ ἐν φωτί ἐστιν, ἀλλὰ μόνον ἑκάστου τὸ οἰκεῖον χρῶμα. ἔνια γὰρ ἐν μὲν τῷ φωτὶ οὐχ ὁρᾶται, ἐν δὲ τῷ σκότει ποιεῖ αἴσθησιν, οἷον τὰ πυρώδη φαινό μενα.[31]

[Not everything is visible in light, but only the proper color of each thing. For some things are not seen in light but produce perception in the dark, such as things that appear fire-like.]

Darkness is something that, in a quite specific way, lets things be seen. In order to establish the dark's difference from daylight, we must draw on a completely fundamental distinction of Aristotelian philosophy: the difference between ἐντελεχείᾳ [actual being] and δυνάμει ὄν [potential being]. Darkness is a δυνάμει ὄν,[32] something utterly positive. Since, in our doctrine of categories, we have not developed such primordial categories, we are unable to comprehend this peculiar structure. Insofar as darkness is a manner of "being away," it must be designated as στέρησις,[33] as the absence of something that should actually be on hand. Darkness' being consists in being *potential* daylight. It would be talking past Aristotle, if one were to say: "Daylight is what lets things be seen; thus, darkness is what does not." The dark also lets things be seen.

The basic concepts of philosophy, such as they run their course in the historical development, are not some property or possession of philosophy that one can hold onto and that stands outside the development. They have become far more our own nemesis insofar as the consideration and interpretation of existing as a whole is pervaded by such concepts that amount to nothing more than a possession of words. They signify the great danger that one philosophizes today in words rather than about things.

Φαινόμενον and λόγος give expression to a fact of the matter. Later the

30. Op. cit., Beta 7, 418b4.
31. Op. cit., Beta 7, 419a1ff.
32. Op. cit., Beta 7, 418b10f.
33. Op. cit., Beta 7, 418b19.

motives in existence itself, on the basis of which φαινόμενον is able to take on the meaning of "illusion," will become intelligible—so, too, it will become understandable how a philosophy that has become superficial and coasts along in words grasps existing entities as an "appearance of something." Aristotle did not have so naïve a metaphysics. And if one attempts today, with the word "appearance" in hand, to offer a critique of phenomenology, it is a groundless endeavor against which I can only protest (compare Rickert, *Logos*, 1923[34]).

Φαινόμενον is what shows itself of itself as existing; it is encountered by life insofar as life stands towards its world in such a way that it sees the world, perceives it at all in the αἴσθησις. Ἴδια αἰσθητά [special perceptibles] are what are perceived in the strict sense of the term. On the other hand, κατὰ συμβεβηκός is perceiving immediately in such a way that from the outset something is originally here along with it. Only in this way are we able to see houses, trees, human beings. If I want to return to the ἴδια, then it is necessary to assume an isolated, artificial attitude. The expression φαίνεσθαι already designates what has been perceived κατὰ συμβεβηκός. If the sun shows itself, then it is here a foot wide, it does not appear so.

Now, the primordial nature of seeing for Aristotle is evident from the fact that he does not allow himself to be misled by the lack of an all-encompassing name for the things that only the night lets us see (thus for fireflies, etc.): ὁρατὸν δ᾽ ἐστὶ χρῶμα μέν, καὶ ὃ λόγῳ μὲν ἔστιν εἰπεῖν, ἀνώνυμον δὲ τυγχάνει ὄν [The visible is color and what can be articulated in a statement, though it happens to be nameless].[35] What matters to him is merely the fact that these things are here, that they are seen and, on the basis of their factual content, lay claim to being taken as existing. The fact that there is no name for these things indicates, however, that our language (doctrine of categories) is a language of the day. This holds particularly for the Greek language and is connected in their case with the basic starting point of their thinking and their formation of concepts. One cannot remedy that by somehow constructing a doctrine of categories of the night. Instead we must go back to a point prior to this opposition in order to be able to understand why the day has this priority.

Thanks to the word-combination παρὰ τὰ φαινόμενα [beyond the phenomena],[36] which recurs repeatedly in Aristotle, the particular character of the claim made by φαινόμενον and what is thereby seized upon emerges. If it is *explicitly* a matter of grasping existence, of retaining it, of securing what shows itself in itself, then we remain in the context of science. In this context the meaning of φαινόμενον comes to a head: what shows itself in itself, with

34. H. Rickert, "Die Methode der Philosophie und das Unmittelbare. Eine Problemstellung" [The method of philosophy and the immediate; a posing of the problem]. In: *Logos*. Internationale Zeitschrift für Philosophie der Kultur. XII (1923/24): 235–280.
35. Aristotle, *De anima*, Beta 7, 418a26ff.
36. Op. cit., Beta 7, 418b24.

the explicit claim of serving as the basis for all further questioning and ex-plicating. What matters for science is σῴζειν τὰ φαινόμενα [to save the phe-nomena]; what shows itself in itself is thereby pressed into a fundamental position.[37] Something of this sort is possible in science. Science has the ten-dency to grasp and demonstrate existing entities in a way that does not leave anything uncovered. To be a scientific person is to be positioned in a specific manner over against the world's being. There are two determinations of this ἕξις [attitude],[38] determinations that, in themselves, belong together: 1. famil-iarity with the things that are subject to the science, ἐπιστήμη τοῦ πράγματος [knowledge of the thing][39]; 2. a certain παιδεία [education],[40] being educated in such a way that one knows how to conduct oneself in the field of scientific investigation. The individual who has the παιδεία can decide quite certainly whether someone who undertakes an investigation is prattling or whether what he is conveying emerges from the subject matter (καλῶς ἀποδίδωσιν [(whether) he conveys (it) well]).[41] On the basis of such παιδεία one must decide what type of investigation is precisely suited to the object. With regard to the pos-sibilities of the investigation, it has to be decided whether, like earlier thinkers, one should posit existing and the determinations of an object's being as sec-ondary and speak primarily of the genesis or not.[42] The answer is easy: only after one has fashioned the basis for the investigation, can one set out to answer the question of the origin and the "why" of the origin.[43] The first thing that needs to be established in building a house is the εἶδος [form][44] and only then the ὕλη [matter]. Εἶδος means to make an impression. This making an impression is the house's being in its surroundings as a house, its look, "face." The φαινόμενον is the entity itself.

§ 2. The Aristotelian determination of λόγος

a) Talk (λόγος) as a voice that means something (φωνὴ σημαντική); ὄνομα and ῥῆμα

In what connection does the concept of φαινόμενον stand to what Aristotle explicates as λόγος? Τὸ φαινόμενον is the being that, in any possible investi-gation, must be appropriated in such a way that it provides the basis for the

37. Aristotelis de partibus animalium libri quattuor. Ex recognitione B. Langkavel. Lipsiae in aedibus B. G. Teubneri 1868. [*The four books of Aristotle's "On the Parts of Animals,"* edited by B. Langkavel (Leipzig: Teubner, 1868).] Cf. Alpha 1, 639b8; 640a14.
38. Op. cit., Alpha 1, 639a2f.
39. Op. cit., Alpha 1, 639a3.
40. Op. cit., Alpha 1, 639a4.
41. Op. cit., Alpha 1, 639a4ff.
42. Op. cit., Alpha 1, 640a10ff.
43. Op. cit., Alpha 1, 640a14f.
44. Op. cit., Alpha 1, 640a17.

inquiry. The expression φαινόμενον is accordingly not a conceptual category, but instead a manner of being, *how something is encountered* and, indeed, encountered in the *first* and, as such, *first legitimate* way. The category "object" was alien to the Greeks. In its place was πρᾶγμα, what one has to deal with—what is present for the concern that deals with things. "Object" means, by contrast, what stands opposite the mere observer who simply looks at it, what is present, after being thematically selected and had as such. Φαινόμενον means the existing entity itself; it is a determination of being and is to be grasped in such a way that the character of *showing itself* is expressed. Τὰ φαινόμενα can be represented by τὰ ὄντα; it is what is always already here, what we encounter the moment we open our eyes. It does not need first to be disclosed, but is frequently covered up. The accent lies, in a completely primary sense, on the character of the "here."

Περὶ ἑρμηνείας [On Interpretation] is not a text but a manuscript that belongs to Aristotle's final period.[45] It grew out of a momentary reflection that did not meet any sort of pedagogical considerations. The observations are made purely in the interest of making distinctions and in no way for the sake of exposition. Λόγος is audible being that means something, it is a voice: Λόγος δέ ἐστι φωνὴ σημαντική.[46] The first question is: What is φωνή? and then: What is φωνὴ σημαντική? and, finally: What is λόγος?

Φωνή (*De anima* II, chapter 8) is a type of sound that is made into something animate, a noise made by something living: ἡ δὲ φωνὴ ψόφος τίς ἐστιν ἐμψύχου.[47] A sound is made when something in something knocks on something: πᾶν ψοφεῖ τύπτοντός τινος καί τι καὶ ἕν τινι.[48] The voice, however, is in and with the being of something living: φωνὴ δ᾽ ἐστὶ ζῴου ψόφος.[49] For this, the voice's being, it is necessary that there is something like a πνεῦμα [breath]. Just as the tongue within a living being has two functions, namely, first, that of tasting and, second, that of enabling speech (something that, to be sure, does not occur in every living being as such), so, too, πνεῦμα has the task of providing the body with inner warmth and, secondly, of facilitating speaking. To have a voice is a distinctive type of being, namely, being in the sense of living. But not every noise emitted by something alive is, by that fact, already a voice (οὐ γὰρ πᾶς ζῴου ψόφος φωνή);[50] one can also produce mere sounds with the tongue, such as coughing. The difference consists then in the fact

45. Aristoteles, *De interpretatione*. In: Aristotelis Organon Graece. Novis codicum auxiliis adiutus recognovit, scholiis ineditis et commentario instruxit Th. Waitz. Pars prior: Categoriae, Hermeneutica, Analytica priora. (Lipsiae 1844). [Aristotle, On interpretation, in *Aristotle's Organon in Greek*, edited by Th. Waitz with the aid of new supporting evidence from codices and with the addition of unedited scholiae and commentary. First part: Categories, Hermeneutics, Prior Analytics (Leipzig, 1844).]
46. Op. cit., 4, 16b26.
47. Aristotle, *De anima*, Beta 8, 420b5f.
48. Op. cit., Beta 8, 420b14f.
49. Op. cit., Beta 8, 420b13.
50. Op. cit., Beta 8, 420b29.

that fantasy is contained in the sound, in the very middle of it (ἀλλὰ δεῖ ἔμψυχόν τε εἶναι τὸ τύπτον καὶ μετὰ φαντασίας τινός [but it is necessary that the one knocking be alive and have some fantasy])⁵¹—then it is a voice. Now, in ordinary language, "fantasy" means splendor, spectacle, appearing like something, thus, a completely objective meaning. Φαντασία—that something shows itself. The sound is a voice (the sound of speech) if, by means of it, something is to be perceived (seen). On the basis of the φαντασία one designates the sound σημαντική.

The λόγος has parts and, indeed, the sort that remain meaningful but only ὡς φάσις (ἧς τῶν μερῶν τι σημαντικόν ἐστι κεχωρισμένον) [as saying (some parts of it—the *logos*—are separately meaningful)].⁵² The parts' manner of meaning something is the mere saying. "The stove gives off warmth" can be broken down into "stove" and "gives off warmth." If I say "stove," then that still means something; it is intelligible, it signifies something. "Gives off warmth" is also already something for itself. But placing it together with "stove" does not yield the λόγος, "the stove" "gives off warmth" (ἀλλ᾽ οὐχ ὡς κατάφασις [but not as an affirmation]).⁵³ It is merely intelligible in the manner of the φάσις [saying], it is not said in the sense of the λόγος that is the συμπλοκή of ὄνομα and ῥῆμα [the intertwining of name or noun and verb].

A name is also something audible that is as such intelligible.

Ὄνομα μὲν οὖν ἐστὶ φωνὴ σημαντικὴ κατὰ συνθήκην ἄνευ χρόνου, ἧς μηδὲν μέρος ἐστὶ σημαντικὸν κεχωρισμένον. ἐν γὰρ τῷ Κάλλιππος τὸ ἵππος οὐδὲν αὐτὸ καθ᾽ ἑαυτὸ σημαίνει, ὥσπερ ἐν τῷ λόγῳ τῷ καλὸς ἵππος. οὐ μὴν οὐδ᾽ ὥσπερ ἐν τοῖς ἁπλοῖς ὀνόμασιν, οὕτως ἔχει καὶ ἐν τοῖς πεπλεγμένοις. ἐν ἐκείνοις μὲν γὰρ τὸ μέρος οὐδαμῶς σημαντικόν, ἐν δὲ τούτοις βούλεται μέν, ἀλλ᾽ οὐδενὸς κεχωρισμένον, οἷον ἐν τῷ ἐπακτροκέλης τὸ κέλης οὐδέν. τὸ δὲ κατὰ συνθήκην, ὅτι φύσει τῶν ὀνομάτων οὐδέν ἐστιν, ἀλλ᾽ ὅταν γένηται σύμβολον, ἐπεὶ δηλοῦσί γέ τι καὶ οἱ ἀγράμματοι ψόφοι, οἷον θηρίων, ὧν οὐδέν ἐστιν ὄνομα.⁵⁴

[A name is a sound meaningful by convention, without time, of which no part is separately meaningful. For in the name "Fairsteed" the "fair" of itself does not mean anything as it does in the phrase "fair steed." But there is a difference between simple names and complex ones. For in the former a part is utterly devoid of meaning, but in the latter the part has some force albeit not separately; for instance, the "boat" in "pirateboat." I say "by convention" because nothing is a name by nature, but only insofar as it comes to be a symbol. Even inarticulate sounds, for instance, those of beasts, are meaningful but none of them are names.]

A word's meaning is not already present on the basis of the way the throat and tongue make speech possible. These are φύσει [by nature], not so a word.

51. Op. cit., Beta 8, 420b31f.
52. Aristotle, *De interpretatione*, 4, 16b26f.
53. Op. cit., 4, 16b27f.
54. Op. cit., 2, 16a19–29.

Words are as one sees fit, κατὰ συνθήκεν [by convention],[55] that is to say, each word first had to come to be as such and has its genesis. The sound of a word does not have a meaning for all time and does not actually have *the* fixed meaning that refers to a subject matter—a word as a whole is drawn, not from a primary, primordial experience of the subject matter, but from pre-conceptions and the nearest at hand views of things. The word's genesis is not born by a human's physiological being, but by his actual [*eigentlich*] existence. Insofar as a human being is in the world and *wants* something in that world and wants it with himself, he speaks. He speaks insofar as something like a world is *uncovered* for him as a matter of concern and *he* is uncovered to himself in this "for him." But the word is thus not here like a tool (οὐχ ὡς ὄργανον[56]), for example, the hand. Language is the being and becoming of the human being himself. In a name, what is named is so named in this naming that it is removed from every time-determination (ἄνευ χρόνου).[57] It is a matter simply of a specific, named "what." That holds, too, for names that refer to something temporal. "Year" does not, indeed, mean this year or the next. No detachable part of a name means something for itself. If I place the parts together, I never come to the unitary meaning. That the specific syllables are together is first established by the unitary meaning. The audible articulation is only intelligible in that meaning. Aristotle: I say this because a word only exists as a word if something audible becomes a σύμ-βολον [symbol].[58] (Σύμβολον in Greek originally signifies rings, broken in two, that spouses, friends give to one another when one of them departs so that, when they meet one another again, the one part is recognized by putting it together with the other part.) The one refers to the other. Σύμβολον makes something else evident, the meaningful word refers to its subject matter. Now, there are sounds that announce something without meaning something, ἀγράμ-ματοι,[59] for example, moaning. These sounds lack the imprint such that one could write or read them (which works only on the basis of meaning).

Λόγος is already used in ordinary language for a fundamental characteristic. With every interpretation of λόγος we already have a specific preconception about the sense of the λόγος. We know in a quite indeterminate way what speech, language is. But we have no sure information about what language meant for the Greeks in their natural existence, how they saw the language. To be sure, Hellenism has a science of language and grammar: a doctrinaire treatment and theory. Every modern conception of language has been influenced by it. There are, in addition, the influences of epistemology, and so

55. Op. cit., 4, 17a1.
56. Op. cit., 4, 17a2.
57. Op. cit., 2, 16a20.
58. Op. cit., 2, 16a28.
59. Op. cit., 2, 16a28f.

forth, such that the question of how a Greek lived in his language is not even posited any more. We must, of course, initially put up with the fundamental [*grundsätzlich*] lack of clarity about the existence of language. But a specific concept of language lies—and must lie—for us at the foundation. We hold it in suspension, that is to say, we concretely shape our opinion about language only to the extent that we have occasion and a basis for doing so. One thing is to be said with certainty. The Greek lived in a special way in the language and *was lived by it* and he was conscious of this. The ability to address and discuss what was encountered (world and self), something that does not need to be philosophy, he characterizes as being a human being: λόγον ἔχειν,[60] to have language.

In *De interpretatione* (towards the end of chapter 3), one finds the following determination:

Αὐτὰ μὲν οὖν καθ᾽ ἑαυτὰ λεγόμενα τὰ ῥήματα ὀνόματά ἐστι καὶ σημαίνει τι (ἵστησι γὰρ ὁ λέγων τὴν διάνοιαν, καὶ ὁ ἀκούσας ἠρέμησεν):[61]

[Verbs themselves, spoken by themselves, are names and signify something (for the one speaking brings his thinking to a halt and the one listening pauses):]

"Whoever says something brings the process of opining to a standstill." When we naturally go along living, then the world is here. We deal with it, we are preoccupied with it. If a word is then spoken, the process of opining is placed before something; in understanding the word I linger with that thing; in meaning something, I have come to a pause. He who listens pauses in understanding the word: ὁ ἀκούσας ἠρέμησεν.[62] In understanding the word, I pause with what it means. To understand something means to have something here, to have it in the manner of understanding a naming of the named. What matters for Aristotle, particularly also in contrast to Plato, is the fact that speaking, when it moves within the language, is something that, as far as its genuine being is concerned, grows out of human beings' free assessment of things; it is not φύσει [by nature].[63] How ὄνομα and ῥῆμα come together in the λόγος cannot actually become a problem at all. Λόγος is, indeed, precisely what is primordial, and ὄνομα and ῥῆμα must be understood as particular modifications of λόγος. It is characteristic of the ὄνομα that it cannot be split up into various characteristics of meaning. The word as name is in the unity of the act of meaning, a unity that we designate "naming something." Now, there are words thrown together that, to be sure, also have a unitary meaning, but in such a way that the elements claim to mean something independent and claim not

60. Aristotelis Politica, Alpha 2, 1253a9f.
61. Aristotle, *De interpretatione*, 3, 16b19ff.
62. Op. cit., 3, 16b21.
63. Op. cit., 2, 16a27.

only to mean something, but to mean it in view of what is meant in the unitary way. The free assessment refers to the act of the creation of language itself and hence does not need to be alive in every performance. That is to say, we do not come into the world with a definite supply of words and we are also not gradually yoked into a definite context.

Ῥῆμα is a word that 1. in its meaning means *time* as well (προσσημαίνει χρόνον[64]); what it means, it means in a temporal manner of being: "being at some time," for example, "will die"; and 2. means it in view of another being (for example, "goes to church"): ἔστιν ἀεὶ τῶν καθ᾽ ἑτέρου λεγομένων σημεῖον [it is always meaningful of things being said of another].[65] Rhematic being is the being that is signified in the ῥῆμα. Ὄνομα and ῥῆμα can only emerge as modifications of the original λόγος. Each is for itself, to be sure, still a meaning; but something is lost. The "how" of meaning changes: out of the κατάφασις [affirmation] the mere φάσις [saying] comes to be.[66]

b) The ostensive talk (λόγος ἀποφαντικός) that reveals (ἀληθεύειν) or conceals (ψεύδεσθαι) the existing world in affirming (κατάφασις) and denying (ἀπόφασις); the ὁρισμός

What is the κατάφασις for Aristotle? Clarification by way of a detour. The λόγος is not in the manner of a tool,[67] but is instead historical and grows by itself, that is to say, from the respective state of the discovery of some subject matter. Not all talking is of the sort that manages to *ostend* or *point out* [*aufzeigen*] something in the manner of meaning something. The only sort of talking that is ἀποφαντικός is that in which something like an ἀληθεύειν [a revealing] occurs: presenting an entity as not concealed or presenting an entity in such a way that, in this ostension, something is "feigned" (ψεύδεσθαι).[68] The *concealing* feigns something in the manner of pointing it out. Ἀληθεύειν and ψεύδεσθαι are the basic ways in which the λόγος as ἀποφαντικός points something out and, indeed, shows an entity as an entity.[69] If the λέγειν is carried out by ἀληθεύειν—revealing—*then* the λόγος is a λόγος ἀποφαντικός; that is to say, not every λέγειν (asking, commanding, requesting, drawing attention to) is "true and false." Each is, to be sure, a way of making something clear—δηλοῦν—but this should not be confounded with theoretically uncovering. Today there is an attempt to understand all knowing in terms of judgments as modifications of it.

64. Op. cit., 3, 16b8.
65. Op. cit., 3, 16b7.
66. Op. cit., 4, 16b27f.
67. Op. cit., 4, 17a1.
68. Op. cit., 4, 17a2f.
69. Ibid.

"If something is thereby posited in addition to it" (ἀλλ' ἔσται κατάφασις ἢ ἀπόφασις, ἐάν τι προστεθῇ [there will be affirmation or denial]).[70] This sentence is interpreted as though a sentence would emerge if additional words are added onto a noun. For Aristotle, πρόσθεσις stands in contrast to ἀφαίρεσις (abstraction); the latter means taking something away from something and putting it, thus taken away, on its own footing. (Geometry, for example, sees the mere spatial form apart from the thing and keeps that form alone in view.) Πρόσθεσις means concretion. But what has been taken away is not added again. Instead, what is posited is posited as an entity (Topics[71]). The κατάφασις is at work beyond the mere φάσις, if what is meant in speaking is meant as a concrete entity. A λόγος is here whenever the speaking is speaking with the existing world. If I merely say "stove," I do not speak on the basis of some existence; rather I set myself off from the existence of the concrete world. I mean something, yet whether there in fact are stoves plays no role for this meaning. Speaking is being with the world, it is something primordial, and is in place prior to judgments. It is from here that the judgment has to become intelligible. In logic there is a tradition of construing expressions like "fire!" as judgments. (By no means is it simply the existence of fire that is supposed to be established here; instead people are supposed to jump out of their beds.) By no means does λόγος entail a plurality of words. The word was originally a naming, but not a naming of a mere name; rather something encountered in the world is being addressed as it is encountered.

Up to this point we have characterized λόγος from three sides: 1. from the side of φωνὴ μετὰ φαντασίας, 2. the significant sound, 3. standing still. Talking is not a property like "having hair." Talking co-constitutes the existence specific to a human being; a human being is in the world in such a way that this entity speaks with the world about it. (The "about" does not mean judging; the "about the world" lies, for example, in the "today" in the request: "please come to me today.")

We have determined φαινόμενον to be what shows itself as immediately existing (the world is meant). In relation to what exists in this way, talking has a special function. The λόγος ἀποφαντικός is the sort of talking with the world, by means of which the existing world is pointed out as existing. (Ἀποφαίνεσθαι is "letting something be seen from itself in its way of existing.") But the λόγος ἀποφαντικός is merely one possibility next to others of speaking about the existing world with words. In De anima Aristotle says that the λόγος is one possibility of being on the part of a human being that aims at bringing him to his highest possible existence (εὖ ζῆν [living well]).[72] From this vantage

70. Op. cit., 4, 16b29f.
71. Aristotelis Topica, Beta 11, 115a26ff; Gamma 3, 118b10ff; Gamma 5, 119a23ff.
72. Aristotle, De anima, Beta 8, 420b20.

point, one might also say that living is identical to *being-possible,* to having quite definite possibilities. Aristotle is speaking here no longer of λόγος but instead of διάλεκτος (speaking with others about something)[73] or of ἑρμηνεία (coming to an understanding with others about something).[74] Here a fundamental definition of human beings emerges for him. Being a human being means the sort of life standing in the *possibility of dealing* with the πράγματα, with the world as the *object of its concern* and, indeed, the sort of being that can *speak.* In its πρᾶξις this entity is essentially characterized as the entity that speaks.

Aristotle lays great weight on the question of the constitutive features of the *unity* of λόγος. For him and for the Greeks generally, the determination of the unity, of the ἕν, alternates with the determination of an entity's specific being. The unity of the λόγος ἀποφαντικός is supposed to be uncovered in two respects: 1. with respect to what is meant; 2. with respect to the factical meaning.

Ad 1. How is the λόγος ἀποφαντικός distinguished from ὄνομα and ῥῆμα? The λόγος here in the sense of λέγειν is to be defined by setting it off from the mere pronouncing of a name or a verb. In contrast to all names is the λόγος πρόσθεσις. What is named, as far as its being is concerned, is undifferentiated. By contrast, what is meant in the λόγος is characterized as existing. Meaning something [*Bedeuten*] in the case of a name is merely entertaining [*Meinen*] it in a formal sense, whereas in the λόγος it is the *ostension, the pointing out of the existing entity as existing.* In the *Hermeneutics* (something that Hegel allegedly discovered)[75] [Aristotle claims]: a verb, spoken merely as a word, is a mere name (Αὐτὰ μὲν οὖν καθ᾽ ἑαυτὰ λεγόμενα τὰ ῥήματα ὀνόματά ἐστι καὶ σημαίνει τι [Verbs themselves, spoken by themselves, are names and signify something]).[76] Something is meant, to be sure, but in this name I am not confronted with the entity and nothing is settled about the existence or nonexistence of what is meant (ἀλλ᾽ εἰ ἔστιν ἢ μή, οὔπω σημαίνει [but whether it exists or not is not signified]).[77] This indifferent being says nothing about the subject matter and about its being as the subject matter: οὐδὲ γὰρ τὸ εἶναι ἢ μὴ εἶναι σημεῖόν ἐστι τοῦ πράγματος [for the "to exist or not to exist" is not a sign of the thing].[78] If I say "stove" and if I understand what I say, then what is so understood is not in any way determined with respect to its specific character of being. Rhematic being says nothing if one

---

73. Op. cit., Beta 8, 420b18.
74. Op. cit., Beta 8, 420b19f.
75. Husserl, not Hegel, is presumably meant; see the Editor's Afterword (p. 247).
76. Aristotle, *De interpretatione*, 3, 16b19f.
77. Op. cit., 3, 16b21f.
78. Op. cit., 3, 16b22f.

takes it merely for itself; in itself, rhematic being is nothing. It is nothing, but signifies in something like a composition (αὐτὸ μὲν γὰρ οὐδέν ἐστι, προσσημαίνει δὲ σύνθεσίν τινα).[79] It is inherent in every verb, in its proper meaning, that it means what is meant by it standing in connection with something else. By means of the rhematic being, a sphere of possible connections is determined. The determination is itself indeterminate insofar as it is not a univocal determination. In the meaning of every verb is a definite reference to connections pertaining to some matter (σύνθεσίν τινα, ἣν ἄνευ τῶν συγκειμένων οὐκ ἔστι νοῆσαι [some synthesis that cannot be thought without what is combined]).[80] A verb actually has a relational character but such that this referential connection and its being are indifferent. In contrast to this indifference to being, existence is meant in every λόγος.

Ad 2. What constitutes the specific *unity* in the case of λόγος ἀποφαντικός? The primordial, unitary λόγος ἀποφαντικός is the κατάφασις, which goes together with the ἀπόφασις, both characterized as ἀπόφανσις (affirmation and denial).[81] Κατάφασις: to affirm something, [taken] from something else, of something. Ἀπόφασις: to deny something this or that, to exclude something else from it. In the ἀπόφασις lies a twofold ἀπό. The two [being *of* something and, on this basis, excluding something else *from* it] do not coincide at all. This entire fact of the matter as it actually exists must be held onto for every further determination; only then can something be denied it or, better, can something else be denied it on the basis of it. Only in this way can one come to some understanding of the problem of negation. These λόγοι are simple because no connection of λόγοι takes place in them as in, for example, the hypothetical sentence: "If it rains tomorrow, I will not go out." Although the λόγος is simple, it does contain a ῥῆμα which speaks in relation to something else. The ῥῆμα does not affect the primordial unity of the λόγος since no naming is contained in the λόγος. "The leaves are yellow" does not contain "are yellow." In the λόγος what is spoken about is held onto as existing. In this way, the λόγος can consist of one word.

What is the standing of the λόγος ὁρισμός (definition) in these connections?[82] Only when viewed from the outside do we have here a multiplicity (human being, living being); in contrast to the ordinary λόγος ἀποφαντικός, the ὁρισμός is distinguished by the fact that what it says and means (for example, "the whole human being is . . .") is attributed to a human being not as existing as something else (given the content of its subject matter, as when yellow is attributed to leaves). Instead, what is said here by the λόγος of an entity is

79. Op. cit., 3, 16b24.
80. Op. cit., 3, 16b24f.
81. Op. cit., 5, 17a8f.
82. Op. cit., 5, 17a10ff.

the entity itself. The existing entity is spoken of here simply in itself (καθ᾽ αὑτὸ λεγόμενον).[83] In the *Metaphysics,* Book VII, chapter 4 (1029b13ff.), where ὁρισμός is analyzed, he progresses farther than anywhere else in the analysis of the immediate. This advanced position is never again attained later.

In speaking, the world's being is here as existing, pointed out from the ground up, taken hold of in itself. Its actual existence presents itself in the act of asserting. The correlation of λόγος and εἶδος becomes fundamental here; εἶδος is the look, that is to say, for the Greeks, a manner of distinguishing itself equivalent to "so it is." What is spoken of as such is also characteristically designated as λόγος and for Aristotle λόγος and εἶδος can be substituted for one another. Εἶδος is the existing entity in the way it looks. In German we say "that is how you look" [*so siehst Du aus*] in the sense of "that is who you are" [*so bist Du*].

c) The possibility of deception, the λόγος ἀποφαντικός and the αἴσθησις

On what is the *possibility of deception, of illusion* based, such that someone could say, "In the world there is only appearance"? Speaking provides the possibility of having the world in its character of being here, that is to say, speaking has within itself the possibility of access and preserving. But the λόγος ἀποφαντικός is not the λόγος in general, not even the decisive λόγος, even if it has the upper hand and the leading role in the history of thinking's self-interpreting in all questions that refer to speaking, the determination of concepts and the interpretation of existence. Unity does not have a merely formal sense for Aristotle and the Greeks, so that everything objective as such would indeed be *one*. The question of unity is closely connected with the question of being, being in the sense of existing. The question of the unity of the λόγος ἀποφαντικός is equivalent to the question: what characterizes the λόγος ἀποφαντικός as *one*? It is *a process of making oneness evident* (ἓν δηλῶν[84]), that is to say, the meaning-function of λέγειν, in which an entity is pointed out as existing, specifies the unitary character of an entity. The individual instances of positing are pervaded by the tendency toward meaning on the part of the sort of λέγειν that aims to point out a specific state of affairs. One would not get at the λόγος, if one were to begin with mere naming. The primordial function of meaning is ostension, to point something out.

In *De anima* Aristotle emphasizes that earlier philosophers paid far too little attention to the fact that a human being spends the greatest part of his time

83. Aristotlelis Metaphysica. Recognovit W. Christ. Nova impressio correctior (1895). Editio stereotypa. In aedibus B. G. Teubneri (Lipsiae 1931). [Aristotle, *Metaphysics*, edited by W. Christ, reprint of the new, corrected impression (1895) (Leipzig: Teubner, 1931).] Zeta 4, 1029b14.

84. Aristotle, *De interpretatione*, 5, 17a16.

in *deception*.[85] Because deceit is so much more at home among human beings than one commonly believes, it is not enough to make deceit a problem only in passing and not in principle. It does not suffice, in regard to the manner in which the world comes to be accessible, to emphasize αἴσθησις [perception] and νόησις [thought] alone; it is necessary to come to an understanding of φαντασία [fantasy], of having something here [*das etwas Da-haben*] [that is not present].[86] Deceit and deception come about on the basis of connections of φαντασία with αἴσθησις and νόησις.

Αἴσθησις is as such a process of offsetting [*Abheben*] something from something else (distinguishing).[87] In selecting something, what is selected is as such offset from something else (πρὸς ἄλλον). Something can be perceived in such a way that, while existing together with others, it is set off from them. The κρίνειν [judging, discriminating] is not formal; rather, in this process of setting something off from others, what is offset becomes accessible and can be grasped as here.[88] This κρίνειν is constitutive not only for αἴσθησις, but also for νόησις. These two possibilities distinguish the human manner of being. A human being is the sort of entity that in its way has the world here by making things accessible to itself in setting them off from one another, the sort of entity who is able to *move about* (κίνησις κατὰ τόπον[89]) in this manner of setting things off from one another and articulating them.

Under what conditions does the basic function of αἴσθησις (which we know as κρίνειν) stand? *De anima* III, 2, 426b8ff. An existing, living entity is characterized by the fact that it is a *being-in-the-possibility* and, indeed, in a definite possibility, capable of something, having about itself utterly definite possibilities, delimited and prefigured possibilities of what it can do and, indeed, what it can do with respect to the world, in which the entity with this capability has its being. (Δύναμις and ἐνέργεια have their origin here. They already appear in Plato, of course, but not yet in their fundamental significance. They belong for Aristotle to the basic categorial determination of being.)

Every instance of perceiving is directed as such at the ὑποκείμενον αἰσθητόν [the underlying perceptible],[90] what is at hand [*das Vorliegende*], what is already here in existence prior to all activities. The ὑποκείμενον is for a Greek something here from the outset. What is at hand need not, however, first be made. A ὑποκείμενον can be perceived, and perceiving constitutes the specific access to what is at hand.

85. Aristotle, *De anima*, Gamma 3, 427b1f.
86. Op. cit., Gamma 3, 427b14f.
87. Op. cit., Gamma 2, 426b8ff.
88. Op. cit., Gamma 2, 426b10.
89. Op. cit., Gamma 2, 427a18.
90. Op. cit., Gamma 2, 426b8.

ἑκάστη μὲν οὖν αἴσθησις τοῦ ὑποκειμένου αἰσθητοῦ ἐστίν, ὑπάρχουσα ἐν τῷ αἰσθητηρίῳ ᾗ αἰσθητήριον, καὶ κρίνει τὰς τοῦ ὑποκειμένου αἰσθητοῦ διαφοράς, οἷον λευκὸν μὲν καὶ μέλαν ὄψις, γλυκὺ δὲ καὶ πικρὸν γεῦσις.[91]

[Each sensation, inhering in the organ as such, is of the underlying sensible object at hand and discriminates the differences in that underlying sensible object, for instance, white and black for sight, sweet and bitter for taste.]

The differences, present as they are in what can be and is perceived, are offset: white and black, sweet and bitter.

ἐπεὶ δὲ καὶ τὸ λευκὸν καὶ τὸ γλυκὺ καὶ ἕκαστον τῶν αἰσθητῶν πρὸς ἕκαστον κρί-νομεν, τίνι καὶ αἰσθανόμεθα ὅτι διαφέρει; ἀνάγκη δὴ αἰσθήσει.[92]

[Since we discriminate the white and the sweet and each of the sensible objects from one another, we perceive by some other means that they differ; and it is necessary that we do this in perception.]

But we also distinguish white and sweet just as immediately as white and black and, indeed, not in merely thinking, but in having these facts of the matter here. One must not introduce the contrast of thinking and sensibility here. The diversity of these facts of the matter is originally perceived. Aristotle asks: In what manner are we placed in the position of simply grasping this being-other? Apparently, it is necessarily through perceiving. For both are, indeed, αἰσθητά. From this point it becomes clear that it does not suffice to cling to the sense of touch for help. For something quite different is involved.

οὔτε δὴ κεχωρισμένοις ἐνδέχεται κρίνειν ὅτι ἕτερον τὸ γλυκὺ τοῦ λευκοῦ, ἀλλὰ δεῖ ἑνί τινι ἄμφω δῆλα εἶναι.[93]

[And it is also not possible to discriminate by means of something separate that the sweet is different from the white, although it is necessary that both be evident to one thing.]

If I linger in perception, then I have the white as such in seeing, the sweet as such in tasting. How do I come to perceive that both are different? Both what is perceived in tasting and what is perceived in seeing must be obvious here relative to one thing; they must be evident here for one thing as what they are. The same requirement holds for the case in which I see "green" and another sees "red." How does it happen that this fact of the matter—that is, indeed, a fact of the matter—is accessible to us in its unitary character and can be so grasped? In the primordial act of perceiving, in its manner of setting

91. Op. cit., Gamma 2, 426b8ff.
92. Op. cit., Gamma 2, 426b12f.
93. Op. cit., Gamma 2, 426b17ff.

something off against something else, there already is a manner of *speaking* (δεῖ δὲ τὸ ἓν λέγειν ὅτι ἕτερον [one thing must say that they are different]).[94] The speaking is one with the manner of perceiving. Speaking is already at work in this distinguishing. Only on the basis of possible communication can one succeed at all to make a unitary fact of the matter accessible to several individuals in its unitary character. The λόγος is at work here as a *communicating* λόγος. By means of it, the world becomes accessible in its unitary articulation. That is the primordial function that the λόγος has insofar as it communicates. If I make an assertion about a specifically perceived fact of the matter, doing so in the public world of existence, then "com-munication" [*Mit-Teilung*] in the precise sense means making what is spoken of so accessible to someone else that I share it with him [*mit ihm teile*]. Now we both have the same thing. Attention should be paid here to the middle-voiced meaning of ἀποφαίνεσθαι. The "middle voice" means: for oneself, for the one speaking himself, such that for him the fact of the matter can be grasped and retained as perceived.

If the λόγος is still at work here, then it is even more at work where the perceiving proceeds naturally as αἴσθησις κατὰ συμβεβηκός. Here *sameness of time* is required, the temporal existence of speaking along with what is perceived in perceiving. That I can perceive what is in this way [i.e., κατὰ συμβεβηκός] perceivable of the world is grounded in the fact that I am contemporaneous with what is to be perceived (ἐν ἀχωρίστῳ χρόνῳ [in unseparated time]).[95] Temporality is not something optional, if one wants to perceive something in the world. For, in the sense of perceiving itself and of what is perceived, there already is the fact that it is perceived as now existing. If, for example, I give expression to a perception, there lies therein, at least tacitly, that what is perceived is *now* here. Time is not deduced for Aristotle; both time and its sameness are equally retrieved from the fact of the matter itself.[96]

The difference between "white" and "black" in perceiving does not enter in through an argument. It becomes alive in *speech*, and αἴσθησις is a κρίνειν. It has struck some as strange that a λόγος should be found in simple perceiving and some have imposed on Aristotle the view that perceiving is already a judgment. Also, the αἴσθησις is characterized not directly as λόγος but instead as something like a λόγος.[97]

1. Αἴσθησις is an ἀλλοίωσις: "a becoming different."[98] Insofar as a human being, concretely alive in his world, perceives something and the αἴσθησις in the human being is here as a manner of being and comporting himself to his

94. Op. cit., Gamma 2, 426b20f.
95. Op. cit., Gamma 2, 426b28f.
96. See Appendix, Supplement 3 (p. 224).
97. Aristotle, *De anima*, Beta 12, 424a27f.
98. Op. cit., Beta 4, 415b24; Beta 9, 416b34.

world, Aristotle designates αἴσθησις an ἀλλοίωσις. In perceiving, the one perceiving becomes himself someone different insofar as, in perceiving, he now takes up a stance towards his world in a definite manner.

2. Αἴσθησις is a πάσχειν, being affected.[99] The aspect of ἀλλοίωσις is made more precise. By means of the perceiving, something takes place in the one perceiving; in the perceiving something happens precisely to the one who is perceiving.

3. Αἴσθησις is a κρίνειν.[100] In the manner of setting something off against something else, the look is explicitly appropriated. But the αἴσθησις does not leave behind the manner in which it is brought about. To be sure, Aristotle designates the same connection of such κρίνειν as a definite manner of speech (λόγος τις).[101] The λόγος has the function of pointing out the perceived as such.[102] This fact of the matter, namely, that of being different, is appropriated in the specific manner of speaking. Perceiving has a distinctive manner of speaking. It is itself one that speaks of many.

4. Αἴσθησις stands in the middle (μεσότης), if we imagine the multitude of colors.[103] Αἴσθησις must somehow stand in the middle, it must not be fixated on one color, it must be able to look at both sides. Seeing stands in the middle of all colors and thus can comprehend all colors equally well. The middle accordingly concerns the possible type and manner of being able to grasp something. Perceiving's character of being is δύναμις: the ability to perceive, having a definite possibility, being in such a way that there is a possibility of becoming the being that perceives.[104] To have the possibility [of perceiving] constitutes a quite specific manner of being of something living. All the determinations hitherto named are to be understood from the standpoint of this basic determination.[105]

Αἴσθησις is present in the sort of being that has *language.* Whether or not it is vocalized, it is always in some way speaking. Language speaks not only in the course of the perceiving, but even *guides* it; we see *through* language. Insofar as language is taken up in a traditional and not in a primordial sense, it is precisely what *conceals* things, though it is the same language that precisely has the basic function of ostension. In this way it becomes understandable that in the existence of a human being, insofar as he has an *existence,* because he has *language,* the *possibility of deceit and deception* is also present.

99. Op. cit., Beta 5, 416b35; Beta 11, 424a1.
100. Op. cit., Gamma 2, 426b10.
101. Op. cit., Beta 11, 424a27f.
102. Op. cit., Gamma 2, 426b20ff.
103. Op. cit., Beta 11, 424a4.
104. Op. cit., Beta 5, 417a13.
105. See Appendix, Supplement 4 (p. 224).

d) The three aspects of ψεῦδος. The factical existence of speaking
as an authentic source of deception. Circumstantiality and
elusiveness of the world

Aristotle speaks about ψεῦδος in *Metaphysics,* Book V, chapter 29.[106] There
he discusses what is expressed in multiple ways and what is said with a
diversity of meaning. Aristotle distinguishes ψεῦδος in three respects: 1. ὡς
πρᾶγμα ψεῦδος, a false being that concerns the genuine being of πράγματα.[107]
We designate and speak of things as false: "false gold"; 2. λόγος ψευδής: the
λόγος, talk, speech is false;[108] 3. ὡς ἄνθρωπος ψευδής: a human being is
false.[109] Ψεῦδος thus befalls the world, speaking, the specific being in the
world, and entities themselves.

The readiness to set things off from one another is already as such an
ostending (thus, not a judging); an existing entity is to be shown as an existing
entity. The potential that has a specific range of things that can be set off from
one another, indeed, each instance of setting one thing off from another is, in
its tendency to point something out, a means of establishing, of determining
something *as* something. This definite something construed as the one in contrast to another. It is something other on the basis of a specific character of
the subject matter. "White" is in itself something other than "black." In this
manner of setting one thing off from another, the "than" or "as," the "being-
other-than" or "not-being-as," is made explicit, whereby the being-other need
not itself be thematized. The theme is the color itself, grasped with a distinctive emphasis, and set off as such. The *critical "than" or "as"* [*kritische
"als"*] springs forth in the field of perceptibility: blue other than red, blue as
not red. That is not, however, the full "as" [*das volle "als"*], to which, in
addition, the *"as" as demonstrative* [*"als" als aufweisendes*] belongs. This
doubling of the "as"-character is covered up by language. The ἀποφαντικός-
as is evident in all speaking. But in all speaking the critical "as" is also
present.

How is the possibility of ψεῦδος grounded in λόγος itself? Ψεῦδος is the
ostensive presenting of something as something. Hence, it is more than merely
concealing something without presenting it as something other than it is. In
what respect can a *matter* [*Sache,* πρᾶγμα] be *false* with respect to its being
as a matter?

τὸ ψεῦδος λέγεται ἄλλον μὲν τρόπον ὡς πρᾶγμα ψεῦδος, καὶ τούτου τὸ μὲν τῷ μὴ
συγκεῖσθαι ἢ ἀδύνατον εἶναι συντεθῆναι, ὥσπερ λέγεται τὸ τὴν διάμετρον εἶναι

106. Aristotle, *Metaphysica*, Delta 29, 1024b17–1025a13.
107. Op. cit., Delta 29, 1024b17f.
108. Op. cit., Delta 29, 1024b26.
109. Op. cit., Delta 29, 1025a2.

σύμμετρον ἢ τὸ σὲ καθῆσθαι. τούτων γὰρ ψεῦδος τὸ μὲν αἰεί, τὸ δὲ ποτέ. οὕτω γὰρ οὐκ ὄντα ταῦτα.[110]

[One meaning of the "false" is the false thing and of this, one sense is in not being together or not being able to be together, as in the case of the diagonal being commensurable or of you sitting. For of these one is always false, the other only sometimes and, in this way, they are not beings.]

1. One possibility of being false lies in the fact that the specific content of characters does not allow them to be brought together on the basis of the states of affairs in which they figure.

τὰ δὲ ὅσα ἐστὶ μὲν ὄντα, πέφυκε μέντοι φαίνεσθαι ἢ μὴ οἷά ἐστιν ἢ ἃ μή ἐστιν, οἷον ἡ σκιαγραφία καὶ τὰ ἐνύπνια. ταῦτα γὰρ ἔστι μέν τι, ἀλλ᾽ οὐχ ὧν ἐμποιεῖ τὴν φαντασίαν. πράγματα μὲν οὖν ψευδῆ οὕτω λέγεται, ἢ τῷ μὴ εἶναι αὐτά, ἢ τῷ τὴν ἀπ᾽ αὐτῶν φαντασίαν μὴ ὄντος εἶναι.[111]

[The second sense concerns those things which, though existing, appear by nature to be either something other than they are or things which do not exist, for instance, a sketch or a dream. For these things are something but not the things of which they produce an appearance. Thus, things are called false if they do not exist or if the appearance coming from them is of something that does not exist.]

2. There are entities that, in their specific manner of being, have the peculiarity of presenting themselves as something that they are not or as characterized in a way that they are not. Thus, here the possibility of deception lies not primarily in a wrong conception, but in the entity itself.

How then does it happen that there can be talk of a ψεῦδος in this case where the fact of the matter designated as false does not exist at all? How is the possibility of a ψεῦδος supposed to obtain here where the relevant fact of the matter in no way exists? How does language come to characterize a non-being as a false being? An example of this is the way the diagonal of a square can be presented by a definite proportion. The facts of the matter initially give the impression that they are measurable. In what we encounter, there is a definite expectation that it has its being in this or that respect on the basis of something in the matter at hand. Yet, as soon as it becomes evident by demonstration that such existence is impossible, this character is taken to characterize its being.

Each of the three meanings of ψεῦδος views a fact of the matter in a definite respect but in such a way that the others are also considered. Thus the πρᾶγμα ψευδές points here to the λόγος ψευδής.

---

110. Op. cit., Delta 29, 1024b17ff.
111. Op. cit., Delta 29, 1024b21ff.

ἑκάστου δὲ λόγος ἔστι μὲν ὡς εἷς, ὁ τοῦ τί ἦν εἶναι, ἔστι δ᾽ ὡς πολλοί, ἐπεὶ ταὐτό πως αὐτὸ καὶ αὐτὸ πεπονθός, οἷον Σωκράτης καὶ Σωκράτης μουσικός.¹¹²

[The logos of each thing is, on the one hand, one (the "what it was to be" of it) and, on the other hand, many since the thing itself and the thing affected are the same somehow, such as Socrates and a musical Socrates.]

For each existing entity as such, there is a single λόγος in terms of which I can speak of the subject matter itself in its being, ὁρισμός. It is the way of speaking of a subject matter by means of which it is pressed into the boundaries of its being and determined. Then there are λόγοι by means of which I can speak of the subject matters in many respects.¹¹³ We see things in terms of the circumstances (αὐτὸ πεπονθός) in which we have something to do with them. This *circumstantial character* of the state of affairs allows for many λόγοι that speak of them. ὁ δὲ ψευδὴς λόγος οὐδενός ἐστιν ἁπλῶς λόγος [The false logos is simply the logos of nothing].¹¹⁴ They are then the sort of λόγοι by which I speak of a subject matter in such a way that what I say of it is something that I get not from it alone but in regard to something else with which I am already acquainted. These various regards themselves, in terms of which I can speak of a subject matter in multiple ways, lie outside the subject matter itself. What I look towards is something that I must draw into consideration, if I am determining the matter. Such a λόγος is never simple. The simple λόγος is that by means of which I determine the subject matter itself; I do not step away from it.¹¹⁵ The *second* meaning of ψεῦδος is the λόγος ψευδής. Aristotle works here with a distinction to the effect that there is a single manner of addressing each entity, when it is taken in its factual content and in its manner of being: the ὁρισμός. Along with this single λόγος, fitted to the entity, there is an array of free-floating λόγοι. This accounts for the fact that there is such a thing as *deception*. He uses the occasion to single out a much-discussed question of the tradition, namely, that there can be no contradiction if there is only one specific manner of speaking of each entity. Insofar as there are only λόγοι that respectively apply to their subject matter, there is no contradiction. Contradiction transpires only in a quite specific dimension, not where it is about the subject matter itself, but instead where one talks around it.

ἔστι δ᾽ ἕκαστον λέγειν οὐ μόνον τῷ αὐτοῦ λόγῳ, ἀλλὰ καὶ τῷ ἑτέρου, ψευδῶς μὲν καὶ παντελῶς, ἔστι δ᾽ ὡς καὶ ἀληθῶς, ὥσπερ τὰ ὀκτὼ διπλάσια τῷ τῆς δυάδος λόγῳ.¹¹⁶

112. Op. cit., Delta 29, 1024b29ff.
113. Op. cit., Delta 29, 1024b30.
114. Op. cit., Delta 29, 1024b31f.
115. Op. cit., Delta 29, 1024b32.
116. Op. cit., Delta 29, 1024b35ff.

[It is possible to speak of each thing not only according to its logos, but according
to another logos, sometimes quite falsely, but other times truthfully, for instance,
speaking of eight as a double according to the logos of two.]

It is possible to address any particular existing entity, not only through the
manner in which it is itself accessible, but in any respect regarding other
entities. The many λόγοι generally deceive, one can say; but it can also be the
case that one is on target.

The third meaning of ψεῦδος, as Aristotle speaks of it, is the ἄνθρωπος
ψευδής [the false human being] (τὰ μὲν οὖν οὕτω λέγεται ψευδῆ, ἄνθρωπος δὲ
ψευδὴς ὁ εὐχερὴς καὶ προαιρετικὸς τῶν τοιούτων λόγων . . . [these things, then,
are called false in this way, a human being is called false who readily and
deliberately makes such logoi]),[117] and this is the προαιρετικὸς, someone who
resolves to conceal the state of affairs, such that it is inherent in his existence,
someone who instills such ways of talking in others. His manner of behaving
is such that on principle he misleads those with whom he speaks.

How are the three meanings of ψεῦδος dependent upon one another? To
answer this question, let us consider the concrete λόγος of a human being
who lives in a world, the πράγματα of which can be spoken of as ψεῦδος. We
transpose the meaning of ψεῦδος into the sphere of *factical existence*. A human being, in speaking about the existent world such as he encounters it, can
lie. Πρᾶγμα, the human being, and the λόγος are the *three respects* that speak
to a *distinctive, fundamental phenomenon* [*Grundphänomen*] that was not seen
by Aristotle. Let us take the meaning of ψεῦδος in this primordial sense and
do so in order, from this vantage point, to render intelligible the fact that
people designate things falsely. We want to understand how it comes to pass
that things are designated in this way. For the understanding of the analysis,
it is necessary to hold fast to one fact of the matter [*Tatbestand*]. *The factical
existence of speaking as such, insofar as it is here and solely insofar as it is
here as speaking, is the genuine source of deception.* That is to say, the existence of speaking bears in itself the possibility of deception. The lie lies in
the facticity of language [*Faktizität der Sprache*].

Let us now attempt—insofar as it is possible—to get closer to what the
facticity of speaking is. It takes place within the sphere of human beings
existing in a world they share. Speaking as such, the factical character of
speaking, is conceived from the outset as follows: *something* is spoken about.
This speaking-here-and-now is taken in the sense that it has the tendency to
say something; it stands in public display. In this way, speaking is here, from
the outset, with the existence of human beings who speak and it is taken,
from the outset, as an ostension of something. It makes the natural and vital

117. Op. cit., Delta 29, 1025a1ff.

claim of saying something. Solely by virtue of the fact of vocalization, something is announced and the possibility thereby presents itself of *hiding* something in existence, insofar as I say something other than I am thinking but what I say presents it other than it is here. The facticity of lying lies in this basic possibility of speaking. A mendacious person is capable of explicitly resolving to hide. He speaks in such a way that what he says hides the fact of the matter about which he is making an assertion. Here the remarkable fact presents itself that someone who lies must be acquainted with precisely the fact of the matter about which he is making an assertion. Only if I am acquainted with the fact of the matter, am I in the position to lie properly.

It is not necessary that this explicit tendency of a life of hiding things is present. One can point to a way of living that does not live in the tendency to conceal objects but instead only talks so in that direction in public. This *talking-in-that-direction* deceives simply by virtue of the fact of talking itself. The real opposite to talking is not talking falsely, deceptive talking, but remaining silent. The tendency explicitly to deceive can recede but in such a way that the talk, more or less consciously, is carried on in a state of unfamiliarity with the subject matters. That is the specific manner of articulating things by means of several λόγοι. The possibility of deception lies here also in the sort of utterance that is at work in a *faulty seeing* where the latter is motivated, not by a carelessness in observing, but by the manner in which the existing entity lives and encounters the world itself. The talk can be such that it has the positive tendency to present facts of the matter as they actually are; but it speaks within the context of a faulty way of seeing, the facts of the matter are not genuinely appropriated. By means of language itself we live in a completely determinate conception of things. (Nietzsche: "Every word is a prejudice."[118]) We will make clear what the sources are from which deception and talk's possibilities of deception can spring. It is possible to take the existing world in diverse respects.

Next to the circumstantial character of talking, a further motive for the fact that we see in a faulty way or do not always speak of the facts of the matter as such lies in the manner of the world's being that I designate its *elusiveness,* namely, that the facts are here in an utterly peculiar character of not being here. The elusiveness is something that lies in the being of the world itself, the phenomena of which include the daylight and darkness with which we have become acquainted. That there is fog, for example, is not some insignificant fact that one can draw upon as an example at some point in episte-

---

118. F. Nietzsche, *Menschliches, Allzumenschliches. Ein Buch für freie Geister.* [Human, All Too Human. A Book for Free Spirits.] Zweiter Band [Second volume]. In: *Nietzsche's Werke* (Großoktav). Erste Abteilung, Bd. III [First division, volume three] (Stuttgart 1921). Zweite Abtheilung: Der Wanderer und sein Schatten, [Second division: The wanderer and his shadow,] Aphorismus 55, S. 231.

28		Introduction to Phenomenological Research

mological investigations. Elusiveness is a feature proper to the existing world as existing. Things can elude us and that is not to say they disappear. The elusiveness of things comes to life by virtue of the fact that we encounter them circumstantially. We do not see the things as subject matters in the sense that they are an object of a scientific investigation. This existence of things is much richer and affords much more fluctuating possibilities than have been thematically prepared. Because the world in its riches is only present in the respective concreteness of living, the elusiveness is much more encompassing and, with it, the *possibility of deception* is at hand. The more concretely I am in the world, the more genuine the existence of deception.

But how then does it happen that one designates the things themselves as a deception? Hitherto we have only stressed that the deceiving lies in speaking. How does it come about that existing things are designated as false? Why are we not satisfied with speaking of the nonexisting as nonexisting? Why do we say here, with an excess of meaning, "false"? If someone says: "The commensurability of the diagonals with a square's side does not exist; this being is false," one must not take such a sentence in isolation. Instead one has to take it in the context from which it is drawn. Mostly, these sides are generally known to be measurable; they are regarded as measurable and give this impression. Yet in fact they are not at all. This, their not-being that awakens the definite impression, is designated as false. This specific impression that such objects make is disappointed. Thus, it is evident that also this use of the expression ψεῦδος in regard to things (insofar as they do not exist) is grounded in the unitary context of which we are speaking. We must also see these things in a context. Already in the process of articulating, insofar as speaking has the tendency to be ostensive, there is the impression that there is something of the sort within a field where there is something measurable. Yet in this case of speaking the fact is that the speaking is not ostending, pointing out an entity. Instead it is of the sort that only opines that about which it speaks. It means the facts of the matter merely as such. Here is the phenomenon of nominalization and neutralization in Husserl's sense.[119] We can articulate sentences as merely opined or meant. Insofar as talk of this sort is directed at the impression closest at hand, what it says is false. It is genuinely deceiving.

Here you see the *difference* between *deceit* and *dream*. A dream has some existence on the basis of which it deceives. The λόγος as apophantic λόγος is, if taken in its factical existence, the sort of thing that contains within itself the possibility of deception. Insofar as λόγος can characterize a human being's

---

119. E. Husserl, *Ideen zu einer reinen Phänomenologie und phänomenologischen Philosophie, Erstes Buch: Allgemeine Einführung in die reine Phänomenologie.* Zweiter unveränderter Abdruck. [Ideas for a Pure Phenomenology and Phenomenological Philosophy, First Book: General Introduction into Pure Phenomenology, second, unaltered printing.] (Halle an der Saale 1922), S. 248 and S. 222. (Hereafter: *Ideen I.*)

existence, it pervades a human being's entire dealings with his world, all seeing, interpreting, articulating.

e) Speaking and the world in its possibilities of deception. The shift of the meaning of φαινόμενον into illusion

This λόγος that bears within itself the fundamental possibility of deception accounts for the fact that all perceiving is in danger of being mistaken insofar as it is dominated by *language*. That is to say: φαινόμενα, as existing in the factical world, are that over against which a human being mostly finds himself mistaken. In other words, what at first only presents itself, doing so in that straightforward manner, is now something that only appears so, something that *seems [scheint]* so. It is no accident that for Aristotle, φαινόμενα, as the basis for further research, means the existing entities themselves, but can also mean: "what only appears so" (φαινόμενον ἀγαθόν [what appears good]).[120] This *shift of the meaning* of the word φαινόμενον—that first means "the existing entity itself showing itself" and then means "what only appears so," thus not actually existing—this shift of meaning, insofar as it is in the sphere of dealing with the world, points to the basic fact that in existence itself error and deception are interwoven in a completely fundamental way and do not merely surface in the world as some defective property that one has to overcome.

Insofar as *speaking* exists as vocalizing, it is *capable of deceiving*. Indeed, taken as existing in a *world* that *in its specific character of being* presents *possibilities of deception,* speaking is capable of deception in the sense that in the world's existence as a whole there is an inner connection that is deception's possibility of being. Insofar as speaking is here in the world, it stands in a definite regard that is taken without any further reflection at all. Human existence is taken here in this respect, namely, that by means of speaking something is said. Speaking in itself makes a claim to communicate. Now, speaking so exists that the one speaking has various possibilities of hiding himself in speaking as such: 1. the possibility expressed, in which the one who is speaking speaks with the explicit tendency to lie; 2. the possibility such that one intends, through speaking, to pretend that the speaking involves some sort of acquaintance with the subject matter. Even where a tendency to the opposite of lying is present, the possibility exists of deceiving through speaking and words.

This *speaking* with its *possibilities of deception* stands as such in a *world* which presents *possibilities of deception* of its own. The world is capable of deceiving, first, by virtue of its circumstantial character and the fact that the

---

120. Aristotle, *De anima,* Gamma 10, 433a28f.

objects with which we deal are present for us concretely in a respective setting so that an assortment of possible ways of discussing them presents itself. The world is capable of deceiving, second, by virtue of its elusive character, obscured by fog, darkness, and the like. Facts of the matter of this sort are inherent in the manner of being of the world itself. There are, in addition, possibilities of being that deceive on the basis of their specific being, such as *dreams* and so forth. For speaking, furthermore, the danger exists that it is here with other speaking, that it becomes a form of parroting [*Nachsprechen*], that it is a manner of speaking along [*Mitsprechen*], a peculiar dominance that language exercises insofar as it suppresses dealing with the subject matters. In this way, an *abundant interweaving of possibilities of deception* becomes evident *as a possibility of being, interwoven with the existence of speaking and the existence of the world*. Let us note that speaking is precisely what hides the subject matter. Thus, the existing world is hidden and encountered in a specific manner of passing itself off, insofar as speaking and opinions about things factically guide our access to what is first here. Insofar then as the world exists with this possibility of showing itself, this possibility is inverted into the opposite: to pass itself off as something. The *appearing of something* in the original sense of showing itself becomes the *illusion* of it. It is important, for substantive reasons, to understand this possibility of the shift of the meaning of the term φαινόμενον into the meaning of something that only appears so.

f) Σύνθεσις and διαίρεσις as the realm of the possibilities of the true and the false[121]

It remains for us simply to ascertain the extent to which Aristotle was explicitly aware of the fact that the field of deception is where things are given in terms of a specific conception, that there are no grounds for the possibility of deception where things are approached straightforwardly, but instead where the world here has the character of being such-and-such. περὶ γὰρ σύνθεσιν καὶ διαίρεσίν ἐστι τὸ ψεῦδός τε καὶ τὸ ἀληθές [For the false and the true are about synthesis and division].[122] In a sphere where there is something such as *being-together* and *being-taken-apart,* there are *both* the true *and* the false.

ἡ μὲν γὰρ αἴσθησις τῶν ἰδίων ἀεὶ ἀληθής, καὶ πᾶσιν ὑπάρχει τοῖς ζῴοις, διανοεῖσθαι δ' ἐνδέχεται καὶ ψευδῶς, καὶ οὐδενὶ ὑπάρχει ᾧ μὴ καὶ λόγος.[123]

[For the perception of the special perceptible is always true and proper to all animals. But it is possible to think also falsely and this is not proper to anything without logos.]

121. See, in addition, the Appendix, Supplement 5 (p. 225).
122. Aristotle, *De interpretatione*, 1, 16a12f.
123. Aristotle, *De anima*, Gamma 3, 427b11ff.

Perceiving of the specific, proper facts of the matter is always such that it presents the perceived in itself. The ψεῦδος is only on hand where there are λόγοι (διανοεῖσθαι δ' ἐνδέχεται καὶ ψευδῶς [but it is possible to think also falsely]).[124] A connection exists between the necessity of the world's constitution as determined by a manifold of possible perspectives and the possibility of deception. The one speaking always speaks to something in a certain respect. Purely to see is, like the mere naming of something, to approach something straightforwardly. I allow it to remain simply as given. I see the color in the sense of taking something straightforwardly. ὅταν δὲ ἡδὺ ἢ λυπηρόν[125]— αἴσθησις: that is to say, if, by contrast, we perceive something delightful or painful, then the perceiving is a speaking that conceives the things *as* something (κατάφασις or ἀπόφασις). When it encounters something delightful, perceiving is sudden. The perceiving and the taking delight by seeing are thereby one. This unitary perceiving is in the middle here (τῇ μεσότητι [in the mean]).[126] Insofar as *this* perceiving is the most primordial, insofar as the things of the world are πρακτά, πράγματα [practical things, affairs] the natural access is a ἥδεσθαι or λυπεῖσθαι [pleasurable or painful].[127] As long as one clings to certain types of experiences, to psychology and so forth, one does not see these facts.

124. Op. cit., Gamma 3, 427b13.
125. Op. cit., Gamma 6, 431a9.
126. Op. cit., Gamma 6, 431a11.
127. Op. cit., Gamma 6, 431a10.

Chapter Two

Present-day phenomenology in Husserl's self-interpretation

§ 3. Recapitulation of the facts of the matter gathered from the interpretation of Aristotle. Anticipation of the predominance of care about the idea of certainty and evidence over freeing up possibilities of encountering fundamental facts of the matter

To *recapitulate* the *result* of our analysis, it must be said that we have established: 1. specific *facts of the matter* that point to the existence of the world and the existence of human life. The state of the matter has led us to a phenomenological characterization of the world and to a specific orientation of the one existing [*Daseiendem*] and it has done this in the sense of a) a distinctive sort of being that shows itself in itself, and b) the λόγος-character as an existing possibility of human life. There is a connection here insofar as the λόγος qua apophantic has the possibility of pointing out what shows itself. These facts of the matter, the existence of the world and of life, became so obvious that certain possibilities became apparent in them. 2. The existence of the world can abruptly turn around into something self-dissimulating, the λόγος can be of the sort that disguises existence. This connection reveals a fate that resides in existence itself, the fact that present there with its being is the possibility of deception and lies.

The aim of the interpretation up to this point has not been to make the development of a term [i.e., "phenomenology"] intelligible in some anecdotal form. The aim was instead to awaken interest in the matter, indeed, in such a way that the direction in which things were heading did not become transparent at first. We have to learn how to read and listen in the manner of waiting.

The background of the interpretation continues to be rooted in the matter at hand insofar as its concern is to make intelligible what is today known under the rubric "phenomenology." That can only mean: making intelligible the sort of *matters* treated in this discipline—what sort of matters present-day phenomenology claims to work on. In order to obtain this sorting, we need a *horizon of matters*. Against this horizon we will have to decide on the extent to which the *facts of the matter of present-day phenomenology* are still connected with what *we* have pointed out about the matter.

In order from the outset to characterize the development in which Aristotle shaped the basic constants of philosophical research, allow me to say the following. Subsequent developments in establishing the facts of the matter of philosophy and the motivation behind the various paths on which these facts were worked on have been *guided by the predominance of an empty and thereby fantastic idea of certainty and evidence*. This predominance of a specific idea of evidence predominates *over* every *genuine effort to free up the possibility of encountering the genuine matters of philosophy*. *Care about* a specific, *absolute knowledge*, taken purely as an idea, predominates over every question about the matters that are decisive. That is to say, the *entire development of philosophy reverses itself*. Beginnings of this development arc already present in Aristotle and the Greeks and they are not accidental, e.g., the notion that the existence of the world as it presents itself is taken to be the specific world of illusion, so that in the future all decisive questions of philosophy are gathered purely from the idea of securing an absolute certainty, together with the tendency to surmount the existence of the world as something contingent. Let us add the observation that this development stems, not from a science's attempts to procure its distinctive manner of access to its subject matter, but instead from an idea that existence fabricates for itself, to a certain extent from an intelligence that has gone crazy.

Through the interpretation of the components of the term "phenomenology," we were confronted by quite definite facts of the matter of existence: the *world's being* and life as *being in a world*. In these two respects we saw at once that the world's being has the character of *showing itself* and that life's being entails a basic possibility of *speaking* about existence in such a way that being *is pointed out* by means of speech. The world's being and life's being have a quite *specific connection* with one another, thanks to *speaking's being*. The existence of the world in showing-itself in this way can turn around into a manner of *presenting-itself-as* something else. *Life is, in itself, capable of concealing the existing world*. Thus, both existence's possibilities and life's possibilities reveal existence to be endangered in a specific way, one that we expressed by saying that existence bears in itself the possibilities of deception and lies.

If we cling solely to the results of the analysis without reference to the theme "phenomenology," then we seem to have made no progress, but instead to be abruptly confronted with specific facts of the matter. However, to understand the connection, i.e., to understand the being and character of the matter that *phenomenology* works on, an orientation to a *horizon of the matter* is needed. I gave a clue for considering an utterly peculiar *reversal*. The predominance of care about the idea of an empty and thus fantastic certainty and evidence, prior to every attempt to free up the possibility of an encounter with specific, fundamental facts of the matter has led to shunting aside what was *originally* a *theme* of the consideration. Indeed, it has led to shunting it so much to the side that not only was the *thematic field* lost sight of but, what is worse, the choice of perspective was not guided by a certain *appropriation of the matters* at hand but instead by a *definite idea of science*—that the idea of a definite sort of knowledge determines the theme rather than, vice versa, that a definite composition of the matter indicates the possibilities of working on it scientifically.

By this means, a traditional idea of the introduction into science of any sort is fended off. [For this traditional idea,] it is not a matter of getting some empty cognizance of what the "object," what the "method" of the science in question is. The method is supposed to emerge during the critical confrontation with the subject matters. The traditional idea of determining and developing a research project works toward determining the "object": the object is such and such, this specific domain of science is [accordingly] worked on by means of specific methods. This sort of orientation is disregarded here.

But if we look closer and ask what we have gained up to this point in regard to the facts of the matter, something surprising presents itself. We have regarded existence in view of a peculiar sort of *self-showing*. We have learned nothing about the character of its *content* but instead have seemingly laid down an empty determination. We have not gathered what an object is. We have learned of a determination regarding *existence*, one that characterizes it in its *how*: *how it shows itself in itself* and *how*, based on this, *it hides itself*. It is just the same with the characterization of the λόγος. We have merely learned of the λόγος a specific, already characterized *manner* of its *being*, that of one time *pointing out* existence *itself*, then *disguising* it. This existence was not determined in terms of its content in the sense of a natural being or of an historical reality but instead in a seemingly empty way: only *how it exists*. By having emphasized these characteristic determinations of existence (namely, that what matters is *how* it exists), we have, in the interpretation, already gone beyond what was comprehensible to the Greeks in the context of their examination of existence.

If we compare this *how-character* [*Wie-Charakter*] of existence with others that the Greeks knew, then we see that they are concerned with *determinations of what* things are [*Was-Bestimmungen*]. There are various respects in which existence is characterized, respects rooted in the matter at hand: 1. Πράγματα, the things which "one" [*"man"*] has to deal with. The entity is accordingly addressed in this respect.—2. Χρήματα, the things insofar as they are used for needs that the existence of the world itself motivates and requires.—3. Ποιού-μενα, the things in the world that are produced, that are made and are available as ἔργα [devices] for 1. and 2.—4. Φυσικά, the existing things of the world that are not produced but instead are in themselves, *coming to be* on the basis of their specific being but capable at the same time of being that out of which something can be produced (wood, iron) and thus having a relation to 3.—5. Μαθήματα, the sort of entities that have the specific character of being able to be learned and concerning which there is a kind of knowing that can be communicated to everyone without their thereby having a practical relation to matters.—6. Within each of these characterizations and the being named by them, there are paradigmatic things which have the peculiar character of being that is designated οὐσία. However, in order to see the connection of οὐσία and the other concepts of being, it should be noted that this seemingly so abstract philosophical concept stands for possessions, property, what is lying around me at home, the "homestead" [*"Anwesen"*].

In *our* interpretation we did not encounter these categories of the world. We heard only of φαινόμενα. Οὐσία provides the basic character of the entity insofar as it is: *presence* [*Anwesenheit*]. It is also meant, implicitly, in the concepts of "thing" that have been noted. The *nearest sort of encounter* of the entity yields the φαινόμενα in terms of the formal *how-character* of that sort of encounter. Φαινόμενα then is precisely the being addressed in all these characters, but is this being only in *the* respect of *showing itself*. We have gathered this characteristic determination from the interpretation and established it for our further consideration. The closest sort of encounter of entities and the unfiltered grasp of them in this sort of encounter must in some way be *phenomenologically* decisive.

§ 4. Consciousness as the theme of present-day phenomenology

We now have to pose the question: What is the *theme* or the *context of being, pertaining to the subject matter*, that is the object of *the* research that *today* is designated *phenomenology*? At the start allow me to give an utterly formal determination of it in connection with the position that Husserl has advanced farthest up to now in the *Ideas to a Pure Phenomenology and Phenomenological Philosophy*. According to this text, phenomenology is the *descriptive eidetic science of transcendentally pure consciousness.*[1] This determination is important for us simply as an indication that *consciousness* is the theme examined in phenomenology. For us the question arises: How does what is designated as consciousness come to enjoy the peculiar prerogative of providing the theme of a fundamental science such as phenomenology claims to be? Are we in a position to make this peculiar prerogative intelligible? To make it intelligible on the basis of what we have become acquainted with up to now? And to do so in such a way that we show that the field of being that is named "consciousness" does not come to enjoy this position of priority accidentally or arbitrarily but instead that this prerogative of it is grounded in distinctive *possibilities* that *existence* bears within itself and that are already

1. Cf. E. Husserl, *Ideen I* [Ideas I], 139.

prefigured in Greek philosophy? If we succeed in demonstrating this, then we will see that these transformations [*Wandlungen*] themselves are grounded and motivated in our existence itself, and that the history that offers us such possibilities and transformations is not something contingent and remote that lies behind us and that we occasionally draw upon to illustrate our opinions. We will see, instead, that in *history's transformations* we encounter nothing other than *our own existence*.

For that reason, the present consideration is not an historical narration but a concrete look at quite *definite possibilities of our own existence*. If these are set forth and seen together with the aforementioned, we acquire with it the basis for a *fundamental differentiation* to be made at the beginning of our investigation.

a) Greek philosophy without a concept of consciousness

How does it become understandable that something like *consciousness* is philosophy's theme? This question becomes fundamental for us the moment we remind ourselves that the Greeks are unacquainted with consciousness or anything like consciousness. In Greek philosophy there is no concept of consciousness. At the same time, to be sure, it must be said that what, among other things, is conceived under *today's* specific, phenomenological concepts of consciousness is already found precisely among the Greeks. In the course of the analysis of perceiving, for example, Aristotle saw that we co-perceive a seeing itself as being [*Seiendes*]. We have an αἴσθησις [perception] of seeing.[2] He asks himself what kind of perceiving it is that we perceive the seeing and the like with. So, too, in the case of νόησις, the question arises: Does the thinking [*Vermeinen*] that thinks the perceiving have the same character of being? Both questions are left undecided. From the standpoint of the specific facts of the matter of research today, we can call this a much more fundamental insight into this context than the rash decision underlying the orientation of modern psychology, namely, that the perception of seeing, that of thinking, and so forth are a matter of one and the same thing, the inner perception.[3] However one intends to decide these things, perceiving how one conducts oneself has become a theme of the examination. What is perceived here should not be interpreted as an experience or mental existence in the modern sense. In spite of this fact, later Greek philosophy displays an acquaintance with what is today designated "consciousness" or "self-consciousness"—an acquaintance not on the path of philosophical reflection,

2. Aristotle, *De anima*, Gamma 2, 425b12ff.
3. See the Appendix, Supplement 6 (p. 227).

but drawn instead from the natural experience of what we today call "conscience" (συνείδεσις) in a very accentuated sense. Thus, it enters into the Christian consciousness of life and it undergoes a further explication in theology. But what was so designated is in no way an object of consideration. That something like consciousness would become a theme of an investigation is out of the question for the Greek and Christian consciousness.

b) Phenomenology's breakthrough in Husserl's *Logical Investigations*
and their basic tendency

In order to understand the thematic field's turnaround from *the entity that the world is* to the *entity that is consciousness of it*, it is necessary to sketch the features of the end-station, i.e., present-day phenomenology, as it becomes necessary for our examination. The research that we designate "phenomenology" appeared for the first time under the explicit title *Logical Investigations*.[4] These investigations move within the framework of a traditional discipline called "logic." From a purely personal standpoint, these themes were obvious ones for Husserl since he was driven from mathematical investigations to logical considerations in an effort to understand the distinctiveness of mathematical *thinking*. The *Logical Investigations* are not motivated by the ambition of working out anything like a new textbook in logic. Instead, the principal purpose is *to make the objects with which logic is preoccupied into the theme for once in such a way that research related to this is put into a position of being able actually to work on subject matters—that the specific objects of this discipline* are brought *to a specific intuition that identifies them*. "Intuition" here means simply: to make present to oneself the object in itself, just as it presents itself. The basic tendency of these *Logical Investigations* is to make this "presentation" one that is methodically secured. Such a tendency could only be genuinely effective through research that *discloses the subject matter*. The "results" of these investigations are so replete that they have born fruit in contemporary philosophy in a way that can no longer be measured today. Even the very ones "stimulated" by the investigations are only slightly

---

4. E. Husserl, *Logische Untersuchungen*. Erster Band: Prolegomena zur reinen Logik. Dritte, unveränderte Auflage (Halle a. d. S. 1922). Zweiter Band: Untersuchungen zur Phänomenologie und Theorie der Erkenntnis. I. Teil (I.–V. Logische Untersuchung). Dritte unveränderte Auflage. Halle a.d.S. 1922. Zweiter Band, II. Teil: (VI. Logische Untersuchung): Elemente einer phänomenologischen Aufklärung der Erkenntnis. Dritte, unveränderte Auflage. Halle a.d. S. 1922. [Logical Investigations. First volume: Prolegomena to Pure Logic. Third, unchanged printing (Halle an der Saale, 1922). Second volume: Investigations towards the Phenomenology and Theory of Knowledge. First part: (First–Fifth Logical Investigation). Third, unchanged printing (Halle an der Salle, 1922). Second volume, second part: (Sixth Logical Investigation): Elements of a phenomenological clarification of knowledge. Third, unchanged printing (Halle an der Saale, 1922). See Editor's Afterword, p. 249.]

conscious of the extent of their effect. The entire course of our examination starts from the *prospect of getting at the matters themselves*, working its way through a merely verbal knowledge to the things.

c) The orientation of Greek philosophy and the question of its reversal

How then does it come to this, that *consciousness* establishes itself as the field of research? From the definition of phenomenology, it follows that consciousness, subject to a quite specific *purification* [or cleaning: *Reinigung*], becomes the object of philosophy. Consciousness does not come to be a possible theme for research without further ado. What motives are to be given for this need to purify consciousness in order for it to become the possible object of a fundamental science? There are two questions that have to be answered: 1. How does it come about that *consciousness* is set up as the theme? and, 2. How does it come about that it is *in need of a purification*?

In order to understand the peculiarity of this examination, we must constantly keep in mind what we gathered in connection with the Aristotle-interpretation. Through enumeration of certain categories in terms of which the Greeks characterized being, we should have gained a first look at what motivations were decisive for them in their research. These various categories of being undergo a distinctive and principal examination in the philosophical work of the Greeks. From the type of analysis of the being that is thus addressed, we necessarily come closer to *Greek philosophy's orientation*. We want to see what of it remains at work in later philosophy.

The manifoldness of entities is first divided by the Greeks into the sort of entity that always is and the sort of entity that can also be otherwise. For this division it is characteristic that it is a matter of the entire domain of entities. This basic division is, for its part, at work in the *four basic determinations of being*, determinations that for Aristotle do not somehow lie in advance in a system but instead are vital motivations in which the research moves:

1. τὸ ὄν τῶν κατηγοριῶν [the categories' being];
2. τὸ ὄν δυνάμει–ἐνεργείᾳ [potentiality's being–actuality's being];
3. τὸ ὄν κατὰ συμβεβηκός [the being of what is attendant to something else];
4. τὸ ὄν ὡς ἀληθές [the being as true].[5]

As for 1., it is conveyed by the view taken toward the λόγος. Κατηγορεῖν [to prove] is a stronger form of λέγειν [to say]: to demonstrate something with certitude to someone. The category works in constant orientation to that possibility of existing that is characterized as speech, a possibility in which the

---

5. Aristotle, *Metaphysica*, Epsilon 2, 1026a33ff.

world existing around it is "here" ["da"]. As for 2., it is drawn from a specific comprehension of *life* itself insofar as "being-alive" means being-a-possibility. Both [potentiality and actuality] only refer to life as existence in a world. "Life" is itself thereby conceived as a worldly happening [*weltlich Vorkommendes*] that has the peculiarity of being *authentic* in its being-present-as-finished [*in seinem Fertig-anwesend-sein*]. In Greek ontology, which is an ontology of the "world," it is precisely "life" (as being in the world) that furnishes the distinguishing characters. As for 3., it encompasses both, namely, the existence of the world and of life. The [Greeks'] gaze rests upon circumstantial aspects insofar as precisely these aspects make up the peculiar character of being. As for 4., it concerns a basic phenomenon of existence that, for the Greeks, is not further characterized. Nevertheless, the Greeks were ahead of present-day epistemology on this point. It arose in view of the peculiar feature that the world is "here" ["da"]—that an entity is in a world, a world which is "here," opened up.

Thus we see that, on the whole, all four directions are drawn from the fact of the matter of *being in the world*. Nothing about consciousness surfaces, although there is in Aristotle something like a treatise Περὶ ψυχῆς [*On the soul*]. How does it come to a *reversal* so radical that what is called "consciousness" comes to be the theme of all philosophy?

§ 5. *The theme of "consciousness" in the* Logical Investigations

a) The *Logical Investigations* between a traditional orientation and primordial questioning

Let us first take an external approach in order to see how the work initially appears. In one respect, what is undertaken in the *Logical Investigations* is entirely *traditional*; in another respect, something *primordial* and utterly remarkable lies beneath its surface. The *Logical Investigations* are intended to be the kind of preparatory labors that for once first seek to bring the object of this discipline into view, just as if it appeared that sciences devoid of any object at all were being pursued. Not only does this appear to be the case; *it is the case* that merely verbal concepts are clung to and exchanged for one another. What, then, is science?

Alongside this inquiry, however, much of the orientation here is traditional. There were powerful tendencies in philosophy at that time to give logic and epistemology a scientific foundation by building them onto a psychology. Insofar as the first work of phenomenology is carried out partly in connection with these tendencies, partly in critique of them, a specific traditional orientation is present. But the distinctive feature of the *Logical Investigations* lies in the way in which a foundation for logic is sought, namely, by aiming to make present to oneself a fact of the matter in which all of logic's objects can be found and investigated, in such a way that logic would have a completely determinate milieu in which to move. Psychology's field of objects at the time was not the "soul" and certainly not the ontological determination of "soul" relative to the being of something living. Instead, its field of objects was *consciousness*.

> b) Ideal meaning and acts of meaning; emptily meaning something
> and meaning-fulfillment; consciousness as the region of experiences;
> intentional experiences as acts; consciousness as inner perception

We want to make clear to ourselves, from the standpoint of the subject matter, how the attempt to work on specific objects of logic demands that one *secures* and brings into view what is designated by *consciousness*. Following tradition, logic has as its theme: concepts, judgments, inferences. They are something meaning-compliant [*Bedeutungsmäßiges*] that stands in some connection with the linguistic expression, a connection that is not something contingent. For all thinking and knowing, all theoretical research are set down in "assertions." Hence, in the investigation of logic, interest is directed at *theoretical thinking*. A definite type of thinking is preferred and is, at bottom, the theme exclusively. Insofar as this theme is set down in assertions and is connected in a quite peculiar way to what complies with meaning and to experiences of thinking, the task consists in seeing this entire complex in its primordial unity, in order to acquire the possibilities of researching these facts of the matter in specific respects.

At that time Husserl had a quite odd, long since abandoned theory, descended from Brentano. Over and against the plurality of possible *acts of meaning* that can grasp a meaning, meaning is an *ideal unity*, a species over against the concrete individual instances (acts). Thus, Husserl speaks of the *ideal meaning* as the species for the individual instances of the acts that respectively mean [*meinen*] this meaning [*diese Bedeutung*]. In the first years of phenomenology, this theory plays a great role. On the supposition that we are to look for such ideal meanings, the entire traditional conception of abstraction, as Husserl learned it from Brentano (who for his part had taken it over from the Scholastics) establishes the necessity of making concretely present the respective experiences in which the meanings are present [*da*]—of making present the subjective realization of them (Husserl).[6]

One can establish the following distinction in acts of meaning: 1. acts in which an empty understanding occurs; 2. the sort of understanding of meaning

---

6. E. Husserl, II. Logische Untersuchung [Second Logical Investigation], op. cit., 141.

that can develop into the sort that is oriented to the meant state of affairs itself and fulfilled by it. *Emptily meaning something [Leeres Meinen]* and *fulfillment of meaning [Bedeutungserfüllung]* are *acts*. For a genuine understanding and, at the same time, for an orientation regarding when such acts are presentational [*vorstellig*] at all, we need to come to some understanding of what is to be understood by "act." Acts are identical with the *intentional experience*. An act delimits a determinate genus within the *entire sphere of experiences*, a sphere that is designated as *consciousness*. Consciousness stands for nothing other than a region of specific events that have the character of experiences. The concept of consciousness must be understood in this *regional sense*. Husserl still holds fast to this understanding today. Under the title "consciousness" a definite category of objects is delimited. The question is, what entities that are experiences can be designated or characterized as consciousness? These belong to the region of "consciousness." All these objects have one quite characteristic manner in which they themselves can be grasped. This sort of access is designated *inner perception*. I am conscious of these experiences. The entire region of experiences is that of which it is possible for me to become conscious in immanent perception. Consciousness in the sense of inner perception as the perceiving of the immanent is immediately related to the first concept of consciousness as a region of experience.

Within this region there is a specific class of experiences: acts, experiences that as such *are directed at something*. Linguistic practice is now such that today even an individual act is designated "consciousness-of-something."[7] After the *Logical Investigations*, Husserl restricted the concept of act. There are intentional experiences, e.g., the so-called "background experiences," that are not acts. Acts are the sort of intentional experiences that are distinguished by the explicit *ego*-cogito. The concepts of consciousness thus all stand in an internal connection with one another and were simultaneously vital in the work of philosophy at the time. Consciousness is the regional title for the entire stock of the soul's experiences [*seelischer Erlebnisse*] which become accessible as such through consciousness in the sense of inner verification. They become accessible in such a way, to be sure, that this inner verifying is able to find a distinctive class of experiences that are characterized as "consciousness-of-something" (see the Fifth Logical Investigation, § 1 ff.).[8]

To understand the following considerations, it is necessary for us to keep in mind as a criterion, for the sake of orientation, *the direction in which Greek philosophy considers things*. The *entity as world* and *life's being* make up the [Greeks'] thematic field. These objective features are interpreted in such a way that in the explication itself specific *characters of being* emerge, so that

7. See the Appendix, Supplement 7 (p. 227).
8. E. Husserl, V. Logische Untersuchung [Fifth Logical Investigation], op. cit., § 1ff., S. 345ff.

one can say the following. The Greek interpretation of existence remains *within existence*, and this interpretation is this existence becoming explicit through the explication. In contrast to this orientation to a specific state of affairs, *modern philosophy* will distinguish itself in a completely different way. Its theme is *consciousness*, purified in such a completely determinate way that it is obvious that what comes initially into purview requires a specific *re-working* in order to satisfy the claims issuing from this conception of philosophy.

Husserl's distinctions sometimes leave the impression that they are a matter of verbal distinctions and he has been reproached for this. That is the primitive but dominant image of what happens in the *Logical Investigations*. Consciousness as a region is characterized 1. through the access to it: inner perception, and 2. by the fact that this region contains in itself that specific class of experiences, the acts that are completely fundamental for the structure of consciousness. This *region of consciousness* is the *theme of the phenomenological examination* and, indeed, with a view to a clarification in an epistemically critical sense [*erkenntniskritisch*]. This is to say, the basic elements of logic are to be brought to such clarity that they form a secured foundation for all further construction of knowledge. The clarification of the basic phenomena of logic, carried out through their installation into the region of consciousness, has the character of a clarification in an epistemically critical sense.

§ 6. The care about already known knowledge, in which consciousness stands

In the wake of these first attempts to familiarize ourselves provisionally with the theme of phenomenology in its initial breakthrough, let us put to ourselves the question: 1. What kind of being, determined by what *characters of being*, is this region called "consciousness"? 2. How does it come about that precisely *this* region with these specific characters of being, procures for itself a *prerogative*, in such a way that it becomes the theme of a science that later characterizes itself as philosophy's fundamental science?

a) Care and its possibilities of disclosing, holding onto, and shaping what it takes care of; its commitment to and loss of itself in what it takes care of

How do we grasp *consciousness* objectively in order to be able to make out, on the basis of it, something like a differentiation of its characters of being? The determination of the characters of an entity's being becomes possible through the interpretation of the *care* in which such an entity is located as this determinate entity. More as a clue for understanding what follows, it should be said: the interpretation has as its theme the manner of *taking care of something* [*Besorgtsein um etwas*]. With the interpretation of taking care of something, this "something" itself becomes evident as *that which the care is specifically about*, that around which the care revolves. It reveals itself in the manner in which it is "there" [*"da"*] in the care; what possible being it has as something encountered in and for this care becomes evident from this manner of being present. Care is nothing subjective and does not feign what it takes care of; care allows it rather to come to its genuine being. If the entity is interrogated relative to the care disclosing it, then what is to be investigated is not the manner of being comprehended [*Weise des Erfaßtseins*] but instead precisely the way of encountering the entity such that it has been freed up, unencumbered, from its own standpoint [*Wie des freigegebenen Von-ihm-selbst-her-Begegnens des Seienden*].

For this determinate being called *consciousness*, the task is first to become acquainted with the *care* in which it is located. Such an interpretation entails seeing the possibility of the specific care in terms of its very being. Solely as a clue to care's being, it may be said that, precisely *as caring*, it first *discloses* what it takes care of and, in its specific manner of being, *holds on* in a specific way to the existent disclosed by it as such. What is disclosed and thus held onto by a care is *shaped*, explicated by it. This explicating is not some theoretical philosophy of what is disclosed. Every care has its distinctive way of shaping what has been disclosed. What is shaped becomes for care what it *commits itself to*. This commitment lies in the very sense of taking care of something. Ultimately, what care commits itself to is something in which care *loses itself.*

b) Care about already known knowledge

The task, therefore, is to interpret this specific being, *consciousness*, in its specific sort of presence and the corresponding tendency of working on it *on the basis of the care* in which it is itself located. The task entails first characterizing this care in a rough way and, indeed, in such a way that we establish it on the basis of concrete facts of the matter.

For this, it is necessary to ask: In what way is the theme "consciousness" present in contemporary philosophy? Seen from the outside, phenomenology has its field of objects in common with the philosophical discipline that is designated as *psychology*. In the introduction to the *Logical Investigations* Husserl himself characterized phenomenology as descriptive psychology.[9] Insofar as consciousness is the theme for him in the sense that it pertains to a

---

9. E. Husserl, *Logische Untersuchungen*. Zweiter Teil: Untersuchungen zur Phänomenologie und Theorie der Erkenntnis. (Halle an der Saale 1901), erste Auflage, Einleitung [(first edition), Introduction], § 6, S. 18f.

clarification in an epistemically critical sense, the work of phenomenology occupies a position within the same orientation [*Tendenz*] as the critique of knowledge, dominant at the time. Insofar as Husserl emphasizes that the theme of his investigations is given in advance in the fact that there are sciences, particularly the mathematical natural sciences, his tendency in treating problems is exactly the same as it is for the "Marburgers."

In the midst of these two *traditional traits*, the *psychological* and the *scientific-theoretical*, both of which are at work in a particular way in the *Logical Investigations*, something *primordial* becomes apparent. What is primordial is that, in the course of working on consciousness in the direction of a clarification in an epistemically critical sense, what matters above all is *to bring* what is to be worked on *into view as it is in itself*. Something completely primordial is at stake: the elevation of the phenomenal facts of the matter, in relation to which, on the one hand, prior philosophy was burdened by categories drawn from natural science and, on the other hand, the critique of knowledge based itself on Kant and was not free enough relative to the matter itself to cut loose from the Kantian way of posing questions.

The question now is: *What care motivates the shaping of consciousness as the theme* and, indeed, with the specific tendency of working on a clarification in an epistemically critical sense? Let us recapitulate for ourselves the context in which "consciousness" comes to be established as the thematic core. The focus dwells on instances of knowledge, specifically scientific instances that are designated in the sense stressed as consciousness-of-something: experiences of meaning, including meanings of assertions of theoretical thinking. From this vantage point, we also understand the priority which what is entitled "consciousness" gains over all other experiences. In itself, it is, indeed, monstrous to designate love a "consciousness-of-something." The care consists in shaping the thematic field for *theoretical knowing*, just as it factically is as *science*; for science insofar as it emerges as a possible context of achievement in the *culture* and is laid claim to as the foundation of a culture grounded on science.

The tendency to work on consciousness in the sense of clarifying it in an epistemically critical way makes this care even more evident. In what regard is theoretical knowing posited? In regard to *the knowing. The care is directed at already known knowledge* because knowledge is supposed to take over the task of *securing* existence and the culture. The aim in *phenomenological research* is for this care about already known knowledge to reach a *basis in the matter* [*sachlichen Boden*], from which the *justifiability* of all knowing and cultural being can become genuine [*echt*]. Even this distinctive explicitness of care about already known knowledge, formally expressed by the phrase "it aims at the matter itself" [*"es geht auf die Sache selbst"*], even this care about the matter proceeds within a tendency that is completely determined. We will have an opportunity to examine the maxim "to the matters themselves"[10] since the most narrow-minded dogmatism *can* hide behind it. By means of these more formal hints, care is merely determined at first as *care about already known knowledge*, led back to a basis in the content of the matter, a basis on which the work of securing is founded.

We are obliged to show that this care is in fact at work. Let us try, not to speak through Husserl's work in detail, but instead to listen to it where it *speaks of itself*, where it articulates itself critically in contrast to contemporary philosophy. Every proper criticism, which takes its stand in the matter itself, as such shows, in the way and manner it defends itself *against something*, *what* is *at issue* for it.

§ 7. Husserl's polemic with contemporary philosophy in the essay "Philosophy as Rigorous Science" and the care about already known knowledge at work in it. The general aim of this essay

This sort of *polemic with contemporary philosophy* is available to us in Husserl's "Philosophy as Rigorous Science."[11] This work comes ten years after the *Logical Investigations*. In the interim, phenomenological research had come to be clarified further, so much so that this research could be shaped systematically and inserted into the work of philosophy. As for the specific care that we determined to be characteristic of setting the field of consciousness apart, we will have to look and see whether this care is actually expressed. The examination will open up for us yet a further horizon of the matter.

Possibilities of concern can serve at the same time as clues to establishing what is under that care. Possibilities of care can be characterized as follows (see above p. 43). A specific care has the peculiar character of 1. *disclosing* and bringing into the realm of existence what it revolves around; 2. *explicating* concretely what has been disclosed in the manner in which it is there; 3. *holding on* in a definite manner to what has been explicitly elaborated; 4. *committing itself* to what has been held onto, that is to say, making specific principles from what has been held onto as normative for the objects of concern of other cares; 5. *losing itself*, setting what is in its specific care up so unconditionally that every sort of care is principally motivated by it.

10. E. Husserl, *Logische Untersuchungen*. Zweiter Band: Untersuchungen zur Phänomenologie und Theorie der Erkenntnis. I. Teil (I.–V. Untersuchung), dritte Auflage. (Halle an der Saale 1922), Einleitung, op. cit., § 2, S. 6.
11. E. Husserl, "Philosophie als strenge Wissenschaft" [Philosophy as Rigorous Science]. In: *Logos*. Internationale Zeitschrift für Philosophie der Kultur. I/3 (1910/1911): 289–341.

If a care is itself explicated in terms of the aspects mentioned, then it also provides an access to what we designate as a care's specific *restlessness*.

If we conceive phenomenology in terms of the concrete breakthrough that it makes with Husserl, we then gain some insight into factual constants of a thoroughly positive nature in the context of this seemingly critical consideration. The *result* of the interpretation to be conducted should be given from the outset. The concrete care that leads to shaping consciousness as such as the thematic field, holding on to it, and setting it up principally as the further theme of philosophy is *care about already known knowledge* and, indeed, such that the knowing of knowing is identified and identifiable from a definitively *secured basis*. With Husserl's essay in hand, we will now have to establish that a concrete care about already known knowledge is in fact the general motivation for the distinctive role that consciousness plays. For this purpose, the *general aim* of the essay will be characterized first.

As the title says, the aim is not somehow to project a program but instead generally to sharpen consciousness for the *idea of a philosophically rigorous science*. Underlying the essay is the conviction that even the *idea* of a philosophy as rigorous science has been lost, so that the essay is faced with the *task* of first bringing this idea itself to light and then lending it the proper impact by putting forward concrete parts of such investigations and their method. The task posed is accomplished, not in a thematic presentation, but instead by way of a *critique*. It is directed first at a falsification of the idea of philosophy in general and then at an enfeeblement of this idea. This conception is suggested by an historical distinction. In the modern era from Descartes to Kant and in part even in the case of Fichte, a specific idea of scientific philosophy is vital. Immediately after this, the idea of a scientific philosophy underwent a weakening in Romanticism. To be sure, it is necessary thereby to acknowledge the peculiar fact that Hegel had this same hope of finally making philosophy into a scientific philosophy and that what matters to him, just as it does to Husserl, is making philosophy *teachable*. Husserl makes Romantic philosophy responsible for a reaction that can be characterized a) as *naturalism* and b) as *historicism*.

A twofold ruination of philosophy in the sense of a rigorous science ensues from these two tendencies, insofar as they dare to break into the field of philosophical labors. For the idea of philosophy here, the guiding *criterion* is formally whether philosophy has come so far that it can lay down an objectively communicable, doctrinal content that is binding for all times. To the extent that it cannot, it is not a rigorous science. (By way of supplementing these remarks, it is noteworthy that today Husserl has a much more positive attitude towards Fichte as well as Hegel and would no longer write these sentences against speculative idealism.)

We have to transfer the examination's center of gravity to the inquiry that concerns us. We want to get clear about the *character of being of consciousness* as the theme of philosophy. It first needs to be shown that the care mentioned is at work in the elaboration of "consciousness" as the thematic field. Attention must be directed at the critique and it must be asked: 1. *What* does the critique look like? a) *Against whom* is it directed? b) In *what way* is the critique in this direction conducted? 2. What *motives* lie behind this critique? Why precisely are *naturalism* and *historicism* themes of critical consideration and why are they such themes in the way characterized, a way that is to be designated a *clarification of the problems*? 3. How does it become apparent from these motives what actually matters to the critique, the *care* that is at work in shaping the critique with respect to its means? 4. In connection with the characteristics of the care of knowing given thereby, we have to look and see to what extent this specific care *explicitly* stands out in the essay. 5. Finally, we have to consider how, on the basis of the care thus identified, consciousness is determined with respect to its *character of being*. At the same time we will see the limits of our examination. By restricting ourselves to Husserl's essay exclusively, we are not in a position to learn why at all it came to this, that consciousness became the theme of philosophy.

§ 8. Husserl's critique of naturalism[12]

a) Naturalization of consciousness

What does the critique look like and against whom is it directed? Against naturalism and historicism. We have to make clear to ourselves how in general the expression "naturalism" comes to be coined and what one has in mind when something is designated as such. Naturalism coincides with the discovery of nature. Analogously, historicism grew out of a discovery of history. The discovery of nature in question is the discovery of it as the object of a special science, the mathematical science of nature. Naturalism is a consequence of this discovery of nature. That is to say, the type of being and object in the context of nature becomes the guide to the content in comprehending *every sort* of being and objectivity. Accordingly, the *specific rigor of the mathematical science of nature* serves as the criterion for every domain of being and epistemic determination of it. The question is the extent to which a determinate *idea of a science and object* of this sort has in fact *expanded*

12. For §§ 8–12, see E. Husserl, "Philosophie als strenge Wissenschaft," op. cit., Naturalistische Philosophie [Naturalistic Philosophy]: 294–322.

to the thematic field of philosophy, in what sense the objective field of philosophy and its method are subjected to the idea of the mathematical science of nature.

The basic character of this science, apart from its rigor, is distinguished by the fact that its results can be formulated in laws. A law-likeness [*Gesetzmäßigkeit*] that is scientific in the eminent sense is called "universally binding." The *binding character* of these propositions is so predominant and at the same time so imposing in human existence that it presents the genuine motive that leads to absolutizing the idea of this science. This nature is not something alien to philosophy since philosophy early on had a tendency to the sort of lawfulness [*Gesetzlichkeit*] that one can formulate as a *normative determination* [*Normierung*]. It is thus no accident that a science that has elevated itself to such rigorousness, as natural science has, makes this task its own and that the specific objects of philosophy succumb to natural science.

The first aspect of the effect of naturalizing philosophy lies in the fact that this same naturalist tendency leads to the *naturalization of consciousness*. (This juxtaposition of the idea and consciousness points back to *Descartes*.) How does it come to the naturalization precisely of consciousness, and what does that mean insofar as philosophy's task is to establish the sorts of lawfulness pertaining to modes of behavior in terms of their meaningful connection? The task arises of acquiring the legitimate grounds for the fact that something like consciousness speaks of an object as actually being and identifies it as such. For this justification of the legitimacy of the claims and acts of consciousness, there is need for a study of these connections themselves. A critique of knowing is needed. Being that has the character of the soul or mind [*seelische Sein*], regarded as [part of] nature, is determined in the sense of *natural scientific categories*. The uniform organization of this misunderstanding is what one can designate as *experimental psychology*, insofar as it lays claim to being significant in a fundamental [*grundsätzlich*] way. It never entered into Husserl's mind to say something against experimental psychology as such. [What he does oppose is how] ideal laws are reinterpreted into the sorts of lawfulness pertaining to sheer processes of consciousness. This is done not only in the domain of thinking, but also in the domain of voluntary action. The norms valid here are also reinterpreted into laws of psychological processes. Husserl explicitly stresses that the laws of formal logic make up the exemplary index of all ideality.[13]

13. Ibid., 295.

b) Naturalization of ideas

Next to the naturalization of consciousness, a further falsification of the idea of philosophy as rigorous science lies in the *naturalization of ideas*. For the explanation of the "idea," see the concrete investigations in the *Logical Investigations*, which are concerned with meanings. These are seen as ideal unities in contrast to the multitude of acts that realize them in meaning something. This unity of the sense is an ideal unity of *validation*. On the basis of this ideal unity of propositions, completely determinate modes of lawfulness of their own sort arise. *The* philosophy that looks on everything as natural science reinterprets this specific lawfulness of the sense into a lawfulness of the *natural course* of the process of thinking: the lawfulness of norms and ideas is reinterpreted into a lawfulness of the course of thinking. The idea, the lawfulness of ideas, is not seen at all. The critique at work in natural science is the sort of critique that is made in the course of achieving knowledge in natural science with its focus on the matters involved. As a critique in natural science, it is the sort that is bent on the facts of the matter under investigation. It is absurd, Husserl says, that the critical possibilities of an individual science should include the possibilities of investigating this science purely insofar as it is science. In the latter sort of investigation, a completely fundamental change of object has taken place. Mistaking this niveau is what enabled natural science to claim for itself the solution to epistemological problems and, as a result, to block the path to bringing the specific sort of object that "consciousness" is into view as such, and to clarifying from this vantage point the set of problems that knowledge and acting pose as being in their own right.

In the examination, the critique of naturalism was intentionally isolated from the critique of historicism. The latter will occupy us later and free up the view for a series of new facts of the matter.

Naturalism is, first, naturalism of ideas; second, naturalism of consciousness. [It is] the ideal connection of ideal laws which, when viewed with respect to life's modes of behavior, can be designated as various sorts of normative lawfulness to which the disciplines of theoretical science, axiology, and practical science correspond. The ultimate constant factors, in which these sorts of normative lawfulness are grounded, are ideas. It is characteristic of naturalism not to see the ideas, to be *blind to ideas*. Consciousness is the genuine theme of the critique, consciousness as a theme for epistemological treatment. There is a question whether the natural scientific method can in principle be expanded, the question of how it is in a position even merely to understand, let alone to justify the legitimacy of the exertions of consciousness.

c) Nature's being as experimental psychology's horizon

Let us ask: In what way does the critique seek to demonstrate that naturalism falsifies the impulse towards rigorously scientific philosophy? The clue to an answer is the following. If it turns out that natural science with its own means of positing objects and working in general cannot attain philosophy's field of problems, then any philosophy making use of this natural scientific method in any way is thereby doomed. *Experimental psychology* is nothing other than a scientific discipline that, in its manner of positing objects and idea of law-fulness, takes over the method of natural science.

A fourfold task presents itself: that of 1. characterizing the specific scientific status of mathematical natural science; 2. characterizing the scientific tendency of experimental psychology; 3. establishing philosophy's domain of problems; and 4. characterizing the discipline that treats this domain of problems satis-factorily (the scientific status is characterized with a view to the adequate way of seeing the type of object involved and then with a view to the type of treatment motivated by that way of seeing it).

The object of natural science is nature as physical nature, as the unity of a completely determinate, thingly being. As the basic character of this being, it is given that each thing in the sphere of being is perceivable as identically the same in a variety of diverse, direct perceptions. At the same time, this being of the natural thing is of the sort that this identifiable sameness of it is per-ceivable by a plurality of subjects. This thingly being is intersubjectively iden-tifiable as being of a certain sort. Every one of these entities has, as one says, its determinate properties in the temporal and spatial expanse of things and stands at the same time in an entire complex of causal series. Each property of a thing is nothing other than a possibility, following under a causal law, of specifically regulated alterations of this thing in the context of nature as a whole. Thus, each thing is principally determinable in the context of nature by going back to the functional connection of relations among things. This specific thingly unity is exhibited in appearances.

This distinctive *being of nature* is the unarticulated *horizon* into which the facts of the matter are gathered that *this psychology* vaguely and arbitrarily takes up from the tradition: fantasy, perception, representation. These basic phenomena do not themselves then become psychology's theme but instead, in connection with them, the facts of the matter are worked over in such a way that determinate regularities and law-likenesses are pinned down. These laws also bear within themselves the basic concepts from which they emerged, but with the same lack of intelligibility and differentiation. This basic defi-ciency of psychology is grounded in the predominance of the natural scientific manner of examination which looks for regularities of events and skips over the appearing thing. Psychology accordingly overlooks the fact that its specific domain is no such domain as that of natural science.

Today the objections made by Husserl already hold less since phenomenological work has penetrated into psychology and essential changes have become evident. Nevertheless, the changes are such that there is no hope at all of arriving at a new determination of psychology. The results of phenomenological work and use of terms have merely been taken over, but there is no purification of the science conducted from the standpoint of phenomenology.

d) The peculiar being of consciousness as the true object of philosophy and the method of discerning essences to acquire universally binding propositions

In contrast to *nature's being*, *consciousness* has this peculiarity, that there is nothing of the sort in it like an identity that is maintained in several direct experiences. This is principally excluded from the domain of mental being. Each perceptible experience is fundamentally [*grundsätzlich*] no longer the same, the moment it is allegedly perceived again. This nonidentifiability of an entity with the character of consciousness goes so far that it also holds for the same subject. The things of nature, by contrast, have an intersubjective identifiability. That is the concrete basis for the fact that the being of the mental is designated a "stream" and "flow." These are not trivial, popular labels; instead the reasons for them lie in the *peculiar manner of being of the mental* itself. This mental being that is thus characterized in regard to its perceptibility is principally the sort of being that does not exhibit itself via appearances; instead it is itself thus, as it appears, the object. Philosophy's object is never nature, but instead always a *phenomenon*. It is noteworthy that Husserl in the *Logical Investigations*, where he researches in a concrete, phenomenological fashion, directly rejects the use of the term "phenomenon." This peculiar being "consciousness" is a monadic unity, a unity that is characterized by the fact that it lies in a temporality that has a dually infinite horizon. Each entity of this domain of being can be pursued in the direction of an endless past and likewise in a futurity that is without end.

What *method* must correspond to the being of consciousness so that work on consciousness yields a *discipline* that leads to *universal* and *universally binding* propositions and an *absolute objectivity*? Insofar as this entity is a domain of being that is not nature but instead a phenomenon, the method cannot be that of natural scientific inquiry. Insofar as it is not nature, but has something like an essence, the sole method that leads to firm results is that of *discerning essences*. This method, and it alone, suffices for an examination of consciousness that gets at something other than a natural scientific, rule-like regularity and its determination; the sort of examination of consciousness that has the task of seeing *ideal connections* as ideal and bringing what it has seen into *binding propositions* of the science.

§ 9. Clarification of the problems as purification and radicalization of their bias. The care about securing and justifying an absolute scientific status

In the face of this critical consideration, let us now ask: What motivates this critique, the manner in which it chooses its object and goes through it? How are we to characterize this critical method itself at all? Husserl speaks of the method as a *clarification of problems*.[14]

The critique speaks *against* a *naturalization* in order to acquire a *genuine science of consciousness*. Insofar as this clarification is critique, the very *aim* and *idea of a scientific treatment of consciousness* is *made into something absolute*. The decision [involved in making the critique] is thus at the same time a decision *for* the relevant matter. In the course of this critique, what matters is to acquire the possibility of a *rigorous lawfulness*, the sort of lawfulness that is rigorously objective, binding, and identifiable. The move toward genuine purification of the field of "consciousness" from every sort of matter of fact, a purification that is the basis of a philosophy as rigorous science— this move to a *universally binding character* is the already characterized *care about already known knowledge*.

An experience can never be iterated as the same for a subject. The genuine context of mental being is a succession of experiences, a succession regulated by a specific temporality and having a dually infinite horizon. In relation to the identifiability, one could say that it is intersubjectively identifiable insofar as a being proper to the soul [*ein seelisches Sein*] can be understood unambiguously by a plurality of subjects. But it may not be equated with the intersubjective identifiability of a thing of nature. This mental being [*dieses psychische Sein*] is conceived by psychology, as far as its manner of being is concerned, as coexisting with nature. Mental being is posited as grounded in the being of nature. Each lawfulness is the sort of lawfulness of something that is a matter of fact, and natural science has to do with various sorts of matters of facts. The question is whether there is anything like the possibility of making matter-of-factness as such intelligible by means of matters of fact.

We are not interested in the stance taken toward the being of nature and that of the soul. What interests us instead is the question of what *biases*

14. Ibid., 297; see the Appendix, Supplement 8 (p. 227f).

[*Tendenzen*] are at work *in the critique of naturalism*, the question of what *care* guides both *the choice of the object and the critique*. We maintain first that the care out of which the choice of the object of the critique grows is *care about already known knowledge, care about securing knowledge* on the path of knowing the knowledge, *securing and justifying an absolute scientific status*. Naturalism is subjected to critique because its set of problems and method are bent on placing the normative lawfulness on a scientifically se-cured basis by means of an exact scientific treatment of consciousness. The *critique* is carried out in the manner of *clarifying the problems*. Problems are *taken up* and, with that, a specific *decision* is also made *about what is asked* and what the *tendency or bias* [*Tendenz*] *of the interrogation* is, a decision to *radicalize the bias* that is at work in what is taken up. What matters to Husserl is to bring the scientific bias to natural science radically to end. By taking up the critique as a clarification of the problems, the critique has decided *for* the scientific bias of naturalism. It is carried out in a *purification* in such a way that all the factors capable of endangering the acquisition of an *absolute ev-idence* and *certainty* are thrown out. This purification of the bias renders it absolute.

1. Hence, we next have to envision what *clarifying the problems* means, in order to see, from this vantage point, what the purification of the sets of problems and methods of the naturalistic philosophy looks like and how at every step *care about an absolute scientific status* is at work. 2. It is necessary to see how the *classification of the problems* is taken over in a positive sense from naturalism and how the specific inclination to it and to its method lies therein. 3. It is necessary to see how the *problem of knowing* takes center stage and, indeed, the problem of *knowledge of physical nature*; it is necessary to see that this context of the problem thus provides the *horizon* for the theme of "consciousness." 4. It is necessary to see how in reference to certain *ten-dencies* in *history*, these tendencies are drawn upon in a positive way.

§ 10. Clarification of problems

Ad 1. What is a *problem*? What possibilities lie further in a *clarification of problems*? As we interpret more closely the context of the phenomenon of the "problem," we hit upon phenomena that will later occupy us in a fundamental [*grundsätzlich*] way from the ground up.

Problem is best rendered: theme [*Vorwurf*]. "Problem" is mostly identified with "question." A problem is a question developed and explicitly posited in a specific manner. For illumination of the "problem" itself in its structure, we see ourselves led back to a closer consideration of what a *question* is.

a) The question and its structures

In a *question* we distinguish: 1. the *interrogated*; 2. *what is asked*; 3. the *regard* in which it is asked, *in relation to which* the interrogated is interrogated—what is asked in regard to it; 4. the *manner of the questioning* itself, that is to say, the actual claim of the answer. 5. On the basis of the basic character of these factors we then understand the *connection* between *question and problem*. We further distinguish: 6. *how* something like a question or a problem *is encountered*, whether questioning is something lying around like stones on a path—the manner of being of a "question"; 7. the discussion of the possible modifications of the factors that are determining in a question; the differences between what is interrogated and what is asked, between the regard in question and the manner of the question; 8. the demonstration that a *specific method* is decided on from the outset along with a question and a problem; 9. the connection between a *problem* and the *history of a problem*; 10. the decisive analysis and interpretation of the question as a question in the sense of a *seeking*. The question is a specific manner of seeking. Here it is necessary to show that a "question" is not at all a theoretical phenomenon. [Finally, we distinguish] 11. seeking as a *specific care* of existence; and 12. care itself as a *specific possibility of being* of existence. Only from this vantage point can it be decided what it means to opt for a "problem."

In the concrete question "does an external world exist?" *what is interrogated* is the external world. What is interrogated can itself be brought more or less explicitly into view in the question of the various possibilities into which it is placed. The inquiry can give itself an account, more or less, of what is actually meant by what is interrogated, for example, what "external world" means in relation to a possible "inner world," and so forth. It can, however, also be the case—and that is the rule—that in such questions what is interrogated is *not* regarded *more closely*. It is there, to be sure, as the theme of the question but not from a perspective explicitly appropriating it. Thus, what is interrogated is what is articulated by the question, in our case, the external world.

By virtue of the question, what is interrogated is taken in a certain *regard*; it is asked whether the external world is real. *What is asked about* is not the external world but instead the external world's being real. The question itself accordingly articulates what is interrogated in a certain regard. Depending upon how what is interrogated is itself intuitively envisioned, the questioning shapes what is asked about as such. Hence, the regard in question is that in view of which the external world is interrogated and, in this case, that regard is its reality. To what extent is the regard in question *explicitly* appropriated? ("Regard" is what is meant in looking-upon something, the content in looking upon something.) The same possibility of deception that already confronted us in language lurks in the question. What is interrogated is interrogated in view of something—in view of its being, in the case of the question that we have taken as an example. What is asked as such is for the most part what, without hesitation, we mean by "question." In *what is asked*, therefore, *what is interrogated* is interrogated *as something*. And this "as something," in view of which it is interrogated, is the regard in question; more precisely, what occupies a position in this regard is *what* the questioning is *about [das Wonach des Fragens]*. In a way analogous to what is interrogated itself, that regard is more or less explicitly appropriated in the inquiry, e.g., the concept of "reality" is more or less set down from the outset. The degree to which the regard in question is elaborated and clearly accessible simultaneously determines the possibility of highlighting the characteristic factors in what is interrogated itself, e.g., the external world's characters of being. It is evident without further ado that the elaboration of the regard in question stands in an internal connection with the elaboration of the observable characters of the question itself. At the same time, what has been elaborated about the regard in question presents the possibility of stamping a question into a dogmatic opinion, even though it presents itself as a question.

Genuine questioning, in the sense of being bent on a decision about a question, is determined on the basis of a genuine *tendency toward an answer*—on the basis of how the answer is entertained, pursued, and laid claim to. Characteristic possibilities in this regard are:

a) The tendency of the answer can go towards acquiring answers in the sense of *valid propositions*. One pursues the answer as a proposition and, indeed, as a proposition of the sort that, in providing the answer, enriches and advances the *treasure trove of valid truths* and, as a so-called *result*, can be installed and arranged in a realm of objectively valid items. All scientific propositions, insofar as science is conceived as a system of objective propositions, are truths in this sense. Here there is a distinction in the sense that the propositions as results are transitional propositions of the sort that, as formulations of validities, they provide the further basis for further questioning that takes these propositions themselves as its point of departure. But even here the ultimate tendency of the answer is the tendency towards an ideal possible connection of all valid propositions in general.

b) The answer to a question, however, can also have the fundamentally different orientation that the answering in itself and, with it, even the question are bent on bringing themselves, via the answering, into a specific *basic relation to the entity interrogated*. Hence, they are bent, not on increasing an identical stock of propositions, but instead on bringing the one questioning, in his being, *to* a being and domain of matters, quite possibly precisely because an internal danger exists of being pushed aside by such an entity. This tendency of the answer, to *bring one to an entity as such*, allows for various possibilities. It can be that the very entity, to which the one questioning and answering is to be brought, turns out in the course of the interrogating and answering to be the sort of entity whose *own sense of being* itself is questionable, hence, the sort of entity that on the basis of its specific being demands to be interrogated in such a way that giving answers, just like questioning, means nothing other than establishing determinations of the entity's being. This entails that the entity (the existence [*Dasein*]) *doing the questioning* fundamentally co-determines the being of the entity interrogated, and vice versa. The *answer disappears* in this peculiar sense, it never gets hold of itself, in contrast to the first case where it sets itself down as it were in "objective structures." In this type of questioning, the possibility exists that the answer is an answer precisely when it understands how to disappear in the right way. If the answer disappears and thereby to a certain extent frees up the *way to the entity, it remains in the mode of questioning*. The answer turns back into questioning. What we call *questionableness* is constituted by the way this questioning turns back into ever new questioning. Nothing is settled initially as to whether this peculiar questioning-and-answering refers or not to the enrichment characterized above, in other words, whether it is science or not. One would first have to agree on what sort of questioning and answering is alone scientific. The point of departure of every question, every development of access to things, is determined by these possible manners of answering and the answer's tendencies. It is not possible here to go into the concrete discussion of this connection.

b) The problem and the factors of its being: clarifying the problem as a matter
of co-deciding on what is to be interrogated, what it is asked, the regard in
question, and the tendency of the answer

How does the *problem* stand in relation to the question? What kind of a question is the problem? In the question, what is interrogated is co-posited; it does not come any further to an explicit treatment. The problem is a question posed, the sort of question that is *explicitly* regarded as needing and deserving an answer, a question explicitly posed in accordance with tasks at hand. The *task-character* and, indeed, the task-character for knowledge in the context of research distinguishes a problem from an arbitrary question. Insofar as the task is explicitly conceived in this problem, it is much more a matter of proceeding further in answering. In *posing a problem*, much less time remains to investigate what is interrogated in itself. It is characteristic for it to present itself as something within which everything else is already positioned as well. In this peculiar character of the problem's being lies the necessity of obscuring what is interrogated, an obscuring necessarily grounded in posing the problem. Every problem that is well known and discussed in public is not so much the sign of a thoroughly well-grounded character as it is instead a prejudice of the most dangerous sort, since the problems are as such apt to *obscure matters* insofar as the problem hits upon the answer and depends upon what is asked. In the context of the problem, what is interrogated is only interrogated as something traditionally *taken up* to be interrogated and only interrogated in the regard in question, taken up with the problem itself.

Problems are mostly not present as explicit questions but instead as *question-words*. They point to an understanding, attaching to the words, in specific directions of questioning. The words traditionally carry the inquiry in themselves. These *problem-words* and this peculiar type of existence of problems can be objectified in the historical examination of them; one speaks of a so-called "history of problems," of "locations of problems," "dominant problem-interests."[15] The Marburg school performed a particular service in having awakened the sense for a vital examination of history (within the framework of possibilities at the time), an examination that designated itself then as a history of problems. For this examination of history, there is to a certain extent a specific stock of problems, already discovered by Plato, Kant, etc. From what has been said it should be obvious that there are problems only for *standpoints*; for only then is some regard in question [*Fragehinsicht*] held onto and laid down. A regard in question has in a certain sense become explicit. *There is a history of a problem only on the basis of an explicit, philosophical standpoint.* A *truly* neutral research, by contrast, is only familiar with "matters" as possible sources and motivations for questioning and elaborating the regards in question. A final factor here is that, in each problem, its method is given with it. Something gets settled about a delimited subject of interrogation by means of specific concepts.

On the basis of these just discussed factors, i.e., the *factors of the problem's being*, it is not difficult to come to some understanding of what it means *to clarify a problem*. Clarifying a problem means nothing other than getting a grip on what is interrogated and what is asked as a task and doing so in and with the question. That is to say, *it means co-deciding on what is interrogated, the regard in question, and the tendency of the answer*. This applies, too, to the critical clarification of the tendency of the problem of naturalism.

---

15. On "problem-history," see W. Windelband, *Lehrbuch der Geschichte der Philosophie. Achte, unveränderte Auflage* [Textbook of the History of Philosophy, eighth, unchanged edition]. (Tübingen 1919), IV; N. Hartmann, "Zur Methode der Philosophiegeschichte" [On the Method of the History of Philosophy], *Kant-Studien* 15 (1910): 459–485, passim. On "problem-locations," see N. Hartmann, *Grundzüge einer Metaphysik der Erkenntnis* [Fundamental Features of a Metaphysics of Knowledge] (Berlin/Leipzig 1921), 3, 5. On "problem-interests," see N. Hartmann, "Zur Methode der Philosophiegeschichte," op. cit., 482.

c) Husserl's clarification of the tendency of the problem
of naturalism through transcendental and eidetic purification
of consciousness. Absolute validity and evidence

In *clarifying the problems of naturalism*, Husserl decides on the specific *object* and at the same time on an *exact* scientific *manner of handling* it. The clarification consists in the following: the *consciousness* that has, along with other things, been set down as the point of departure is clarified, as are, at the same time, the *regard in question* and the *tendency of the question*. [This is] the sort of tendency, proper to an exact scientific inquiry, towards what is clarified. [It involves] a *purification* of the object and the manner of handling it. This purification, which is a twofold one, should show us that the previously indicated care about already known knowledge lives in it.

In what sense is consciousness purified, in order, as purified, to become the object of a *phenomenology of consciousness*? Consciousness is posited as a starting point in psychology in such a way that physical being is posited along with it. All these positings of consciousness as a connection of experiences are co-positings of *nature*. In order for facts to be understood in their being-known, the sphere supposedly yielded by such knowing may not be of the same character [as nature]. Consciousness must be purified of every admixture of positings of nature. Nothing like a *human being's* consciousness may be posited in it [consciousness]. Husserl designates as "transcendental" this manner of being free from every sort of positing of nature. This is the one way of purifying the field of objects, purifying it in the sense of *suspending* every sort of positing of nature. The field of consciousness is, in its being, no sort of matter of fact. That this entity is an individual, unique entity is, nevertheless, not suspended. In spite of all transcendental suspension of nature, the being of consciousness is an individual uniqueness of the stream of experience.

Is there a method of working on the transcendentally pure consciousness in such a way that the determinations emerging within it have *intersubjective validity*? What Husserl characterizes as *knowledge of the essence* satisfies this demand. Here, too, it should be noted that the idea of knowledge of the essence grew out of a specific critical delimitation of natural science. This purification is the so-called *eidetic purification* of consciousness. In this twofold tendency toward purification, the transcendental and the eidetic, the *care* involved is at work to secure a field of objects that makes it possible to acquire *absolutely binding determinations*.

By means of the *transcendental reduction*, the theme is first obtained, in relation to which the question can arise: How is a science related to this theme possible? What sort of manner of comprehension must there be for a science to be able to establish itself? What manner of comprehension satisfies the idea of absolute justification?

If one keeps in mind the context of the development of phenomenology purely historically, then it is apparent that in the *Logical Investigations* there was as yet no talk of perceiving essences. In the Second Investigation something like a theory of abstraction surfaces, a phenomenology of comprehending the universal, a phenomenology that investigates the consciousness of the universal solely in the sense of the experience of things and matters. By this means, nothing in principle is settled as to whether such comprehension of a species can be carried over, without further ado, to any field of objects. Yet this expansion occurs in the sense that it is said that comprehension of essences is the only sort of comprehension by the transcendentally pure consciousness, within which propositions binding for all eternity emerge.

It is thus apparent what the decisive motives are from which the *care* springs, the care to *secure* and maintain *an absolute scientific status* in relation to the *transcendentally pure consciousness*. Whether Husserl's declaration that he is determining something about every sort of consciousness, even God's, is justified remains to be decided.[16] The essential, scientifically decisive move within the scientific tendency is a move that Husserl makes as well. *Posing the problem in a purified way is, in spite of this, still naturalism.*

With regard to the designation "transcendental," attention should be paid to the necessity, as far as Husserl's work is concerned, of distinguishing between what it is determined as and established as purely terminologically, and what he accomplished in his actual work. This distinction was not made and he was completely misunderstood because the *Ideas* were viewed only in connection with contemporary philosophy. By attending only to these aspects, one prevents oneself from being able to see what is decisive. What is essential is that here something in general was done, that the *matter* was advanced. The self-interpretation is unimportant. Where something is actually done, it is mostly the case that the one doing it does not realize at all what it is about.

§ 11. Order of the inquiry and clue to the explication of the structure of all experiential connections

a) Orientation toward connections among disciplines: philosophy as a science of norms and values

A second factor that makes this care about already known knowledge apparent is closely connected with the first and is evident from the *order of the inquiry*. The first factor is the idea of absolute validity and evidence. The entire context of the inquiry runs within a definite framework that *is oriented to disciplines*

---

16. E. Husserl, *Ideen I*, 156f.

and connections among disciplines. In place of natural science a new science is supposedly grounded. It is not asked whether such a discipline has any sense at all. Setting up a discipline is guided in turn by an interest in having a discipline; indeed, the fundamental discipline of philosophy is supposed to be acquired. Thus, the discipline that steps into the place of natural science is supposed to become the fundamental discipline of philosophy which is itself again there as the unity of the disciplines. The entire concept of philosophy is oriented to this unity of disciplines for which, as sciences of norms, a grounding discipline is acquired.

In this connection a further traditional constraint of phenomenology presents itself, a constraint that here, too, aims at a rigorously scientific status: namely, the conception of philosophy as a *science of norms and values.* In the entire essay that has been discussed, nothing is said about the object; instead purely the idea of a discipline of it is carried out. Care about already known knowledge shows itself *in this effort* to attain a new scientific status. Interest in the *matter itself* is not even mentioned, except insofar as it is the sort of matter that allows for something of this sort.

b) Theoretical knowing as the clue

The third factor is given in the fact that the inquiry of philosophy and the entire critique does not take its leads from anything like a fundamental [*grundsätzlich*] structure of consciousness. Instead it *takes its leads* from the class of experiences proper to *theoretical knowing* and, indeed, it is the clue to the explication of the structure of *every* connection among experiences. Practical consciousness is always treated by way of analogy. "Something analogous obtains also for evaluating and acting."[17] Hence, theoretical knowing enjoys the primacy, but not somehow in the sense that it is first asked: What is the *primordial* phenomenon of theoretical knowing? *Mathematical natural science* is made, as *prototype*, into the foundation without further ado. The so-called humanities are always determined only on the basis of the contrast to the natural sciences, in relation *to the latter*, by virtue of being-*different*. The idea of science is prefigured by the *idea of mathematics* as science. Once again [there is] a purely formal orientation to the factor of validity. Even the type of *validity of norms* is viewed from the standpoint of the utterly theoretical: "The formal-logical principles are the exemplary index of all ideality."[18] Thus, we may consider it demonstrated, on the basis of these four characteristic factors, that in this entire inquiry care about already known knowledge is in fact what guides the inquiry, providing the problem and sustaining it.

17. See E. Husserl, "Philosophie als strenge Wissenschaft," 290.
18. Ibid., 295.

§ 12. Characteristic factors of care about already
known knowledge in Husserl's critique of naturalism:
back-flash, falling-prey, pre-constructing, ensnarement, neglect

In addition to the factors already mentioned, let us now further ask what this *care itself* looks like, what characteristic factors are invoked precisely for this concrete care. The *care about an absolutely binding character*, in its manner of guiding the critique and positive work, shows a characteristic factor, a phenomenon that may be designated a *back-flash* [*Rückschein*]. This peculiar phenomenon as a character of care lies in the fact that what stands in its care—the objectively binding character that is supposed to be procured—is vitally at work in the care's own concrete *being* itself, in such a way that everything entering into the care's field of view is more closely determined from the standpoint of *this* object of concern [*this* thing taken care of: *Besorgte*].

Everything that the previously characterized care about already known knowledge places among its interconnected tasks is seen in the light of this care. Each question, each matter is taken up from the outset in terms of this specific orientation. Husserl says literally: "The idea of science is, indeed, all-encompassing; thought in terms of its ideal completion, it is reason itself."[19] This sentence is of a scope that can perhaps not be completely taken in at first. The back-flash of the object of concern upon everything that the care is involved with is a characteristic moment of care insofar as it is characterized as knowing nothing of itself.

In caring of this sort there is a peculiar *non*explicitness, in that the care *falls prey* to the object of its concern. The care as such has no time for any sort of deliberation as to whether what it is preoccupied with is not in the end determined by *it* itself. This manner of being pulled in a nonexplicit way by itself is expressed in the character of the back-flash just discussed. What we come to know as *falling prey* to the care enters the picture.

This nonexplicitness that makes it possible for care to be self-absorbed has, nevertheless, a *specific ex*plicitness: that of *pre-constructing* as a peculiar mirroring [*Widerschein*] given with it itself. The care is inexplicit insofar as it lives for the object of its concern; yet it has a peculiar interpretation of itself in the form of a *systematic program*. It fashions for itself a meaning and a sense and an interpretation through the program that it pre-constructs for itself in a completely formal manner. By means of this pre-construction, the care provides itself a quite specific tranquility [*Ruhe*] and the certitude of an objectively binding accountableness. Through *this sort* of pre-constructing of what it is concerned about, the care fashions for itself its specific explicitness.

19. Ibid., 296.

The care is in need of a specific tranquility in order to expend itself entirely on the object of its concern. At the same time, via this pre-constructing, the possibility of the back-flash is heightened. The certitude with which every-thing is given in the sense of the program (and violence is done in this sense to history in its entirety) increases with the development of the pre-constructing as such. The back-flash reaches so far that the possibility of a concrete ethical life is made dependent upon the presence of an ethics as an absolutely binding science. The back-flash's own possibilities of effecting mat-ters are fortified by the pre-constructing. All the tasks that must be completed in the future are prefigured, and everything encountered is determined by the idea of this prefiguring and determined in this direction as belonging in the program.

If one pursues these factors of the back-flash, the pre-constructing, and that characteristic explicitness of the care, something primordial becomes evident, something that underlies this phenomenal connection, a basic phenomenon that is not merely proper to the care but that we will come to know as bound up much more intimately with the character of existence's being. I have in mind the *ensnarement*, the way that the care, insofar as it lives for the object of concern, is what it is precisely by virtue of the fact that *it ensnares itself in itself*. Thanks to this ensnaring of itself in itself, care comes to determine each and every thing from this standpoint.

This self-ensnaring makes for the fact that everything that crosses the path of the care is cared for in such a way that what is not cared for is not simply merely not there but instead is cared for as something that does not have to be there. We see in the ensnarement a further phenomenon that may be des-ignated *neglect*. Each care qua care neglects something. That is nothing that is imposed on care from the outside. What is neglected is precisely what the care itself claims to take care of. We must try to envision this phenomenon for ourselves concretely. We have to examine what sort of phenomenon the neglect proper to the care about already known knowledge is, whether it ne-glects something precisely in the midst of what it claims to take care of. Let us, therefore, ask: What neglect is it that can be seen in this concrete care? By pointing out a specific neglect and, indeed, as neglect on the part of this specific care, we gain a new confirmation of the care-character of this care. We will complete the task of establishing this characteristic neglect by *inves-tigating the second part of the Husserlian critique, the critique of historicism.* We must examine the extent to which a specific neglect on the part of this care can be located in this critique. To this end, we must first ascertain how the neglect already becomes evident here in the critique of naturalism. Only from this perspective will we see that the neglect is not somehow like for-getting. We will see that what is neglected is neglected in the sense of the care. The neglected is not forgotten but virtually banished. The care defends itself against what it neglects.

The theme is consciousness and, indeed, the lawfulness of every possible behavior. This lawfulness is, as such, an ideal lawfulness. It is grounded in the idea that it ought to be secured as a normative lawfulness in such a way that a thoroughgoing and *absolutely objective normative determination of the entire existence of humanity* is attained. The task of the normative science is set up with the aim of regulating and consolidating human existence, i.e., the culture, by means of securing that science. In the foregoing considerations [by Husserl], there has never been any talk of *what* is supposed to be normatively determined; *the entity* subjected to the normative determination is never placed under scrutiny in the same primordial sense. It is even said that such phenomena as the "concrete *I*" and the "soul" are supposed to be put out of play. Thus, what is supposed to be normatively determined does not enter into the realm of the actual theme. If this should be a case of neglect, as claimed here, this does not mean that what is subject to the normative determination must be investigated so that the norm can be fitted to what it is supposed to determine normatively. Rather, the claim is much more a matter of principle. The sense of the norm and normative lawfulness cannot be established as long as one does not envision what type of being is meant by a *normatively determined* and *determinable being*. The possibility of normativity cannot be explained without being investigated as normativity *for* something and, that means, without the "*for what*" being investigated in terms of its structure of being.

The reason, then, why this neglect is in fact present, the reason why the idea of normative determination is discussed with an astonishing insouciance, lies in the fact that the idea of the norm is drawn from a completely isolated perspective that is in turn given in advance by the care about already known knowledge. It is drawn from the fact of the matter of *theoretical judgment*. A theoretical proposition is spoken. The spoken proposition is the basis for the consideration in such a way that the difference between the occasional pronouncement of the proposition and the valid sense of the proposition is stressed. The latter is itself *always* objectively valid while, in contrast to it, the concrete assertion of the judgment in reality changes. Everything that one characterizes as the concrete pronouncement of the judgment is suspended as a murky form of appearance of the valid. On this slight basis, the differentiation of the valid idea and so forth is acquired and transposed, by way of formalizing and analogizing, to every behavior suited to consciousness. Insofar as all interest is directed at the justification of such a validity, all research into consciousness is so conducted that, from the outset, it disregards *what* is supposed to be normatively determined. We have to learn to understand that this neglect is not simply an oversight, a failure to pay attention to something that could subsequently be done, but instead that what is here neglected is *neglected in the manner of a concern for it* [*in besorgender Weise*]. That is the genuine sense of the critique of historicism.

§ 13. Husserl's critique of historicism[20]

The question arises: How does *history* [*Geschichte*] enter at all into the field of view in the context of the theme of consciousness? It was stressed that in this entire period and even today philosophical inquiry is still principally oriented to *science* and to *disciplines*. Hence, history is a theme for a science or group of sciences, history as scientifically known, as an *historical account* [*Historie*].

a) The different basis of this critique

By way of introduction, Husserl says that *historicism* is an overreaching of specific, scientific ideas. The science of history, he says, has to do merely with facts. Its object belongs to the empirical science of facts. At first it is impossible to foresee how this question is supposed to have a connection with the idea of a philosophy as a rigorous science.

Contemporary with the epistemology and so forth at the time, a philosophy comes along that receives its impulse from Dilthey. In the course of his research into the history of the human spirit, Dilthey arrived at basic insights into the accounts given of history. According to Dilthey, the "formation of historical consciousness" gradually leads to destroying belief in the existence of an absolute philosophy, i.e., in the present case, belief in "consciousness-of" as *knowing*.[21] The formation of historical consciousness, far more than the discord among systems, is precisely what motivates the recognition of the impossibility of an absolute philosophy. It should be said that this tendency did not attain the level of clarification that it could have claimed and, as a result, the *Husserlian critique of historicism* from the outset stands *on a basis different from* that of the critique of naturalism. In the case of naturalism, not only does a group of sciences, a theory of science, occupy a position in a much more distinct and conceivable way, but Husserl's interest is also primarily anchored in naturalism's group of sciences, while a thorough study [on his part] of the other group is lacking. As a result, the analysis of how the

---

20. For §§ 13–14, see E. Husserl, "Philosophie als strenge Wissenschaft," op. cit., Historizismus und Weltanschauungsphilosophie [Historicism and Philosophy of World-view]: 323–341.
21. Ibid., 324.

latter group overextends the sense of science becomes precarious, the argumentation more cautious, and at the same time such that it appeals more to feeling than to absolute insights. This critique moves in the direction that has Husserl saying: history, i.e., an historical account, can speak neither for nor against the validity of ideas. Hence, the fact that there has been no philosophy as a rigorous science up to now is no proof against the possibility of the idea of this philosophy. The usual argument is drawn upon: historicism, thought through to its logical conclusion, leads to relativism and this relativism to skepticism.[22]

b) The neglect of human existence, in the deficient care, care about absolute, normative lawfulness

For us the leading question is how *to understand consciousness in its character of being*. This character becomes apparent, if we concretely envision for ourselves the care that revolves around consciousness as a determinate field of knowledge and if we ask *what* in consciousness this care is concerned about. It is necessary to determine the *care at work in Husserl's critique*. Care about obtaining an absolute certitude of knowledge is what determines the entire critique in its selection and handling of themes. In our last discussion, we happened to establish a fundamental factor of the care, a factor that was designated as the neglect in every care. In order to understand this, it is necessary from the outset to heed the fact that the neglect itself is something that is the concern of the care. Neglecting can be characterized as *deficient* caring. A being is deficient if, in the manner of its being, it is detrimental to what it is with and to what it, as an entity, is related. The neglecting is thus itself a care and, indeed, a *deficient care, in such a way, that the care cannot come to what, in accordance with its own sense, it is concerned about.*

One of the things that care takes care to do is to omit something, to leave it out. It is inherent in care's character of being, not merely simply to be, but *to have such and such definite possibilities*. In the type and manner of neglect, we encounter this peculiar movement that lies in the being of every care. Neglecting is not simply a matter of leaving something out; instead, insofar as the care has to do with the object of concern, it also has to do with the object of its neglect. The care takes care that what is neglected remains genuinely neglected and does not get in its way again (whereby, precisely in the neglecting, something that it is allegedly concerned about remains as not neglected). Care blocks its path to what it neglects so that it is in no way disturbed in its neglect.

Let us, therefore, hold on to the following points: What is the object of

22. See the Appendix, Supplement 9 (p. 228).

concern? An absolutely justified, binding character of the norm for the sake of making it possible to shape the culture ideally as the genuine culmination of the idea of humanity. The focal point is an alleged need of human existence, a need that is supposed to be principally removed by the work on the absolute certitude of the norms. Thus, human existence itself is also there in the sphere of what is an object of concern. The question remains: What, then, is neglected? In this care about the absolute certitude of the norm and, at the same time, about elaborating a genuine lawfulness, the task of examining human existence itself does not come up at all. Precisely what, as such, is supposed to be secured does not enter into the theme of the examination. In the first place, it does not enter into the theme in a principal way like everything else does and, in the second place, it is dismissed as being of secondary importance, a *cura posterior* [second-order care]. The full weight of the care rests solely on the normative lawfulness as such. *What is neglected is what is the genuine object of concern: human existence.* There is no inquiry into what it is; instead, the idea of humanity and the concept of the human being are left in a routine sort of contingency. It needs to be shown in more detail what the object of neglect looks like and how the caring is deficient caring, how the care takes care not to let human existence approach it, how it takes care to render human existence innocuous, and to keep it in this innocuous state.

§ 14. Critique of historicism on the path of the clarification of problems

Historicism is likewise considered in greater detail [by Husserl] on the *path of the clarification of problems.* One should think at first that, in the discussion of historicism, the concrete existence of the human being would be encountered. We will see that, through the very way that the question is posed, care is taken that history as such does not come into view at all.

a) Husserl's critique of Dilthey

In the course of the critique of historicism that is likewise made in the manner of clarifying the problems, a specific *world-view* is taken up as Dilthey developed it. Indeed, Dilthey is drawn upon in such a way that he is covered up with a catchword [*Schlagwort*] from the outset. In this critique there is no possibility of even merely understanding Dilthey's work *positively* in any sort of sense. Insofar as this work is from the outset subsumed under the catchword "historicism," the critique proceeds by clarifying detrimental features in Dilthey himself. In this critique of historicism, the obscurities are not clarified but elevated into something that is a matter of principle.

In regard to the question of what historical existence as such looks like,

Dilthey himself failed because he did not have any possibilities of even posing this question. In spite of this, it must be said that the tendency to interpret him in view of any sort of normative philosophy, in order then to put him down as a relativist, is utterly alien to what he is. One has to let Dilthey's work stand as it is. One should not judge him in view of the familiar and usual ideas of philosophy. One has to learn to understand that his work is no empty reflection on history and historical consciousness, that his work was the work of giving an historical account and that in this work something like the possibility of a new and distinctive consciousness of existence [*Daseins-bewußtsein*] first gradually took shape. For Dilthey, life in history was itself an existential possibility that he himself lived, albeit a possibility that did not become totally clear to him since he himself is still caught up in the traditional consideration of history, which I call the *aesthetic consideration of history* under the idea of humanity. This leads to [Husserl's] critique that, to its detriment, takes up the obscurities in Dilthey himself and takes them as the occasion for refutations.

b) Historical existence as the object of neglect

If we look at it in a positive way, we may ask: What does the care about already known knowledge *neglect* in the course of the critique of historicism? Here it needs to be said that the characteristic factor of a back-flash makes itself apparent in a decisive way in the critique of historicism. How does history enter at all into the field of view? History enters as the thematic field for a completely determined task of knowledge. The possibility of seeing historical existence itself, of developing a primordial relationship to historical being, is cut off from the outset. The question of what historical being as such is cannot even appear within this clarification of problems.

History is set down as the *object* of *the science of history*, as a determinate, uniform domain of facts. Insofar as the science of history has specific tasks as part of its examination, history becomes material for the examination of history with respect to these aspects. *Historical existence* is degraded to factual material [*Tatsachenmaterial*] for a specific task. This task is characterized as follows. From the concrete factual material of spiritual existence [*geistigen Daseins*], the aim is to establish the many types of formations as formations of meaning [*Gestalten des Sinnes*]. This examination of a formation has its exact analogies in organic nature. In organic nature, too, there are possibilities of establishing the morphological character of things. The idea behind this consideration of history is a morphology or typology of historical events. As material it moves even more into the role of the unimportant. The respective individual is, indeed, merely the exemplary material for the type. Through this entire development of the idea of an historical examination, *historical existence* is *completely degraded.* Only as an object of the science of history, does history enter into the field of view. The way to the historical as such is cut off. *Care about already known knowledge has excluded human existence as such from any possibility of being encountered.* History is degraded down one more level as a fund of material and collection of examples for philosophical notions. The tendency to get a grip on human existence is severed.

The neglect, the care in regard to what is neglected, is again evident from the fact that it does not simply leave matters at that. Instead, history, thus degraded, is then tolerated in this degraded state for the sake of posing the question of its importance for the idea of a philosophy as a rigorous science of an absolutely justified lawfulness. History is posited in a certain regard without asking whether this regard has any sense at all. This way of posing the question is presupposed. Thus it happens that what is conveyed in positive work [in historical investigation] stands in no connection at all with the claim to mathematical rigor as is demanded for the idea of such a philosophy. Precisely at decisive points, the rigor demanded is missing.

c) Origin and legitimacy of the contrast between
matter of factness and validity

From what and with what *right* is the *contrast between matter of factness and validity* drawn? With what right is this contrast set up as a fundamental [*grundsätzlich*] distinction for the entire consideration of entities?

Even within science Husserl distinguishes science as an objective unity in terms of its validation [*objektive Geltungseinheit*] and science as a factual, cultural formation. Each science is divided up in this way. Insofar as the historical account has to do only with facts, this science intends to study them only in their matter of factness. Hence, from the study of the history of philosophy, from the study of the factual material, it is not possible to make out what the science is as an objective unity in terms of its validation. On the basis of this distinction, not only history but also the science of history is put out of play as insignificant.

The genuine point in question is that of the distinction between the factual and the valid: 1. What is this distinction drawn from? 2. If it is drawn from a determinate, concrete base, can it be extended to every formation of the human spirit?

This distinction is drawn from *theoretical behavior* and *judging.* Distinguished therein are the judging behavior's valid sense and its matter of factness. This distinction is made absolute. Here the neglect makes itself palpable in an utterly fatal sense. A rigorous investigation of the matter is disregarded and a completely banal Platonism is resorted to.

This distinction is not invented by Husserl but instead pervades the entire history of philosophy.[23] The peculiar development of the history of the human spirit [*Geistesgeschichte*] that begins at the outset of the eighteenth century and is designated "the development of historical consciousness" becomes transparent in a concrete way for the first time in Dilthey. But he did not get far because he lacked the training in method that was necessary as a preparation and because the possibility of handling the problem of history in a way completely detached from the science of history remained hidden from him.[24]

The severing of the valid and the factual, in the state in which it dominates in traditionally Platonizing philosophy, is simply taken over without the slightest alteration. In the critique of historicism it is evident that the care and what it is concerned about—absolute validity in the interest of shaping the idea of humanity—put the existence of the human being and genuine interrogation of it out of play.

d) The reproach of skepticism and the care revealing itself therein, care about already known knowledge as anxiety in the face of existence

The critique delivers its main blow by bringing the argument from *skepticism* to bear on historicism, the argument that all historicism, thought through "to its logical conclusion," leads to skepticism.[25] We intend to consider the critique first in three respects: 1. How does the care about already known knowledge make itself evident? 2. How does this care's peculiar need make itself evident? 3. How does the neglect reveal itself in it?

Care about already known knowledge is evident from the manner in which its back-flash (in the back-flash there is always a relative *blinding*) validates itself such that the position of historicism is interpreted in terms of validity. It is claimed that historicism amounts to saying that truths are not in themselves valid but instead only taken to be valid by specific human beings for a specific time. No attempt is made to see whether or not within historicism there is a possibility of determining the truth otherwise. From the outset, demands are made on the position in the sense that the critique itself chooses, such that absolute validity and factically holding-something-to-be-valid are placed in opposition to one another. The back-flash of the care is evident from the fact that the idea of *validity* is posited from the outset as equivalent to the idea of *truth*, such that it is said that if the idea of validity is not made absolutely certain, then there is no science. It could be that the idea of absolute validity is senseless and that science is possible in spite of this or rather precisely for that reason. The entire Husserlian argumentation is a way of

---

23. See the Appendix, Supplement 10 (p. 228f).
24. See the Appendix, Supplement 11 (p. 229).
25. E. Husserl, "Philosophie als strenge Wissenschaft," 324ff.

purely and formally opposing a valid sense to a real, temporal sense. Within these alternatives, no other possibility even appears on the horizon. On the basis of its ensnarement, the care is locked up in what it is concerned about. The critique thus becomes completely unfree.

In this line of argument, the peculiar need [*Not*] of the care becomes palpable. The demonstration proceeds in an utterly peculiar fashion. Following upon the basic refutation is an appendix in which the genuine force behind the argumentation is seen ("by this means, all the sentences that I now articulate will be false"[26]). At this juncture, care about already known knowledge takes a peculiar step: it appeals to what it neglects. In the demonstration, the party to be refuted is shown what existence would be like if there were no absolute validity. With a squinting glance at existence, one is made anxious. In its greatest need, the care appeals to existence as something potentially *uncertain* and appeals to it in order to bump the consideration back away from it. At the juncture of the decisive blow in the form of an argumentatio ad hominem, the critique explicitly takes into its care what it always neglects, claiming for itself what it neglects. By holding out the prospect of a potential existence in this uncertainty, he [Husserl] implicitly urges his readers not to have any part in such an existence. That is the genuine, unspoken sense of every argumentation that believes that, with skepticism, it can make for skittishness. The care about already known knowledge is nothing other than *anxiety in the face of existence*.

e) The preconceptions about existence at work in this care

Quite definite *preconceptions about existence* are at work in this care, though this seemingly radical critique does not give the slightest account of them. Here only three preconceptions underlying the argumentation are enumerated: 1. that the human beings to whom this argumentation is directed are bent on experiencing and preserving the truth at all costs; 2. that truth is validity; and 3. that truth and truth's being can be proven through theoretical deduction and, conversely, that the denial of truth can lead, through a theoretical deduction, ad absurdum.

Ad 1. Is it such a settled matter that human existence wants to become acquainted with the truth at any cost? Or is it not much more important to human existence to evade the truth and in the place of the truth to deceive itself with a phantom? The question is not resolved and must be decided or, better, if undecidable, then it must be *left open accordingly*. Only by researching human existence's manner of being can anything be settled about this. Moreover, what if it should even turn out that we today, precisely on the basis

26. Ibid., 325.

of traditional philosophy, are not in a position at all to make human existence into a theme ontologically? Does the possibility exist at all of penetrating to *existence*?

Ad 2. It is presupposed that truth is validity (within the horizon *of validity*, being-true—the truth is interpreted as *validation*. This is the phenomenon of falling prey [*Verfallsphänomenon*] theoretically absolutized into Plato's "ideas.") Validity is a character of the articulated proposition, the finished knowledge, insofar as it has become *public*, that is to say, insofar as it is oriented to communicability, transmission, and acquisition. Validity is the manner in which the truth is here publicly. This peculiar aspect in which the truth obtains publicly is so constituted that it has already given the truth away. The alleged possession of a validity is not yet warranted at all by the fact that a *specific readiness of access* to the entity that the "truth" uncovers is inherent in truth. What is inherent in truth is not only the readiness of access but also the possibility of *sustaining the encounter of the entity in its primordial character*; the primordial character of our interactions with the entity that we have appropriated to ourselves [is what I mean here] since the entity gets lost again and again precisely on the basis of the sort of possession of it that grinds it down beyond recognition. The equating of truth and validity is not transparent without further ado. Above all, it should be noted that truth, precisely insofar as it is taken to mean validity, obscures the decisive problems of existence. The question is whether the interpretation of truth as validity makes any sense for historical knowledge. That becomes even more questionable in the case of philosophical knowledge and utterly impossible in the case of the "truth" of art and religion.

Ad 3. It is thus evident that where, in the deciding arguments, care about already known knowledge battles against skepticism, it is bent on enabling itself a constant *flight in the face of existence* itself. It takes care to look to *validity* and to *disregard the possible prospect of an uncertain existence*. Today and always the critique of historicism has a particular cogency because of a lack of clarity about the object of the critique itself, namely, because skepticism explains itself with the means which, for its part, it combats. Skepticism is a fruitful rebellion against the trivializing of philosophy; yet it is itself a halfway measure. The division between skepticism and absolutism regarding validation rests on a basis that has not been made clear and the division is to be rejected as a whole. The difference between ideal and real being is not only not identified, but is only drawn from a thoroughly limited sphere in the most peculiar field, the theoretical field. The decisive guides, the concepts of being and being-true, are not grounded in the way necessary for a science that works towards ultimate identifiability. In this way, a fundamental [*grundsätzlich*] neglect on the part of the critique and even of the positive research becomes evident.

This neglect can ultimately be corrected. Much more important than this neglect is the manner in which the argumentation against skepticism ultimately lands in trouble. It must be prepared to conduct an ad hominem argument. The possibility of rigidly holding oneself to what is called "historicism" is pursued to its final consequences and directed in such a way that the prospect of an existence of a specific character affords itself. As a consequence of historicism, the conclusion is necessarily reached that there perhaps no longer is a principle of contradiction—that all propositions that we articulate are false. With this prospect of an uncertain existence, the argument can leave matters at that, on the self-evident presumption that those to whom the argument is directed renounce such a prospect.

The argument against skepticism presupposes further that in a decisive sense it matters to human beings to preserve the truth. That is a sheer presupposition relative to the existence of human beings that has not come into view up to now. In this argumentation there is first this specific preconception about human beings and then the conviction that truth is validity. Truth is given as the validity of a proposition in its specific, public validity or lack of validity. Even this quite secondary aspect is unsuited to serve as a guide. In the decisive argument against skepticism, it is thus evident that care about already known knowledge ensnares itself in itself—that in the decisive moment it resorts to precisely what it flees.

§ 15. Making more precise what care about already known knowledge is

We have rolled out this entire examination of the question of the decisive care underlying the critique so that we have a basis for concretely deciding the following question: *What character of being does consciousness have, the consciousness that has been set up as the thematic field of phenomenological research?* How is this field obtained? Let us envision the care, in order to experience in it and on the basis of the possibilities of its existence the sort of being that the object of its concern has.

Before we proceed to the final way of answering this question, it is important that we make *care about already known knowledge more precise for ourselves and thus pose three further questions*: 1. What does this care interpret the object of its concern as? 2. What is the care about the matters themselves that was earlier assumed to be the characteristic factor in the breakthrough of phenomenological research? 3. In what sense is the care thus characterized care about the rigor of science? These questions are connected with one another. The way of answering the first prepares the way for the others.

a) Care about justified knowledge, about a universally binding character that is evident

Care about already known knowledge is directed at *justified knowledge*, at ultimately valid knowledge that as such, with the circle of propositions and unified complexes of propositions secured by it, constitutes the genuine basis for all science. Care about already known knowledge is care about a knowledge justified by knowledge itself. This knowledge is taken, from the outset, to be *scientific* knowledge. Care about already known knowledge is care about a definite and ultimate scientific status and the scientific status is itself determined to be "binding on all rational beings." A scientific status means a status binding on every discerning person; care about it is care *about a universally binding character that is evident*. The characteristic element in this self-interpretation is the fact that *what* is supposed to be known in this knowledge is from the outset secondary. The care is primarily focused on *fashioning any possible, absolutely-binding sort of knowledge at all*. Connected with this is the fact that, in the concrete examination of science, science is conceived as the unity of a set of problems and method. The care is directed at a questioning that is secured in a definite way. The question itself as question, what ultimately determines the question, decides the answer's tendency toward the proposition's validity in the sense of apodicticity, prior to any interest in the matter questioned. What is interrogated, the matter, first genuinely has its genuine being through the elaboration and correct clarification of the question itself. Thus, philosophy becomes the basic science in the sense that in it the formation of ultimately valid propositions is supposedly enabled. There is always only *the one* question: How can the scientific status with a universally binding character be accomplished? The matters themselves are primarily encountered in this care as problems, as objective connections prefigured in terms of determinate orientations of problems.

b) "To the matters themselves": care about matters prefigured by a universally binding character

Given what has just been said, the phrase "to the matters themselves" [*"zu den Sachen selbst"*] can no longer mean here to envision the matters freely from their own standpoint, *prior* to a determinate manner of question. Instead it means enabling what is interrogated to be encountered *within this set of problems* that *is prefigured in a completely determined way*. Even so, the slogan "to the matters themselves" still has a certain primordial character relative to the constructions of contemporary philosophy. But in view of the sense of this philosophy that is most proper to it, one sees that this call emerged from a care that is unsuited to the matter. This call is nothing other than the demand to lose oneself decisively in care about a *universally binding character*, to envision for oneself only the *matters prefigured in it*, so that this seemingly quite self-evident call "to the matters themselves" leaves outside its purview the much *more fundamental possibility of presenting the entity so freely* that solely the corresponding worthiness of the entity to be interrogated decides what philosophy's primary object is. Such a decision must free itself up in itself for the possibility that this sort of knowledge has nothing to do with an idea of science taken up from mathematics, but that perhaps only the sort of decidability that proceeds from setting the matters free achieves the genuine sense of knowledge.[27]

c) Care about the rigor of science as derivative seriousness; the mathematical idea of rigor, uncritically set up as an absolute norm

We are now prepared to investigate what the demand for the *rigor of science* means for this science itself. Rigor is something procured in a specific *seriousness* relative to a care. Insofar as being able to speak of the freely presented matters is not primarily decisive, but the binding character and the possibility of demonstrating it are, the seriousness concentrates on shaping this binding character. Care about rigor in this case is the seriousness that is directed at *justifiability* and *genuine justification*.

Insofar as this seriousness is grounded in the thus characterized care, it is a *derivative* seriousness. It lacks the primordial character that could bring it to the point of risking everything such that first *what* is known is recognized as the determining factor. Not only here but in our entire history of science, the *mathematical idea of rigor* has been uncritically erected as an *absolute norm*.

This erection of an utterly contingent idea of rigor has issued in an entire complex of questions, for example, "How is the science of history to be brought up to the level of a rigorous science?" A science's possibility of being rigorous cannot be ascribed to it from the outside but instead must be taken and formed from the science itself as a way of uncovering entities. The rigor is not an empty idea but instead something concrete that shapes itself out of the science itself.[28]

From the answers to the last three questions it is evident how the care constantly *ensnares* itself. On the basis of this character of being ensnared in itself, we now understand the characteristic that we earlier laid down about care, concerning which we made the following determination: each care seizes

27. See the Appendix, Supplement 12 (p. 229).
28. See the Appendix, Supplement 13 (p. 230).

upon something, holds on to it, interprets it, commits itself to and finally loses itself in the object of its concern. Ensnarement is a movement inherent in the existence of care.

§ 16. Disclosing the thematic field of "consciousness" through the care about already known knowledge. Return to the historical, concrete instance of the care

Up till now we have basically merely made clear that care about already known knowledge shapes the object of concern in the sense that it *secures* a *set of problems* and a *method* directed at that object. Furthermore, we have seen that the care about already known knowledge refers all possible questioning of a fundamental [*grundsätzlich*] sort back to the thematic field of "consciousness," that care about already known knowledge binds itself to the object of concern. We have seen how the care loses itself in the thematic field of "consciousness," not only insofar as this *basic science of consciousness* as the establishment of an ultimate binding character is determined as a possibility of the culture's existence, but also insofar as the ultimate science of consciousness is characterized as the ἡγεμονικόν [fit guide] of human existence in general, with the result that care's specific way of being lost in the object of concern [i.e., consciousness] reveals itself in this ultimate, basic point of departure. We have *not yet answered* the decisive question of *how care arrives at this object of concern*. Thus, we are faced with the further task of showing that it is this *care about already known knowledge* that *discloses* this *thematic field of "consciousness."*

a) Care's circumspection and aim

In order to understand this final demonstration, a brief preparation is necessary, one that consists in making present to ourselves a factor of care that has not been explicitly emphasized up till now and to do so solely with the help of what we have already made out about care. If we remember a care's neglect, then it is easy to see how care's *circumspection*, as we call it, is at work in this peculiar manner of caring. Every care is, as such, a seeing. That it is a seeing is not an external determination but instead is given with its being. A kind of sight is, along with other things, inherent in being in the sense of being within a world. This kind of sight is there [*da*] as such in each manner of humanly being (of *existence* [*Dasein*]), also in the basic manner of existing, in care. This kind of sight has nothing to do with theoretical knowledge but is, instead, a *kind of accomplishment of existence's basic constitution*, one that ought to be referred to as *uncoveredness* (see the end of the lectures, p. 218, and Part Two, p. 149). These phenomena reside in a primordial dimension that is much more fundamental than what is handed down to us through specific theories. Each care has its definite point of view and the point of view is at work in the exercise of caring [*Sorgensvollzug*] as the respectively performed circumspection [*Umsicht*] of each care, a circumspection that is not contingent but is instead guided by what may be designated the care's *aim* [*Absicht*]. Each step of care is guided by this aim.

What needs to be shown is how the thus characterized care, by virtue of the way it realizes its viewpoint, discloses something specific that is to be taken care of [or with which it is to be concerned: *zu Besorgendes*], *how the care about already known knowledge* thereby in fact *discloses* the *thematic field of "consciousness."* Decisive for us is *how* the care about already known knowledge in general acquires its specific, thematic field; to what extent the care about already known knowledge is suited to disclose and to sustain something like the thematic field of "consciousness." The understanding presupposes an orientation regarding a basic peculiarity of all caring, namely, that it is caring with a certain kind of sight, that it has the object of concern in view in some sense. Caring's kind of sight is a character that is given with existence itself. Existence as *being in a world* (being-in) is being that discloses. What is expressed by the phrase "in a world" is not that two objects are related in some way to one another but instead that the specific being of what is alive is grounded on *having* the world in the manner of taking care of it. We designate this orientation of an entity insofar as it lives, that is to say, insofar as it is *in* its world, as a kind of sight. Each care lives in a determinate point of view towards what it takes care of. The sphere of what is to be taken care of is seen by the care through various possibilities of seeing peculiar to it, possibilities which, for their part, are guided and led by the way of looking upon what is to be taken care of, by the aim.

b) Descartes' research as a factically-historical, concrete instance of the care in its disclosing of the thematic field of "consciousness"

The task now arises for us of understanding something even more primordial, namely, how a specific care that is determined by what it looks towards, its aim, can disclose something that can be taken care of, in other words, how care about a universally binding character *as such discloses and works on a field of being*. Indeed, initially the care about a universally binding character is not related to a specific field of being at all. The question is how the formation of the care leads it to see what it should be decisively concerned about in a specific domain of being towards which it steers itself.

Each care is, in its being, *factical* care, that is to say, the *factical, concrete instance* of its being is inherent in what the care is. Together with other things, *facticity* is inherent in what the care itself is [*Wassein der Sorge selbst*]. That expresses itself in such a way that the care is a manner of existence. Existence is as such factical.

In the course of conducting an original examination of care and its being, we now see ourselves led back to a *respective* facticity. In the elucidation of the care involved, it is important *not* to make it into an object in a way that is *indifferent with respect to being*. The *concrete* manner of being of the care about already known knowledge, in which *consciousness* discloses itself *as a field* [of study], has been patently given to us in *Descartes' research*. At this juncture in our examination, it is necessary to introduce a fundamental [*grundsätzlich*] consideration, namely, the *connection of our examination with the historical*. You may see from what has been said that the return to the *concrete, historical instance of care* is not accidental but is instead demanded by the sense of philosophizing, demanded in the sense that we look for this care in its respectively primordial and historically decisive dimensions. Here Descartes and Husserl are not arbitrary exemplifications of what we assert about care; instead they are *possibilities of care's being* itself. From this it becomes evident that, at the present juncture of our examination, we are cast back from the analysis of the phenomenon of care to *history*, in the effort to gather what the genuine being of this care is and what it discloses.[29]

29. See the Appendix, Supplement 14 (p. 231).

PART TWO

Return to Descartes
and
The Scholastic Ontology that Determines Him

Chapter One

Making sense of the return to Descartes by recalling what has
been elaborated up to this point

*§ 17. The hermeneutic situation of the investigations up to this point
and of those standing before us*

We are faced with *returning to Descartes*[1] because of the current situation of
philosophy itself, yet the peculiarity of the return has not become obvious. In
the way that *Husserl's critique returned to Descartes*, quite specific oversights
took up considerable room, with the result that the manner of the return must
be presented more precisely. We will make *sense of the return* by quite simply
recollecting what has been accomplished up to this point. A recollection is
not simply a retelling, but instead a way of making something clearer to
oneself by running through the path traveled up to this point. By means of
the recollection, what was run through up to this point is set against a horizon
in which the contrasts are sharpened. The recollection must stress more point-
edly the decisive impetuses animating the considerations. The dominant impetuses are determined by 1. *what* is in view from the outset in the entire
investigation; 2. how what is placed in view from the outset is *seen*; 3. how
this undertaking [*Vornehmen*] of a specific theme is motivated from a specific
position, how this type and manner [of undertaking it] determines the *conceptual* explication.

Hence, it is necessary to come to some understanding of 1. the *pre-
possession* [what one has before one: *Vorhabe*], what is had from the outset
for the investigation, upon which the look constantly rests; 2. the *pre-view*
[what one foresees: *Vorsicht*], the sort and manner of seeing what is held onto

1. See the Appendix, Supplement 15 (p. 231). This text immediately precedes the first sentence of § 17.

in the pre-possession; 3. the *pre-hension* [foregrasp, anticipation: *Vorgriff*]: how what is seen in a specific way is conceptually explicated on the basis of specific motivation. These are the factors of the *hermeneutical situation* on the basis of which something is interpreted. Έρμηνεύειν means to interpret in the sense of an interpretation that keeps itself transparent to itself. All the characters of the hermeneutical situation are determined by the categorial *pre-emptiveness* [or fore-going character: *Vorhafte*]. This pre-emptiveness that pertains to these determinations of the hermeneutical situation is a basic determination of existing itself. The possession, the view, the grasp are basic constitutions that arise for existence.

What the investigation itself *has in advance, the pre-possession* [*Vorhabe*] is *being-here*. The *pre-view* [*Vorsicht*], that in regard to which being-here itself is seen as such, is *being*, being-here in terms of its being, in terms of the possibilities and manners of its being. The *pre-hension* [*Vorgriff*] is determined by the fact that the characters of being are *explicated*. Being-here is seen in regard to a genuine possibility of being, with regard to *existence*.[2] This possibility of being on the part of being-here discloses itself only in a radical, hermeneutical questioning. Explication is itself a possibility of being that can be described in a radical questioning that has been traditionally designated "philosophical." In this sense all these characteristics, insofar as they concern existence, are *existentials*. The existentials are quite specific determinations of being that have nothing to do with the usual categories. Categories always apply to factual, worldly domains of being.

The observations made *up to this point* divide into two initially separate observations. The first observation centered around the clarification of the term "phenomenology." The second set out to identify what designates itself with this term today. Both investigations point to a specific uniformity of theme and agreement in method. Both investigations are conducted by interpreting what is given to existence in advance.

Φαινόμενον and λόγος are interpreted with respect to existence: self-showing as a specific possibility of the world, which can turn around into pretending to be something else, whereby the further development into illusion becomes possible. Λόγος as a basic possibility of existence: as a process of addressing and discussing the world encountered.

The second observation was already characterized by the explicit character of the inquiry as the sort of inquiry in which being is what matters. We interpreted the thematic field of "consciousness" with a view to a specific care; we interpreted the formation of the thematic field as a manner of existing.

---

2. [This paragraph is one of the few passages containing both *Existenz* (here translated "existence") and *Dasein* (here translated "being-here" in order to maintain the contrast with *Existenz*, but otherwise usually translated "existence" or "existing").—D.D.]

To be caring [*sorgend sein*] in this manner is a basic type of existence. Thus, in the last interpretation of care about already known knowledge, it turned out that care, the possibility seized upon, is the possibility of being that is indicated in the Aristotle-interpretation.

In the interpretation of care we elucidated it with a view to possibilities of being: back-flash, pre-constructing, ensnarement, neglect. Care about already known knowledge is a flight in the face of existence as such. From here we also understand the further question of what it means that consciousness be-comes the thematic field. *Consciousness as the thematic field comes to pri-macy through a care of existence itself.* Existence flees in the face of itself and gives up the possibility of radically seeing and grasping itself. This is the meaning of the seemingly harmless process of consciousness becoming the thematic field.

§ 18. Becoming free from the discipline and traditional possibilities as a way of becoming feee for existence. Investigation as destruction in the ontological investigation of existence

Both investigations—the elucidation of the term ["phenomenology"] and the characterization of what is designated by it—are *not oriented to a previously given discipline.* These investigations have the peculiar character of leading out from the discipline to a peculiar connection of phenomena: existence. *Becoming free from the discipline for existence itself.* This "becoming free" means seizing the possibilities of making this existence itself the theme of a research determined *by existence itself.* This research is nothing other than a possibility of existence itself.

This task of becoming free for this fact of the matter, existence, is accom-plished in *becoming free from handed down possibilities and traditional types* of determining and classifying this being in the general inquiry of philosophy. We have to make clear to ourselves that all previous research that is related to existence in any sense at all (under the title: stream of experience, reason, life, "I," person, and so forth) reveals a *basic neglect*: a neglect to inquire first of all into the *actual constitution* [*eigentliche Verfassung*] of the very entity that is treated. It must be shown that all previous philosophy, on the basis of its origin, was not in a position to determine this entity more precisely *as existing*, though this entity was taken up as part of philosophy's pre-possession [*Vorhabe*]. What has become familiar under the rubric "philosophy of life" is a *tendency* toward living existence. At bottom, however, precisely the philos-ophy of life shows how little it has understood its very self, its basic task. Life designates a manner of being for which each category from previous ontology is wanting. Dilthey, who developed the greatest possibilities for grasping life, realized them in such a way that he worked reactively and thus obstructed the way to life, obstructing it from himself. With his proclivity for bringing life into view and getting a grip on it, he was inclined to bring life into the same inquiry that had been made of "nature," as it is called; although *he* battled exactly every naturalistic psychology in the most acute way, he continued to labor on *psychology*. Dilthey moved within the same sort of seeing that he defended himself against. He did not manage to free himself, as far as this entire tendency of his is concerned. The transparency of an instinct presents a much greater difficulty than does the certainty of the instinct and sustaining it.

The interpretation of existence is confronted with a peculiar difficulty that can only be established but is not to be overturned: namely, that every attempt to experience existence primordially comes to life out of the *present-day position* of the interpretation and conceptual determination of existence and life. This position is dominated by the *old ontology and logic* that hold as self-evident for everyone today. Hence, the task of freeing up existence itself and acquiring explications of it is necessarily bound up with the task of shaking up present-day existence (that is *ontologically obstructed*) in its obstructiveness, of *dismantling* it in such a way that the basic categories of consciousness, person, subject are led back to their primordial sense. They are to be led back in the sense that one shows, from insight into the origin of these categories, that they emerged on an *entirely different ground* of the experience of being and that, in terms of their conceptual tendency, they are inadequate for what we want to get into view as existence.

Each ontological investigation of existence is as such *destructive*; it stands in an inner connection with what one designates "historical consciousness." The existence, our *present-day* existence, is nothing isolated; this existence is in the basic composition of its possibilities a still-existing [*Nochdasein*], a "being what has been" [*Gewesensein*] of an earlier existence. Hence, for this entire fundamental consideration, *history* is not something arbitrary, something lying behind it and an opportunity for some sort of hustle and bustle in the humanities. Instead, history is something that we ourselves are. By contrast, what is presented to us as a past is not a past at all but rather a paltry present. What matters is *to disclose the past for the first time*. Our historical consciousness (Spengler) is the sort of consciousness that suffocates history altogether.[3] The talk is no longer of history and historical being at all. Each historical orientation must be viewed, not as a contingency, but instead as a definite task that is prefigured by existence itself.

---

3. This sentence is crossed out in the transcript worked over by longhand.

*§ 19. Return to the genuine being of care about already known knowledge
in its primordial past as a return to Descartes*

These determinations, which were given in a completely general fashion, are
to be applied now to the specific instance of the interpretation that presently
occupies us, the interpretation of care about already known knowledge. They
are to be applied in such a way that we ask: *How and in what manner does the
interpretation of care about already known knowledge lead back to Descartes?*

In the interpretation of Husserl we have seen that, with the establishment
of the thematic field of "consciousness," what presents itself is a definite way
of returning to existence, where it is taken in the concrete sense as a specific
exemplification of a universal. Consciousness designates the circle of phenomena that are studied with a view to the structures that apply to *each* consciousness qua consciousness. Being human is only one instance of this universal possibility of being: "consciousness." This context is determined by a
distinction of traditional logic: *genus* and *exemplar* of this genus. In relation
to what we have said so far, it is evident that, with the establishment of the
thematic field of "consciousness," the genuine context of existence with its
possibilities, a context that is historical, is extended into a *formal-logical* context that is not interested in *being* at all, but solely in a formal-logical order.
Through the *interpretation of this research with a view to the origin of the
way it is* [*seinsmäßiger Ursprung*], we will force the answer to a certain extent
[as to why this research is so conducted]. The determinations of the being of
this consciousness will turn out to be the sort that lead back to ancient Greek
ontology and logic. We will see that the novel character that distinguishes
Descartes is novel only in an *external respect,* that what presents itself in
Descartes' case is, to the contrary, no break, but instead a process of seizing
upon a prefigured possibility that we have already considered. The care about
already known knowledge is a possibility of being that *Greek philosophy*
specified *in a definite sense* by way of the absolute primacy accorded θεωρεῖν
among all of existence's possibilities of being.

The recollection is the deliberation on the hermeneutical situation, on the
position of the interpretation itself. The stance of the examination can be
characterized in various directions, as far as its way of being is concerned.
The most important are: what is had in advance, the pre-possession [*Vorhabe*],
namely, what remains in view from the outset, in terms of which everything
that comes into view is interpreted. *Being-here* [*Dasein*] was characterized as
pre-possessing the interpretation.[4] If what the interpretation looks towards is

---

4. [In the rest of this paragraph *Dasein* is again translated "being-here" not "existence," in
order to be able to reproduce Heidegger's way here of relating *Dasein* to *Existenz* ("existence").—D.D.]

characterized as its pre-possession, then contained in this expression is the fact that a *decision* is made—the decision that *being-here* becomes *the focal point of the investigation*. In a genuine examination of the hermeneutical situation and the factor of pre-possession, we are led to give an account of the motives that being-here itself has for deciding for the theme of "being-here." The reduction of the pre-possession into the undertaking [*Auflösung der Vorhabe in die Vornahme*], which pertains to an even more radical level, must be reversed. Being-here has been interpreted with respect to its being, being-here is examined with respect to its character of being, such that being-here's explicit "categories" are drawn from its specific being. More precisely, we will see that what were designated as categories in the previous consideration of being-here no longer come into consideration at all. We will designate being-here's characters of being, taken as being, as existentials and, of course, because being-here, taken as a determinate possibility of being, is named "existence" [*Existenz*] by us. This possibility is not always present; it is the sort of possibility that emerges in the philosophical deliberation. It cannot be set forth absolutely and as the sole possibility of being. We view being-here with respect to the characters of its being. What we observe are these determinations of being as existentials. The connection of these characters as existentials should not be made analogous to any sort of system of categories. The existentials exclude a kind of system in any sense of the term. Their connection is grounded in a completely different manner. What is thus seen in being-here, can be determined conceptually by means of the interpretive differentiation. The structural connection of this conceptual explication is what has been designated the "pre-hension" [*Vorgriff*]. The entire complex of possibilities that is given by means of such an interpretation lies in the grasp [*im Griff*]. "Pre-hension" is merely the synoptic title for the conceptuality that emerges in this explication. For elucidation of the basic character of care about already known knowledge, *of being-qua-disclosing*, it is necessary to go back to the genuine being of care.

Now, it was already apparent in earlier considerations that today *care about already known knowledge* is *dominant* in a peculiar sense and dominates philosophical inquiry. Care about already known knowledge has a dominance that is no longer controllable, a dominance that is *uprooted*, no longer aware of its origin. One lives in and with the tendency to treat consciousness as the basic theme. Care about already known knowledge is no longer capable of seeing its genuine being. It is impossible for care in this, its normal state [*Durchschnittlichkeit*] to get its genuine being into view. One must return to a *genuine being of care in its primordial past*. To return to the genuine being of care, for the sake of determining how in its being it is disclosive, is to return to a *context of research* that bears the name "Descartes."

§ 20. Destruction as the path of the interpretation of existence. Three tasks
for the explication of how, in its being, care about already
known knowledge is disclosive. The question of the
sense of the truth of knowledge in Descartes

The return appears as though it were a matter of turning away from a thematic consideration to an historical one. *Care's being* is an *historical being*, such that it can be uprooted like today's care about already known knowledge, but it is nevertheless historical. For a genuine examination of being, this does not mean that history has disappeared where care is uprooted; it is there in a subterranean way. Thus, we are already led closer to seeing existence as something that is concealed by its own history, by the history of its sort with its manner of interpreting itself. Up to the present day, the nexus of categorial research and logic, exemplified by the Greeks, dominates the perspective on what is designated "existence." Insofar as the goal is to bring existence into view, in each case the necessity grows of freeing existence up from such conceptual overgrowth, an overgrowth that existence itself has developed for the purpose of its genuine explication, but in which a peculiar tendency of existing presents itself today: *self-obstruction* [*Sich-selbst-verbauen*]. Existence has obstructed itself from itself in the entire sphere of its being. Freeing existence up by way of a *dismantling*, a *destruction*, occurs by tracing *concepts* back *to their distinctive origin*. What is accomplished at the same time on this path is the *elucidation of the inadequacy of the concepts for existence*, an elucidation of how existence's self-obstructing is enacted in history. When I designate this peculiar method of interpretation of existence as, in short, a *destructive method*, this can be regarded from four points of view.

    1. The *method of dismantling* is not a universal historical method, but instead a completely specific, concrete path that emerges from the necessities of existence and the categorial research into existence. This path is limited in its effectiveness to this. The destruction appears to be something purely negative. But it should be born in mind that the destruction looks, not for the weaknesses, but instead for the positive, the productive in what it takes up. The positive possibilities of research are kept in view. It is rendered visible, precisely in these possibilities, where they have their limits. What one designates, in short, "theological and philosophical work" falls into the sphere of the task of the destruction. Theological work falls into this sphere because Christian theology has constantly lived from hand to mouth and, in the appropriation of scientific conceptual means, has sought a connection to the respective philosophy, inasmuch as certain problems of existence are also broached in theology. Here is not the place to discuss whether it is possible for a theology to create its own conceptuality without leaning on a philosophy.

In any case, up to now theology has lived only from philosophy. Even Luther's original point of departure was completely smothered in the first ten years after his breakthrough by Melanchthon and the Aristotelian tradition that was taken up again. If attention is directed at what is positive, that does not mean that the destruction is supposed to bring about an improvement in the sense of separating the right from the false. Assessment of the history of existence in terms of truth and falsity is a misunderstanding of the sort of knowledge characteristic of the philosophical and theological sense of truth.

2. The destruction is in fact *critical*. But what is criticized is not the past that is opened up by the destruction. Instead the *present*, our *present-day* existence, falls prey to critique insofar as this existence is covered up by a *past that has become inauthentic*. It is not Aristotle or Augustine who is criticized, but the *present*. Far from dismissing the past, the critique has precisely the opposite tendency of bringing the object of the critique to light in its *primordial* past. Moreover, it aims to do so in such a manner that the primordial type of researching becomes evident and, in our present-day existence, something like a *respect for the history* in which we live out our own fate grows. Thus, the destruction as the critique of the present-day is the critique that makes visible what genuinely and primordially is positive in the past. By this means, the past first becomes visible as something that we genuinely have already been and can be again [*eigentliches Gewesensein und Wiederseinkönnen*].

3. It is evident that the destruction is *historical knowledge* in a genuine sense and is not first in need of a cultivation of systematic inquiry.

4. It must be said, in addition, that the destruction can *never be a way of refuting* of the sort that, by means of the refutation, one's own position is defended. Hence, the destruction may not be *isolated* as a method of historical examination that runs on its own. Instead, it has sense only as *thematically disclosive research into existence* in terms of its characters of being.

What we have thus established, we must apply more precisely in taking the decisive step of *returning to Descartes*. For the purpose of explicating the genuine being of care about already known knowledge, its being-qua-disclosing, *three* tasks need to be accomplished; [we have to show]: 1. that this care is in fact alive in Descartes' work of research; 2. that it is this care that discloses consciousness, and how it does so; 3. that this care's specific being already prefigures specific characters of being of what in general can be and is disclosed by this care.

The first demonstration is purely external: from the essay "On Method,"[5] it

---

5. René Descartes, *Abhandlung über die Methode*. Dritte Auflage. Übersetzt u. mit Anmerkungen hrsg. v. A. Buchenau (Leipzig: Felix Meiner, 1919). [*Discours de la méthode* (Discourse on Method), *AT* VI, 1–78.]

can easily be established that his work is subject to the basic criterion of *clara et distincta perceptio* [clear and distinct perception]. For the actual task at hand, it must be demonstrated *that* it is this care that discloses consciousness and *how* it does so. In connection with this, we are led to envision the care for ourselves in its full makeup and then to determine more exactly what is designated by the title "truth." The *care of knowledge* is oriented to *truth*. In this orientation to the truth of knowledge, a definite *idea of truth* already becomes apparent. We will make the sense of this idea of truth more accessible for ourselves by orienting "truth" to existence itself and asking *in what sense truth pertains to "existence" at all*. It is the Augustinian question of the *relation of veritas* [truth] *and vita* [life]. Due to the orientation of the concept of truth to a specific cognitive care, an orientation that develops historically since the Greeks, philosophy is enmeshed in an impossible question. The idea of truth that we encounter in connection with care about already known knowledge will prove, in its *genuine conception*, to be—not a character of knowing but instead a *basic constitution of life* itself that was torn from its possibility by a type of caring. The starting points for embedding truth in existence already present themselves in Greek philosophy in the term ἀλήθεια. We will first come to some understanding of the phenomenon of truth as it is made possible by the traditional sort of treatment of the concept of truth. Initially, existence as such does not even appear in connection with the phenomenon of truth. Truth is seen as a character of judgments, of theoretical knowing in such a way that truth means as much as *validity*. Specific phenomena are layered around "truth" insofar as knowing is achieved in the manner of articulating what is known, in putting what is known into a proposition, and insofar as this proposition is communicable and requires some comprehension for communication. This entire complex is determined as an epistemological inquiry in the broadest sense.

The precise interpretation of care about already known knowledge on the path taken by Descartes' examination must be oriented from the outset to the question: *What concept of truth and being-true* is placed in the center for Descartes? From there we will learn to understand in more detail how the being, which is conceived as true, is itself. Our examination *centers* on the *phenomenon of truth* from two directions. 1. From the fact that we read off it the type and manner of caring, and learn to understand how the path is prefigured in such a way that care about already known knowledge is realized on the *path of doubting*. 2. Doubting is an explicit type of being that cares about knowledge in the sense of being concerned about a specific idea of truth. The doctrine of being and being-true, the Aristotelian doctrine dominant in the Middle Ages, has passed on to Descartes, so that we are transferred back to the beginning of the examination. After this examination we are sufficiently prepared to explicate existence itself in this direction and to see how far the most advanced attempt in contemporary philosophy of life (Dilthey) gets in its aim to bring life into the grip and conceptuality of philosophical knowing.

The destruction has a negative character in the sense that negation, properly understood, constitutes the genuine character [*das Eigentliche*] of existence itself. Taken in this way, destruction should not be characterized as negative in the sense of logical negation. From the beginning, in what the destruction determines to work on, it does not make the weak sides its theme, but instead what is genuinely positive and viewed as positive from the standpoint of the problematic that drives the interpretation itself. It is no accident that this positive side is not imposed on another way of thinking but is emphasized as itself something positive in the appearances [that philosophies make] since every philosophy is, explicitly or not, about existence. What is brought to the investigation is made, with a view to its positive side, into the theme. Another concept of truth than that popular in science guides the destruction. The destruction is critical; the critique has a positive character by virtue of directing itself at the present within which the destruction is carried out, by virtue of living in the very research that accomplishes the destruction; living in it in such a way that the critique of the historical is nothing other than the critique of the present, a critique such that, through it, the situation of the interpretation itself becomes transparent and critically tilled.

Herein lies, further, the fact that the destruction is not a consideration of history in the usual sense, above all, not in the sense of the history of a problem. The historical orientation of the destruction is from the outset not a manner of running through a series of world-views. The destruction is much more a battle with the past and, indeed, such that this past itself is brought to its *own being* through the genuine objectivity of the destruction. The objectivity of the destruction is such that the past is brought to its genuine being, i.e., to its suitability to redound [*Rückstoß*] on the present itself. Only if the past is brought to the possibility of this redounding, do its objectivity and the way the present is bound up with history emerge. Thus, for the destruction it becomes apparent that philosophical research cannot be reduced to a systematic and historical consideration. The type of research proposed here lies in advance of this distinction; it is much more primordial than the basis on which the historical and the systematic are separated.

Chapter Two

Descartes. The how and the what of the being-qua-disclosing of care about knowledge already known

Let us now make Descartes part of our theme in the following manner. The interpretation is conducted with this slant—its aim is to consider *care about already known knowledge* in view of *how* it is disclosive and *what* it is in *disclosing*. It is knowledge to be established in the traditional sense in terms of possibilities of determination as they emerged through work on the knowledge. The *dominance of theoretical knowing* as the genuine measuring rod of all knowledge is so strong in the development of the history of our mentality [*Geistesgeschichte*] that even the phenomenon of believing is regarded with a view to the phenomenon of "knowledge." A look at the history of theology shows that fundamental disadvantages arise from this dominance.

§ 21. Determinations of "truth"

Insofar as we start from these determinate concepts of knowledge, we have to orient ourselves first regarding the *determinations of "truth"* and to see how determinate possibilities of truth's being in life issue from how an idea of truth is posited.

Truth is 1. taken as *the true*: the entity that is uncovered here in a determinate sort of knowledge. The true is the entity in its genuine, uncovered existence itself; scholastically: verum id, quod enuntiando ostenditur [the true is that which is shown in an enunciating]. In the enuntiando [enunciating], a further truth is already given, in which the sense of truth is determined.

2. The process of experiencing a known entity and originally having it present is enacted in a way that goes hand-in-hand with its being addressed and discussed in the process of experiencing it. The known, uncovered entity is that about which someone *speaks*. The entity as known is present and can be present explicitly as discussed. What is discussed is what is spoken of—articulated [*Das Besprochene ist Gesprochenes—Ausgesprochenes*]. We designate as a *proposition* what is spoken of and uncovered. The proposition is what in itself retains the entity uncovered insofar as it is spoken of. By virtue of the fact that the entity is spoken of as something true, the proposition itself is communicable. As spoken, it is already there in existence. A proposition that keeps an entity articulated and uncovered is a truth that is communicable, that can be assumed or contradicted, that can be rejected.

3. Truth is how such a truth [as a proposition] is itself here, free-floating

to a certain extent, so that it is not regarded at all with a view to the fact that it is said about a determinate entity. The proposition can be here in the manner of being repeated with the claim of endorsing the truth articulated in the proposition. In the public domain, truth of this sort has the manner of being of a *validity*, while the type of demonstration of that validity can change, even be lacking.

4. This validity itself—which is articulated and passed around in various ways and, in being thus passed around, is present—has in itself, in keeping with its origin, the possibility of a peculiar demonstrability. Insofar as a validity is assumed in the sense that the demonstrability itself is valid, the proposition is a right one, a case of *rightness* [or correctness: *eine Richtigkeit*]. Insofar as, in the process of agreeing with the validity, the agreeing is such that what is agreed to shows itself in the direction of [or in the right direction toward: *Richtung auf*] its origin, the validity has in itself the peculiar character of being righted toward its origin as something explicitly appropriated. This factor of rightness can be obscured and lacking and, in spite of this, the proposition can claim to be binding as something that, on the basis of its origin, bears within itself the demand to be affirmed.

5. Insofar as one then determines the binding character of a proposition as what ought to be recognized, the proposition is, insofar as it is present as a valid proposition, *something with the character of an ought* [*Gesolltes*]. If one takes the proposition in the manner of an ought and one determines the ought as a value, then one designates truth as a *value*.

From the demonstration of these diverse possibilities of the existence of what we determined at the outset as the true, it should be clear that *the true* has *determinate possibilities* of being present in life. These diverse possibilities exhibit ever-growing distances from what actually constitutes the true: from the entity itself in the manner it is uncovered.

If we begin with the last possibility, *truth as value*, then there is nothing there of the original sense of truth. The philosophy of value distances itself so much from the sense and being of the true that the path to exhibiting the genuine sense of truth is definitively blocked. This path that we have described is not a contingent one or one established for the purposes of a destruction. This *path of distancing* is the path that history has made and trod, the path on which the interpretation of the entity as true moves. Therein lies the fact that the propensity for the just-presented, manifold ways of interpreting the true is already laid down in Greek philosophy. Apart from the fact that the Greeks did not take seriously the original sense of being-true, the true was oriented from the outset as the determination of a proposition. This orientation was reinforced by the fact that theoretical knowledge has a particular significance in the development of Greek philosophy from the beginning. The subsequent fate of the idea of truth was ultimately determined from this point on.

Only once does a new attempt to give the idea of truth a new sense arise: in the New Testament and, in connection with it, in Augustine. This new sense is naturally not explicated by the Evangelists expressly; instead it would have been theology's task to explicate an original sense of truth of this sort by means of an explication of belief. It failed. Even Kierkegaard's "Paradox" is nothing but the result of the fundamental failure to interpret the idea of truth.

§ 22. Three possibilities of care about already known knowledge: curiosity, certitude, being binding

We have treated knowing in a specific sort of consideration in terms of care about already known knowledge. There is now need for a *more exact orientation* about the *care of knowing*. This remark suggests that care about already known knowledge constitutes only one *definite* possibility, the *other* possibilities of which we now have to look into.

The care of knowing can be characterized in terms of three possibilities: 1. the care of *curiosity*; 2. the care for *certitude*; 3. the care about *being binding*.

1. The care of knowledge can disorient itself initially and primordially by not allowing itself to be satisfied with having known a specific portion of the entity that is present in life. What matters to this care of knowing is precisely to develop the possibility of penetrating ever further in knowing regarding a specific region of what is known. The care of knowing ensnares itself in itself. To this care of knowing it no longer matters *what* it knows and still less the *sort of being* of what it knows. It is interested solely in this, *that* ever-new possibilities of knowing are at hand. Thus, precisely the care of knowing presents the peculiar character of ensnaring-itself-in-itself [*Sich-in-sich-selbst-verfangen*] that we specify as *providing-for-itself* [*Sich-versorgen*] in a twofold sense. a) The care of knowing provides for itself as *curiosity*; that is to say, it is entirely absorbed in itself, in such a way that being able to see is all that matters. With this, the lack of receptivity for the genuine appropriation of the entity grows. The reigning sort of interest today in everything, even religion and religiosity, is a feeble offspring of this new care. b) The care of knowing provides for itself in the sense that it does not need anything else. It provides for itself; it is *not needy*. Insofar as it is not needy, it fails every time the demand is made to take seriously what it has known.

2. The care of knowing is the care for *certitude* [*Sicherheit*]. In this type of care, what matters for knowing is for it to be executed in such a way that

the *knowing* and the *known* in this being-known are *known*. The knowing itself is conveyed into a determinate manner of being known. Care about already known knowledge: the peculiar character of this care is the extent to which it matters to the care to possess the knowing itself, to present itself as evident; insofar as what alone and primarily matters to this care is *evidentness* [*Einsichtigkeit*], it comes to display a particular interest in methodological considerations. The specific *primacy of methodological considerations* is characteristic of today's type of knowing. Here, too, it ensnares itself in itself. First, it must be concerned with the certitude of the possible knowledge, so much that it takes into account a failure to see, in relation to the entity that is supposed to be known. Precisely in this connection, there emerges a specific blindness for *what* is actually supposed to be known. Method in connection with the care for certitude is thereby taken in a completely determined sense: as the path to the acquisition of the greatest possible *evidence*. Method in the genuine sense, by contrast, must have the sense that the *path to the matter itself* is opened up and secured.

3. The care about *being binding* goes together for the most part with one of the first two named manners of knowledge. It is out not merely to enable more and more knowing or to know with more certitude and with absolute evidence but [also] to establish a dominance of knowing as such, where knowing manages to assert itself in a way that takes precedence over all other possibilities of existence and determines them. It is characteristic for the care about being binding to pass beyond knowing itself in a peculiar manner, such that this care, if it speaks of itself, says: "The propositions of knowledge bear the stamp of eternity."[1] What is evident in this [remark] is an arrogance of the knowing, over against itself, such that this knowledge in this care systematically covers up its own possibilities of existence. An exponential indicator [*Exponent*] of the arrogance of this care of knowing, gone to the farthest extremes, is the manner in which this care critically engages historicism.

The respectively dominant concept of truth stands in connection with these diverse possibilities of caring. If these connections are together in their unity as already present historically and still dominating today, then it becomes apparent that the present is unprepared, in the broadest sense thinkable, for a question like: *What does the truth of life and existence mean?* Both "pieces," truth and existence, are in no way elucidated. But one is of the opinion that one has the means at hand to make something out about this.

We have to see where the *present-day* dominance of the care of knowing has its *source* and which origins it is uprooted from today. We will consider care about already known knowledge because it appeared at a decisive *turning-point of the history of philosophy*. Descartes is a decisive turning-

1. See E. Husserl, "Philosophie als strenge Wissenschaft," op. cit., 337.

point only in the way that the present-day interprets itself and its history under the dominance of theoretical knowing, although Descartes is actually thoroughly medieval.[2]

With our determination of the true, we have not drawn on the concept of truth that Husserl has set down in the *Logical Investigations*.[3] Husserl is oriented toward the sense of truth as the truth of a proposition and, indeed, truth is determined as the fulfillment of an intention. Truth consists in the fulfillment of what is at first emptily meant.

We now have for ourselves a definite connection with the care of knowing, corresponding to the diverse meanings of truth. A characteristic feature of the care of curiosity is that something comes under that care only insofar as it is new. The care about being binding is characterized by the fact that, unlike the care of curiosity and the care for certitude, it does not seize one-sidedly upon one determinate possibility of existing [*Existenzvollzugs*]. Instead what is characteristic of care about being binding is the fact that in a peculiar way it passes beyond knowing itself, such that the knowing in an emphatic sense belongs to the basic possibilities of existence. One must pose the question of what manner of being in existence itself is caring in the sense of knowing [*das Sorgendsein im Sinne des Erkennens*], such that in the caring these definite possibilities of unfolding are there in keeping with its being [*seinsmäßig da sind*].

2. See the Appendix, Supplement 16 (p. 233).
3. E. Husserl, VI. Logische Untersuchung [Sixth Logical Investigation], op. cit., 115ff.

Chapter Three

Descartes' determination of falsum and verum

§ 23. Preview of the context of the question

We have to interpret Descartes' work with respect to three questions. The second question reads: What actually is the *field of being* that *care about already known knowledge discloses*? The third question is the question of *how* the care about already known knowledge, being as it is, has here this field of being, with this determinate character of being. The second question is the decisive one. With the answer to it, the third question is dispatched as well.

What is it that care about already known knowledge holds onto in its care? 1. What do "true" and "false" signify, what does it mean that the care about already known knowledge is out for *truth*? 2. What "being" is it that is designated as *being in truth* or as *being in error*? What kind of possibility of being within existence is expressed by the fact that one says: [this is] grasping truth or erring? To grasp truth or to err are considered with respect to what they are *in existence*. What consideration of existence does Descartes lay as the foundation? 3. What *path* is prefigured by this now-illuminated being of care? It will be apparent that, along with this path's character of being, quite determinate possibilities are already prefigured as to what it can encounter, what it can disclose.

We will orient ourselves first on the concept of *falsum* and, more precisely, we will pose the question: How does the necessity arise for Descartes of explaining the falsum as such? What determinations does he draw from the phenomenon of the falsum? What factors does he take over from the tradition and the contemporary philosophy?

The falsum is initially determined as *error*, and error as such is characterized as *malum* [evil]. This is a determinate manner of not-being, in accordance with the traditional consideration of it as *non esse* qua *privatio* [non being as privation]. This consideration necessarily casts light on the *verum* as well. The falsum is, indeed, nothing other than the *cavendum* [something to be guarded against], something that the care of knowing has to avoid. Through the determinate concept of cavendum, a determinate view of the verum is already at work. It must be asked whether Descartes determines the verum in the same fundamental [*grundsätzlichen*] direction. Up to now, this has generally been denied and it has been maintained that Descartes attributes the falsum to the voluntas, the verum to the perceptio as the theoretical [the false to the will, the true to perception as the theoretical]. We will see, however, that the characterization of the verum proceeds in the same way as that of the falsum. Hence, it will have to made intelligible that the necessity of ascribing the *falsum* to the *voluntas* and the *veritas* to the *ideas* or to the correlative conception, the *perceptio*, in fact obtains on the basis of this peculiar interpretation of verum and falsum. Through closer interpretation of the verum and falsum, we will glean the determinacy that the care is working towards if it wants the verum. The orientation to a specifically interpreted verum and falsum across the domain of being of subject matters decides the extent to which consciousness in some sense or other is disclosed by the care about already known knowledge and established as a domain of being. Why *being-true* [*Wahrsein*] also decides about *being* will only be intelligible by returning to the ontology in which the entire Cartesian investigation is conducted. The interpretation must be lead back to the contexts of its origin [*Ursprungszusammenhänge*]. In this return to the *ancestry* [*Herkunft*], we will only treat the main way-station and even this not very thoroughly. We will consider the fundamental sources [*Quellen*] for this explication: Thomas, Anselm, Augustine with a brief glance back at Aristotle.

§ 24. The cogito sum, the clara et distincta perceptio, and the task of securing, in keeping with being, the criterion of truth

Descartes names his investigations "de prima philosophia" [those of first philosophy].[1] The idea of *prima philosophia* is Aristotelian. The designation of Descartes' investigation in this sense arises from the fact that he saw quite clearly that he moved in the ambit of ontologia generalis. Thus, it is not a prima philosophia in the modernized sense; instead the title bespeaks a consciousness of the connection with ancient ontology's inquiry.

Accordingly, we first have to orient ourselves concerning the concept of the *falsum*. Before we begin the actual interpretation, it is necessary to ascertain the context of the Fourth Meditation within the *Meditations*. The connection of the questioning and the motives should be discussed in order then to enter into a closer examination of the explication of the falsum.

Descartes found something that is true and this something that appears with the cognizance of being-true, is the *cogito sum* [the I think, I am] or, better, the *res cogitans qua ens* [the thinking thing qua being]. *Cogitatio* is equivalent to *intentio* ["Thought" is equivalent to "intention"].

1. Descartes, *Meditationes de prima philosophia.* Curavit A. Buchenau. Biblotheca Philosophorum Vol. I. Sumptibus Felicis Meineri. (Lipsiae 1913). [Edited by A. Buchenau (Felix Meiner: Leipzig, 1913).]

Cogitationis nomine, intelligo illa omnia, quae nobis consciis in nobis fiunt, quatenus eorum in nobis conscientia est.[2]

[By the term "thought," I understand all those things which occur in us, while we are conscious of ourselves, insofar as, in us, there is consciousness of them.]

Descartes characterizes the concept of cogitatio in such a way that it roughly coincides with the concept of *intentional experience*, currently used in phenomenology. The res cogitans is thus something that *is* as a variety of such possibilities of experience. With the grasping of the res cogitans' being, the criterion for the evidence of this grasping is also grasped at the same time. For the cogito means: *cogito me cogitare.*

Sum certus me esse rem cogitantem, nunquid ergo etiam scio quid requiratur ut de aliqua re sim certus? nempe in hac prima cognitione nihil aliud est, quam clara quaedam et distincta perceptio ejus quod affirmo; quae sane non sufficeret ad me certum de rei veritate reddendum, si posset unquam contingere, ut aliquid quod ita clare et distincte perciperem falsum esset: ac proinde jam videor pro regula generali posse statuere, illud omne esse verum quod valde clare et distincte percipio.[3]

[For the cogito means: *I think that I am thinking.* I am certain that I am a thinking thing, do I not therefore also know what is required for me to be certain of any thing? For in this first thought, there is nothing other than a certain clear and distinct perception of what I affirm; which would plainly not suffice to make me certain of the truth of the matter if it could ever happen that something which I perceived so clearly and distinctly was false. So I now seem to be able to lay down as a general rule that everything which I perceive very clearly and distinctly is true.]

This connection must be kept in view, namely, that with the grasping of the *cogito sum*, the *clara et distincta perceptio* is given at the same time. By "cogitatio," Descartes does not mean experiences simply insofar as they are directed at something but insofar as they have in themselves at the same time a *consciousness of themselves.* He says: If something that I grasp in this manner, namely, by means of the clara et distincta perceptio, could be false, then I could not rely on this criterion. Descartes assumes the criterion in order to *justify* it. The difference between the Cartesian and the modern orientation amounts to the fact that the criterion as such does not suffice for Descartes. He says: In the course of articulating a proposition such as cogito sum, I experience that my assent is drawn to assent to the proposition thus grasped. But Descartes says: For the foundation of knowing, I cannot rely upon an obscure connection of being drawn to what I grasp; I must have secured the clara et distincta perceptio itself in terms of being. The *regula generalis* [gen-

2. Descartes, *Principia Philosophiae*. In: *Œuvres de Descartes*. Publiées par Ch. Adam & P. Tannery (Paris 1897ff.). Tome VIII (Paris 1905). Pars prima, § 9, 7 [*AT* VIII, 7].
3. Descartes, *Meditationes de prima philosophia*. Meditatio III, 33 [*AT* VII, 35].

eral rule] is to be justified as a possible absolute criterion of knowledge. Modern philosophy has characterized Descartes' proof as a relapse into the old metaphysics. But one must ask whether Descartes did not in fact see more radically in that he sought a further justification of the criterion. (Husserl has concentrated all his work of the last years on justifying the idea of absolute evidence on the basis of itself.)

This task of justifying the criterion leads Descartes to become clear about the falsum. It should be noted briefly how the *analysis of the falsum* is determined by the necessity of *securing* the criterion of knowledge *in accordance with being*. I have given the criterion, but only obscurely. I must seek to press on to the proof. Up till now I have merely the cogito sum, no inference, but a uniform representation, a co-perceiving of the sum in the cogito. In the course of descending-into-myself, I find that I am a *res finita*, thus *imperfecta* [a finite, thus imperfect thing], that I cannot, therefore, have the ground of my existing in myself. So I am led, in the course of the consideration of myself, to demonstrate a *ground* of my existence. How does Descartes go from the analysis of this inner givenness to determining that it is *God* who has given me the existence from which everything positive in me then stems? I find in me a definite idea of God as infinite, which as an idea is a *realitas objectiva* [objective reality]. If God exists and what is positive in me stems from Him, is created by God, that is to say, is *true*, then everything that comes about in me is, qua being, a *verum*. Hence, the *clara et distincta perceptio* that co-constitutes my genuine, created being, the *perfectio* of my existence, is true. If, then, God exists and I owe my existence to Him, then He cannot be the cause of my deceiving myself. The question now arises: If my being stems from God, *whence* comes the *error*? Only if I have proven that the error can*not* stem from God, in accordance with His being, is the criterion of all knowing justified in accordance with being, and the possibility open, at the same time, of the falsum as malum in ens creatum [the false as an evil in created being].

If we place Descartes' meditation in the context that was characterized in determining the destruction, then the foregoing remarks are meant to say: we seek to establish *what supposition of existence* [*Ansatz von Dasein*] lies in what one today means by *consciousness*. It cannot be a matter of establishing a determinate character of being of this sort of object. The important thing is that one makes intelligible in all detail what connection these determinations have with the foundation. All fundamental [*grundsätzlichen*] determinations, such as those of inner perception's privileged evidence or those of the person's specific type of being, are *uprooted* from the ground they stem from. They no longer have genuine authority of themselves, but impose themselves instead. Any attempt to investigate the current philosophy of life with respect to its foundation must come to naught. Prior to every further determination,

we must make clear to ourselves: What does "being-true" mean? We will
proceed from the falsum and investigate in more detail how it is determined
[and], in the process, which means of determination come to be applied as
categories of being. From this vantage point, the ground for the verum is
conveyed at the same time. From this vantage point, the character of the res
cogitans becomes apparent. Descartes is very definitely conscious of the fact
that the analysis of verum and falsum is of fundamental importance for his
Meditations.[4] Here you already see a quite definite *concept of being-true*, one
that is oriented primarily not to the judging but to *the entity itself*. The clare
et distincte perceptum is verum [what is clearly and distinctly perceived is
true]. At the same time, what the genuine sense of falsehood consists in will
be unraveled. The entire investigation is undertaken to justify the sorts of
knowledge found in modern natural science. It determines the theme of the
Fourth Meditation. *Error*, to be sure, is in that case the issue—but not the
sins, the error boni et mali [error of good and evil]. The determination of sins
as error tips off that a human being's genuine being is seen in failing, in error.
Error is at issue but in a sense that is restricted in an utterly specific way,
namely, in terms of *ideae speculativae* [speculative ideas], of theoretical comprehension and knowledge. In this connection Descartes emphasizes the fundamental significance of the sense of verum et falsum.

§ 25. Descartes' classification of the variety of cogitationes. The judicium as the place for the verum and falsum

In order to gain a concrete idea of the place where verum and falsum make
their appearance, we have to come to some understanding of how Descartes
classifies the variety of cogitationes. You will see from this that Brentano is
essentially determined by Descartes' classification. In the Third Meditation,
Descartes undertakes such a classification:

> Nunc autem ordo videtur exigere, ut prius omnes meas cogitationes in certa genera
> distribuam, et in quibusnam ex illis veritas aut falsitas proprie consistat, inquiram.[5]

> [Order, however, seems now to require that I first divide all my thoughts into certain
> genera and that I inquire in which of them truth or falsity properly consists.]

The division of the variety of things pertaining to the soul into certain classes
is required in order to say something about the verum et falsum. He wants

---

4. See the Appendix, Supplement 17 (p. 233).
5. Descartes, *Meditationes de prima philosophia*. Meditatio III, 35f. [*AT* VII, 36f.].

thereby to make out those cogitationes in which truth or falsity actually consists. *Verum esse* [to be true] is a determinate *being* of a determinate cogitatio, as *falsum esse* [to be false] is a determinate *not-being* of a cogitatio. The first thing that needs to be settled is which cogitationes come into consideration for this at all.

Quaedam ex his tanquam rerum imagines sunt, quibus solis proprie convenit ideae nomen [some of these, to which alone the name "idea" properly applies, are as it were images of things][6]: one class of cogitationes is designated *idea tanquam rerum imagines* [as it were, images of things]. A whole swarm of errors is bound up with the term *imago* insofar as representations were taken as pictures of something external. But imago rei [the image of a thing] must be conceived much more formally in the sense that an idea is something like the imago rei. It provides something for seeing, *exhibits something*. Representing is the basic function of the idea.

> Aliae vero alias quasdam praeterea formas habent, ut cum volo, cum timeo, cum affirmo, cum nego, semper quidem aliquam rem ut subjectum meae cogitationis apprehendo, sed aliquid etiam amplius quam istius rei similitudinem cogitatione complector; et ex his aliae voluntates, sive affectus, aliae autem judicia appellantur.[7]
>
> [But others have beside this certain other forms: for when I want, when I fear, when I affirm, when I deny, I always apprehend something as the subject of my thought, but include in my thought something more than the likeness of the thing; and of these, some are called volitions or emotions, but others are called judgments.]

The idea has a forma, something constitutive of its being. It consists in exhibiting [*darstellend*], while other cogitationes are other forms; they exist in other ways. In affirming, willing, denying, rejecting, I have cogitationes but in these cogitationes there is something there, a subjectum (ὑποκείμενον), that lies there from the outset as apprehensum [apprehended]. Each cogitatio, be it an idea or not, is apprehending. But in these [more complex] cogitationes I seize upon even more of what is given. In actually grasping something, I am directed at what is apprehended; in willful behavior or in being overcome, I am drawn (affectus) by what I grasp or I judge, i.e., I give my assent, I say "yes" (judicium). Here is the root of Brentano's classification: *presentation* (idea), *judgment* (judicium), *emotion* (affectus), a classification that has exercised a far-reaching influence on the development of phenomenology. *Voluntas* [will] has a *double-meaning*. It means, first, each actualization of a possibility in the soul and, second, specifically willful behavior. In our consideration we will see which concept of voluntas plays a role here.

6. Op. cit., 36 [*AT* VII, 37].
7. Ibid. [*AT* VII, 37].

Jam quod ad ideas attinet, si solae in se spectentur, nec ad aliud quid illas referam, falsae proprie esse non possunt, nam sive capram, sive chimaeram imaginer, non minus verum est me unam imginari quam alteram.[8]

[Now as far as ideas are concerned, considered alone in themselves, I do not refer them to something else; they cannot properly be false; for whether I imagine a goat or a chimera, it is no less true that I imagine the one rather than the other.]

If I see an *idea* solely as such and the idea, what is presented therein, does not refer to something else, but instead I merely envision the content presented as such, then the idea cannot be false. For whether I have a goat or a chimera as the "content" of the idea, both are true; no idea is false if I take it only as presented. My presenting of what is presented, my having the idea present is, namely, true. The concept of truth is primarily oriented not at the content of the idea, but at the imagining itself. Insofar as I am a presentation, this my being-qua-presenting [*Vorstellendsein*] as an actual being is true. We can only establish why this being qua being is true by going back to the tradition.

Nulla etiam in ipsa voluntate, vel affectibus falsitas est timenda, nam quamvis prava, quamvis etiam ea quae nusquam sunt possim optare, non tamen ideo non verum est illa me optare.[9]

[Also in the will or emotions no falsity is to be feared, for although I may be able to opt for depraved things, even those things which never are, it is not, nevertheless, thus not true that I opt for those things.]

Insofar, then, as my imagining is a being that always remains true, even *willing* and the *emotions* are never false. It can be the case that I wish something which does not exist at all; in spite of this, my wishing is thus a being, whether the wished exists or not. What matters is the being of the cogito as such.

. . . [S]ola supersunt judicia in quibus mihi cavendum est ne fallar:[10] The only things remaining are *judgments*, towards which I must be on guard that I am not deceived. That means, therefore, that if verum means "esse in the sense of the cogito," the being-onhand [*Vorhandensein*] of a cogitatio as res, then falsum must mean "non esse of a cogitatio." On the basis of the way judgments are, they have the possibility of being and not being. Now one can say that, like ideae et voluntates, they are always true, since they in fact come about in my consciousness. They can turn into the opposite. [But] as long as I consider ideae solely in themselves, indeed, ideas that provide the funda-mentum for the judicium, I cannot fall into error.

The determination of the idea as true in itself goes back to Greek philos-

8. Ibid.
9. Ibid.
10. Ibid.

ophy's determination that the αἰσθητά as such are always true. The proposition that Aristotle limits to grasping in the most immediate, sensory sense and to specific manners of grasping on the part of νοῦς is transferred quite universally to any possible grasping at all.

It cannot escape Descartes that a *certain falsity* obtains even in ideas as such. He explains this falsity through a distinction. There are diverse ideas: 1. those innate in me (ideae innatae), 2. those coming to me from "outside" (ideae adventitiae), 3. those produced by me myself (ideae a me ipso factae).[11] These ideas are distinct insofar as it is diversely difficult to establish in individual cases whether what they present is "true" *extra mentem* [outside the mind], that is to say, *is* actual. Although genuine falsehood (*falsitas formalis* [formal falsity]) cannot come about in the ideas, there is a *falsitas materialis* [material falsity] in them.[12] The falsitas formalis is proper only to judgments that have the possibility of non esse verum [not being true]. This falsehood pertains in no way to the idea. Its esse is only to present [*praesentieren*] something. If something is presented, this suffices for the idea's being. The idea is false if it displays something that is not the case as if it were so. In the case of an idea of warm and cold, if I feel the cold and feel the warm and then, relative to this idea, want to become clear about its truth and falsity, that is to say, whether the coldness is a genuine being of the cold or not, whether being cold is a determinate being of warmth or the reverse—I cannot decide, if I have warmth or coldness, which of the two is the genuine being. The question of being in regard to extra mentem esse [extra-mental existence] is oriented to a specific conception of being, but it is certain that these ideae present me with something. Each idea is, as an idea, rem repraesentans [representing a thing]. If I come to say "Cold is a privatio of warm," and determine, on the other hand, that the idea of cold presents something real to me, then I must say that the idea is false insofar as the actual consideration of being shows me that the cold is a non esse. "The idea is materially false" means it is a possible material that, taken up into a judgment, becomes the possible falsehood of a judgment.

§ 26. *The distinction between the idea as repraesentans aliquid and its
repraesentatum; realitas objectiva and realitas formalis sive actualis
[the distinction between the idea as representing something and what it
represents; objective reality and formal or actual reality]*

The idea itself, then, presents *possibilities of distinctions* and these become important. What is it in an idea, what is found, what is referred to in a

---

11. Op. cit., 37 [*AT* VII, 37f.].
12. Op. cit., 46 [*AT* VII, 43, 46].

judgment, as being related to something extra mentem? In order to explain this, Descartes uses a distinction handed down to him *by the tradition*, a distinction that can be characterized as that between *realitas formalis* [formal reality] and *realitas objectiva* [objective reality].[13] If Descartes wants to see this consideration through, then he must show the existence of God on the basis of consciousness. He does this by showing that in consciousness there is an idea with a completely idiosyncratic character, an idea that has the character of a realitas objectiva.

The orientation in regard to Descartes' basic division of the variety of cogitationes is important because a concept of being-true and being-false, a concept that is of fundamental [*grundsätzlicher*] importance for us, has already made its appearance. The judicium [judgment] remained as the sole genus of cogitationes that can also be false. He thereby draws attention to a manner of being of the cogitatio as cogitatio, from which the judicium is also not excluded. The judicium has the possibility of a defectus [defect], just because it is equated with the ideae et voluntates [ideas and volitions] precisely in this respect, namely, that it occurs in the res cogitans. Only for this reason can it happen that, by non verum esse [not being true], the specific being of the judgment breaks off from the other ideas. The entire consideration runs its course to show: 1. what the *being of the judgment* is constituted in; and 2. what the *determinations of being* are that allow for something like a *defectus*, the defectus that makes up the ratio formalis, the genuine being of the falsum.

What the judicium is, we only know negatively: it is that cogitatio, in whose being falsitas is grounded, in keeping with the way things are [*seinsmäßig*]. Descartes does not come to discuss falsitas and veritas with the aim of simply putting forth the criterion of evidence by an appeal to an obscure awareness of its irresistible intelligibility. Instead he comes with the aim of rigorously proving this criterion. It must be shown that the res cogitans' being, insofar as it is an actual being, excludes every error. It must be shown not only that the res cogitans, insofar as it is, is created by God, but also that what really occurs in it as error is something that cannot stem from God.[14] This leads Descartes to the explication of the falsum. Insofar as falsum is in consciousness, it needs to be proven that it cannot stem from God. We do not want to consider Descartes' proof of God at length, but only the point around which the consideration turns.

For this purpose, we must briefly come to some understanding of how Descartes is able to move out beyond consciousness from the ground on which he stands, namely, that he knows: cogito sum, i.e., how with the same evidence

---

13. Op. cit., 41 [*AT* VII, 40].
14. Descartes, Meditatio IV, 61 [*AT* VII, 60f.].

he can show that something outside (extra mentem[15]) exists. The question is: Where do the points of departure for going beyond consciousness to the affirmation of a *being extra mentem* lie? We have already heard that the idea, in the way that it actually is, is itself true, that the idea is what we designated as knowing. Theoretical grasp of being lies primarily in the field of the idea. Let us now ask: How does Descartes come to posit an esse extra mentem on the ground circumscribed by the cogito sum? In order to make this path intelligible, Descartes introduces a distinction within the sphere of ideas.

> Nempe quatenus ideae istae cogitandi quidam modi tantum sunt, non agnosco ullam inter ipsas inaequalitatem, et omnes a me eodem modo procedere videntur.[16]
>
> [For insofar as these ideas are only certain modes of thinking, I am not aware of any inequality among them and they all seem to proceed from me in the same way.]

We can consider all ideae, each percipere of an idea, in one respect in which they are all alike. There is no dissimilarity among any of the ideae insofar as I consider them as manners of the cogitare [to think] itself—insofar as I take the idea simply as a cogitatio, as repraesentans aliquid nehme [as a thought, as representing something]. Each idea qua idea is an esse cogitans [thinking being]. However, insofar as I consider the ideae with respect to the *repraesentatum*, I find a difference: sed quantenus una unam rem, alia aliam repraesentat, patet easdem esse ab invicem valde diversas [but insofar as one idea represents one thing, another idea another thing, it is clear that they are quite diverse among themselves].[17]

The question now is: What, more precisely, is the factor in view of which the ideae are different from one another? The repraesentatum is considered in terms of the sense of being possessed by what is represented itself: the representing of a stone, of a geometrical object, of God. They are repraesentata [what are represented]. They are considered with respect to their *modus essendi* [mode of being]. This manner of being is the *realitas objectiva*. Here "objectiva" still has the original sense of what is held opposite, of what is presented. Realitas objectiva is a res' being insofar as it is a res repraesentata [a thing represented] in an idea. There is a *diversitas* [diversity] among the ideas with regard to the realitas objectiva. The realitas objectiva among the ideas can be diverse in the manner of the *majus* and *minus* [more and less]. The entities that are present with the content of their being can be diverse with respect to their content. Descartes gives examples of this:

---

15. Cf. Descartes, Meditatio III, 40 [*AT* VII, 39. Descartes writes "extra me," not "extra mentem."—D.D.].

16. Ibid. [*AT* VII, 40].

17. Ibid.

Nam proculdubio illae quae substantias mihi exhibent, majus aliquid sunt, atque, ut
ita loquar, plus realitatis objectivae in se continent, quam illae quae tantum modos,
sive accidentia repraesentant:[18]

[For it is beyond doubt that those ideas which exhibit substances to me are something
more and, as I might say, contain more objective reality in themselves than those
which represent only modes or accidents:]

Such ideae, which represent substantias, majus repraesentant [represent more]
than those which exhibit only accidentia. The distinction between majus and
minus is shown in the distinction between substantia and accidens, a distinction that is taken from Greek philosophy, insofar as the superiority in being
of οὐσία over συμβεβηκός holds fast there. The ground from which this distinction is gathered is no longer present here.

Within the substances, a distinction is made between the substantia *finita*
and the substantia *infinita* [finite substance and infinite substance]. Among the
ideae, I have one that exhibits an ens realissimum [a most real being]; insofar
as, in the same act, I consider myself as res finita [a finite thing], that infinite
substance presents itself as *creator*.[19] That is, to start with, the stock [*Bestand*]
of what Descartes can point to as stock within the res cogitans.

How is the being of what is represented in the realitas objectiva of the idea
secured through the givenness of such an idea? For the purpose of making
evident the actual onhandness of what is presented as the realitas objectiva of
the idea, general *axioms* from the Scholastics are drawn upon, axioms that
are briefly formulated: non posse aliquid esse [the impossibility for something
to be] in the sense that it comes from nothing (fieri a nihilo[20]). Everything
that is must have come into its being from somewhere. This *causa* is necessarily such that it must be at least equal to the effect's character of being, if
not even superior to it. Hence, something cannot be brought into being by
aliquid minoris realitatis [something of less reality]. Descartes introduces these
axioms shortly before the decisive consideration.

[A]tque hoc non modo perspicue verum est de iis effectibus, quorum realitas est
actualis sive formalis; sed etiam de ideis, in quibus consideratur tantum realitas
objectiva.[21]

[And this is perspicuously true not only of those effects of which the reality is actual
or formal, but also of ideas in which only the objective reality is considered.]

A new concept of realitas thus surfaces: *realitas actualis sive formalis*. The
realitas formalis is that very mode of being that represents the actual being

18. Op. cit., 40f. [*AT* VII, 40].
19. Op. cit., 41 [*AT* VII, 40].
20. Ibid.
21. Ibid. [*AT* VII, 41].

of the object qua being. It must be carried over to the idea. The ideae are what they are by virtue of yielding something represented [*ein Vorgestelltes geben*]. In this way, he then applies the previously given, general ontological axiom to the realitas objectiva of the ideae.[22] The realitas objectiva, the content of whose being is represented, is in need of the corresponding causation. Descartes secures this reflection of his in a twofold way by showing that it would be perverse to believe that the axiom could not obtain because one would have no realitas formalis in the ideae. Descartes acknowledges that the actual being of the realitas formalis does not flow over into consciousness. That does not keep him from applying the axiom about causation since the realitas objectiva is not simply nothing but instead a something.

> Nam quamvis ista causa nihil de sua realitate actuali, sive formali in meam ideam transfundat, non ideo putandum est illam minus realem esse debere, sed talem esse naturam ipsius ideae, ut nullam aliam ex se realitatem formalem exigat, praeter illam quam mutuatur a cogitatione mea, cujus est modus; quod autem haec idea realitatem objectivam hanc vel illam contineat potius quam aliam, hoc profecto habere debet ab aliqua causa in qua tantumdem sit ad minimum realitatis formalis, quantum ipsa continet objectivae.[23]

> [For although this cause transfers nothing of its actual or formal reality into my idea, it should not be thought that, therefore, this cause need be any less real; for the nature of an idea is such that of itself it requires no other formal reality than what it borrows from my thought, of which it is a mode; that this idea, however, contains this or that objective reality rather than another, it certainly must have this from some other cause in which there is at least as much formal reality as it itself contains objective reality.]

From the fact that the realitas formalis is not found realiter in the realitas objectiva [that the formal reality is not found really in the objective reality], one may not infer that the cause of the realitas objectiva would not have to be just as real as the cause of the realitas formalis. Although the cause does not transmit any of its actual realitas into my consciousness, one should not believe that it must, therefore, be less real. The idea not only has the modus essendi as realitas formalis [the mode of being as formal reality] qua cogito, but has, in addition, a realitas formalis that causes the realitas objectiva.[24] The realitas objectiva accrues to the ideae qua ideae [the ideas as ideas] themselves and because this [objective reality] accrues to them on the basis of their nature, the being of the idea itself demands the realitas formalis of the res repraesen-tata [the formal reality of the thing represented]. Even if no overflowing of the realitas formalis is to be found, it would still be wrong for me to believe

---

22. Op. cit., 42f. [*AT* VII, 41].
23. Op. cit., 42 [*AT* VII, 41].
24. Ibid. [*AT* VII, 41].

that the cause of the idea would need less realitas. To elaborate the actual proof further is superfluous.

> [N]am quemadmodum iste modus essendi objectivus competit ideis ex ipsarum natura, ita modus essendi formalis competit idearum causis, saltem primis et praecipuis, ex earum natura.[25]
>
> [For just as this objective mode of being comes with ideas by their very nature, so the formal mode of being comes with the causes of ideas, at least the first and principal causes, by their very nature.]

The realitas objectiva of an idea demands for itself as cause a res of realitas formalis [a thing of formal reality], the being of which is there in the realitas objectiva. Insofar as I have the *idea of God* and I myself as imperfectum cannot have caused this idea, I myself must have been caused by this esse perfectum. Application of the general Scholastic proposition: God is Himself His being (Deus est entitas essendi sui). It becomes clear that Descartes transfers the axioms of the cause of esse naturale [natural being] in a simple, formalizing manner to being in the sense of the entity represented as such. He is able to do this because the "objectivity" itself inheres in the ens formale [formal being] of the idea: it *is*, indeed, as a way of letting [something] be seen. Along with its being, something's being-sighted [*Gesichtetsein*] also *is*. The being-sighted *of . . .* "is" what it is; with its *of which* [*Wovon*], the presence of . . . "in" the *perceptio*—is a being of the respective "of which." If this is God, then this presence cannot "be" from me, that is to say, it cannot be produced by me as res finita [a finite thing]. This demonstration is trenchant if one takes the esse of the res cogitans, of the cogitare [the being of the thinking thing, the being of thinking] completely for an idea, that is to say, if one understands it as *ens creatum*. For us that means that Descartes sees in the being of the res cogitans a twofold being, in which the distinction between *esse repraesentatum* and *esse repraesentans* [between being represented and being qua representing] collapses.[26]

We have come to some understanding of an important factor of the ontological basis of Descartes' determination of consciousness and we have done so, to be sure, in view of a distinction that he makes for the idea. He separates two manners of being of the idea: 1. its manner of being as a cogitatio (modus essendi mutuatus a cogitatione [the mode of being borrowed from thought]), 2. the modus essendi objectivus [the objective mode of being], the being of what is represented as represented. This distinction within the idea is the basis from which Descartes comes, by means of ancient ontological principles, to the evident claim of the existence (onhandness) of what is presented. Each

---

25. Op. cit., 43 [*AT* VII, 42].
26. See the Appendix, Supplement 18 (p. 234).

realitas objectiva demands of itself a causa, the character of whose reality corresponds to the entity that is given in the realitas objectiva. Each cause qua cause is real. Being in the sense of a causa is a realitas formalis. The result of this train of thought, constructed in part with the distinctive emphasis on the clara et distincta perceptio of the idea of God and with the principles of traditional ontology, is that Descartes *reduces a twofold being to one uniform dimension* within the res cogitans: the *esse* of the *cogitare* and the *esse* of the *cogitatum*. Both are one esse animi [being of the soul], a being that, as such, is initially independent of the body's being. Descartes reduces [*nivelliert*] the realitas objectiva and the realitas formalis of the idea itself and this reduction is, of course, possible because the cogitare qua cogitare [thinking qua thinking] and the cogitatum qua cogitatum [the thought qua thought] are evidently given in the same manner, because they can be identified as something (aliquid) on hand. In regard to the *esse verum*, both types of being are ultimately identical. Both entities are, that is to say, they are created, created by God, that is to say, verum. On the basis of this determination, it becomes clear that here the criterion of clara et distincta perceptio takes over the function of reducing the characters of being. That points to a distinctive manner of exercising the care about already known knowledge. We encounter it where two diverse manners of being are reduced within consciousness, in such a way that both are subjected without restraint to causal consideration in the sense of the Scholastics.

§ 27. The question of the being of the falsum and error

We get a further clarification of the *esse* of the *res cogitans* through the interpretation of the *esse* of the *falsum* and the *error*. We will not pursue Descartes' actual train of thought; we will only see how the question of the falsum was set forth and explicated.

a) The constitution of error: intellectus and voluntas as libertas; Descartes' two concepts of freedom

God is not only in a positive sense the cause of the idea that I conceive. Even more, God can also not be the cause of an entity (the errare [erring]) that is likewise in me.[27]

> Deinde, ad me propius accedens, et qualesnam sint errores mei (qui soli imperfectionem aliquam in me arguunt) investigans, adverto illos a duabus causis simul

27. See the Appendix, Supplement 19 (p. 234).

concurrentibus dependere, nempe a facultate cognoscendi quae in me est, et a facultate eligendi sive ab arbitrii libertate, hoc est ab intellectu, et simul a voluntate.[28]

[Then, looking more closely at myself and investigating of what sort my errors may
be (which alone betray some imperfection in me), I notice that they depend upon
two simultaneously concurring causes, namely, the faculty of knowing that is in me
and the faculty of choosing or freedom of the will; that is to say, they depend on
the intellect and, at the same time, on the will.]

The cause [of erring] lies in the coexistence of the *facultas intelligendi* [faculty
of understanding] and the *facultas eligendi* (*libertas arbitrii*) [faculty of choosing (freedom of the will)], in short, in the intellectus simul cum voluntate
[intellect at the same time with the will]. Descartes then shows that each
facultas qua facultas cannot be the sufficient ground of the error. The facultas-
character is a positive sort of being and, as *esse positivum* [positive being], it
is an *esse creatum* [created being]. As such, it is a *bonum* [good]. Qua facultas,
the being of the falsum cannot be a malum [an evil].

Nam per solum intellectum percipio tantum ideas de quibus judicium ferre possum,
nec ullus error proprie dictus in eo praecise sic spectato reperitur.[29]

[For through the intellect alone I perceive only ideas about which I can make a
judgment and, properly speaking, no error at all is found in it, viewed precisely in
this way.]

Descartes advances some customary objections and then refutes them. The
intellectus qua facultas and as *ens creatum* is a *bonum* [The intellect as faculty
and as a created being is a good].

[Q]uamvis enim innumerae fortasse res existant, quarum ideae nullae in me sunt,
non tamen proprie illis privatus, sed negative tantum destitutus sum dicendus, quia
nempe rationem nullam possum afferre, qua probem Deum mihi majorem quam
dederit cognoscendi facultatem dare debuisse.[30]

[For although innumerable things may possibly exist, of which there are no ideas
in me, properly speaking, it should not be said that I am deprived of them but,
negatively, only that I lack them, since I can offer no reason by which I might prove
that God ought to have given me a greater faculty of knowing than He did.]

Now, one could say that since errors in fact occur, why did God not create
me so that an error can never occur in me? For this, our intellectus would
necessarily have to be constituted like God's, that is to say, it would have to
be unlimited in relation to the possibility of comprehensible objects. But it is
limited and not everything that it conceives is conceived by it with a clara et

28. Descartes, Meditatio IV, 64 [*AT* VII, 56].
29. Op. cit., 64f. [*AT* VII, 56].
30. Op. cit., 65 [*AT* VII, 56].

distincta perceptio. Hence, a mistake? No. For the limitedness of my intellect is no *privatio* [privation]. My present makeup can be determined as *carentia* [lacking] only in relation to the ideal of God's constitution. Insofar, however, as I cannot lay claim to this infinity, my being-finite is no deficit. I cannot lay claim to more. Such is Descartes' characterization of the facultas intellectus [faculty of the intellect].

This type of proof is necessary because at the same time human perfection still lies in the intellect for him. To be sure, he says that the perfectio lies in the *voluntas* [will], but the explication of the voluntas as *facultas eligendi* proceeds, following Thomas, in the direction of the intellect.

> Nec vero etiam queri possum quod non satis amplam et perfectam voluntatem, sive arbitrii libertatem a Deo acceperim, nam sane nullis illam limitibus circumscribi experior.[31]
>
> [Also, in truth, I am not able to complain that I received an insufficiently ample and perfect will or freedom of choice from God for I do not experience it being circumscribed by any limits.]

The facultas eligendi is a facultas that is not enclosed by any limits. By contrast, the *imaginari* [imagination] or *memory* is limited. In these cases I can form ideals that go beyond what I find in myself.

> Sola est voluntas, sive arbitrii libertas, quam tantam in me experior ut nullius majoris ideam apprehendam; adeo ut illa praecipue sit, ratione cujus imaginem quandam, et similitudinem Dei me referre intelligo.[32]
>
> [It is only the will or freedom of choice that I experience in myself to be so great that I do not apprehend the idea of any greater faculty; such that it is principally by reason of this faculty that I understand that I bear in some way a certain image and likeness of God.]

I can imagine a greater possibility of imagination but not a greater possibility of my will, which is absolute in a certain manner. In regard to my will, I experience my similarity with God.

Here the characteristic connection with the tradition confronts us, a connection that we encounter whenever distinctively human being is introduced: faciamus hominem secundum imaginem et similitudinem Dei [let us make man according to the image and likeness of God].[33] It is no accident here that Descartes points to the fact that the being of my will demonstrates my being

---

31. Ibid. [*AT* VII, 56].
32. Op. cit., 66 [*AT* VII, 57].
33. Bibliorum Sacrorum iuxta Vulgatam Clementinam nova editio. Curavit Aloisius Gramatica. [New edition of the Sacred Bible, to which the Clementine Vulgate edition is attached. Edited by Aloisius Gramatica.] (Mediolani 1914). Liber Genesis I, 26: "Faciamus hominem ad imaginem et similitudinem nostram."

as the sort that is an imago et similitudo Dei. To be sure, I must acknowledge that the voluntas Dei [will of God] surpasses my voluntas, but the respects [in which God's will surpasses mine] do not affect the ens formale [formal being] of the will.

[N]am quamvis major absque comparatione in Deo quam in me sit, tum ratione cognitionis et potentiae quae illi adjunctae sunt, redduntque ipsam magis firmam et efficacem; tum ratione objecti, quoniam ad plura se extendit, . . .[34]

[For although the will in God is incomparably greater than the will in me, both by reason of the knowledge and power that are adjoined to it and render it stronger and more effective, and by reason of its object, since it extends to many more things, . . .]

1. In relation to the *ratio cognoscendi*, in view of the transparency of the willful act, I am at a disadvantage opposite God. 2. With regard to the possibility of executing what is willed by Him, He also has a greater potestas [power]. 3. *ratio objecti*: In view of the possibility of the objects willed by Him, God's will is superior to mine. If, on the contrary, I consider the *willing purely in itself*, it is evident that it is not greater than mine:

non tamen in se formaliter et praecise spectata major videtur, quia tantum in eo consistit quod idem vel facere, vel non facere (hoc est affirmare vel negare, prosequi vel fugere) possimus, vel potius in eo tantum quod ad id quod nobis ab intellectu proponitur affirmandum vel negandum, sive prosequendum vel fugiendum ita feramur, ut a nulla vi externa nos ad id determinari sentiamus.[35]

[nevertheless, viewed formally and precisely in itself, the will [[in God]] does not seem greater [[than the will in me]] because it consists only in the fact that we are able to do or not do one and the same thing (to affirm or to deny, to pursue or to flee), or rather it consists merely in the fact that we are drawn to what is proposed to us by the intellect to be affirmed or denied or pursued or fled, but in such a way that we do not feel ourselves to be determined to it by any external force.]

In what, then, does the *esse formale* of the voluntas [formal being of the will] consist? *Posse idem facere vel non facere*: being able to do and not to do one and the same thing set before us as such constitutes libertas.

With this determination, Descartes has a *traditional determination of freedom* in mind, a concept of freedom that can be characterized as an *absentia coactionis et determinationis* [absence of being forced and determined]; he has the actual elementary school concept in mind: the absence of being specifically tailored to something. In contrast to this concept, Augustine grounds the concept of freedom in the fact that the *determinatio* is the constitutive factor of libertas, that the determinatio, instead of being a deficiency, is the

---

34. Descartes, Meditatio IV, 66 [*AT* VII, 57].
35. Op. cit., 66f. [*AT* VII, 57].

will's genuine manner of being as a *free will*. Here the genuine art of finessing one's way through something, as is frequently the case for Descartes, makes its appearance. He determines libertas as *absolute indifferentia*, quod facere et non facere idem possumus [as absolute indifference, that we are able to do and not to do one and the same thing]. He thereupon gives the determination of voluntas as if it were a second determination in which he conceives freedom in such a way that it is a libertas in the sense of *absentia coactionis* [freedom in the sense of the absence of being forced] but in spite of this is a *determinari* [being determined]. To be free is not the mere indifferente, the ability to do one thing or the other, but instead *determinatum esse ad aliquid quod propositum est ab intellectu* [to be determined to something that is proposed by the intellect] in the sense of an affirmandum vel negandum sive prosequendum vel fugiendum [something to be affirmed or denied, or pursued or fled]. Thomas says: appetitus nihil aliud est quam quaedam inclinatio appetentis in aliquid [appetite is nothing other than a certain inclination of the desire for something].[36] Thus, being bent on something definite, not indifferently having possibilities at hand, is proper to the voluntas. Each inclinatio is an *inclinatio in aliquid* [an inclination to something], each esse qua esse is a bonum, thus each *inclinatio* is inclination as such to *bonum*.[37] Descartes says:

> Neque enim opus est me in utramque partem ferri posse ut sim liber, sed contra quo magis in unam propendeo, sive quia rationem veri et boni in ea evidenter intelligo, sive quia Deus intima cogitationis meae ita disponit, tanto liberius illam eligo.[38]
>
> [For in order that I may be free it is not necessary that I be capable of being drawn to either side; on the contrary, the more I am inclined to one side, either because I understand clearly the proportion of truth and goodness in it or because God thus disposes my innermost thinking, the more freely I choose it.]

In order to be free, it is not required that I can move in both directions, but rather: *quo magis in unam propendeo eo liberius* [the more I incline to the one, the freer I am]. Here the Augustinian concept of freedom comes to the fore: the more primordially the propensio [propensity] is for the bonum [the good], the more authentic the freedom of acting. An acting that places itself completely under God's will is absolutely free. It is this *libertas* that Descartes has his eye on here and that he applies to the *clara et distincta perceptio* in a manner quite characteristic in the perspective. I am genuinely free if I go towards what I understand. I live in a propensio in unam partem

---

36. Sancti Thomae Aquinatis Summa theologica. Vol. II, complectens primam secundae. [St. Thomas Aquinas, *Summa theologica*, volume 2, containing the first part of the second part.] (Parma 1853). In: *Opera Omnia* [Complete Works] (Parma 1852ff.), Tom. II. Quaestio VIII, articulus 1 [volume 2, question 8, article 1].
37. Ibid.; see, too, question 13, article 6.
38. Descartes, Meditatio IV, 67 [*AT* VII, 57f.].

[propensity for one part], namely, in the direction of what agrees with what is known clare et distincte [clearly and distinctly]. An utterly characteristic manner of being motivated is present in being-free in the genuine sense. By contrast, the indifferentia, the formal posse [the indifference, the formal possibility], is precisely not freedom but instead the infimus gradus libertatis [lowest grade of freedom].[39]

In these propositions that appear to be set forth so utterly self-evidently and freely, the entire contemporary background reveals itself. This rejection of the indifferentia as esse liberum [indifference as being free] is a blow against the Jesuits and a bow in the direction of the Port Royal.[40]

b) The concursus of intellectus and voluntas [the concurrence of the intellect
and the will] as the being of error. Theological problems
as the foundation of both concepts of freedom

Error has its being in a *concursus* [concurrence],[41] which is not seen with respect to God but with respect to two possibilities of behaving that are given to the human being itself. The facultas eligendi et intelligendi [faculty of choosing and understanding] are simultaneously concurring causae [causes]. From this fact the question then arises of examining this peculiar *simul esse voluntatis et intellectus* [simultaneous being of the will and the intellect] more closely. What does it mean: "the *intellectus* and the *will are with one another* at the same time"? This simul esse [being at the same time] must be such as is designated as a being-together of both, of the sort that is predetermined by its own being. This voluntas, being-together with the intellectus, must yield the sort of being that bears within itself the possibility of a *defectus* [defect]. It must exhibit the sort of being that is genuinely just as it is supposed to be. For only if a *debitum* [debt] is there in a being, does the possibility exist of speaking of a *carentia* [lack]. The being of error resides in this being-together and not, by contrast, in the intellectus' being as such qua facultas or in the voluntas' being qua facultas. That is out of the question for Descartes insofar as human beings are created with this constitution by God. Even if knowledge on the part of human beings is limited, one cannot say they do not have something that they should. Nor is it any more possible to designate the voluntas as such as something negative. I myself experience the will as something infinite and understand by this that it can direct itself at everything in the manner of facere et non facere posse idem [being able to do and not to do one and the same thing]. The *perfectio voluntatis* [perfection of the will]

---

39. Ibid.
40. See the Appendix, Supplement 20 (p. 234).
41. Op. cit., 64 [*AT* VII, 56].

lies in the fact that the voluntas can direct itself at everything in the sense of being able to and being able not to [*Könnens und Nichtkönnens*]. A specific sense of freedom provides the measure for the determination of the infinity of the voluntas: *libertas voluntatis* [freedom of the will] in the sense of *indifferentia* [indifference]. In the passage where Descartes passes over to determining the positive character [of the will], he *begins* with the characterization of libertas in the sense of *indifferentia*. The further determination then connects up with it seemingly without a break. He speaks of a being-free, in which a *determinatio* is on hand *ad prosequendum vel fugiendum* [to pursue or flee].

These *two concepts of freedom* with which Descartes operates have their *basis in theological problems* that preoccupy theology since Augustine and were being discussed in a particularly lively fashion precisely at the time that Descartes wrote the *Meditations*. The entire theological discussion within which the problem of freedom appears is the question of the connection between *grace* and *freedom*. The fact of being-free is indubitable for the theological inquiry. *That* the human being is free is not a veritas naturalis [natural truth], but a dogma. Any opinion that doubts freedom is heretical. By contrast, the *natura* voluntatis et libertatis [nature of the will and freedom] is questionable within the theological discussion. *How* freedom of the will is to be understood, that is controversial. And, indeed, the question of the sense of being-free on the part of human beings moves in two directions that one can designate for short as *Aristotelian* and *Augustinian*. A *twofold absentia* is necessary for being free in the *Aristotelian* sense: an absence of both *coactionis et determinationis* [being forced and determined]. For *Augustine*, precisely a *determinatio in summum bonum* [determination towards the highest good] is constitutive. Insofar as the will is directed at the highest good, it is not subject to a servitudo [servitude]. These two determinations remain controversial up to the present day.

The general problem is this: 1. How must the sense of God's *grace* and its manner of working be determined so that the human being's freedom is not destroyed? 2. How must *freedom* be determined so that it can submit to God's grace without canceling itself? With this, the possibility of a *mediating* standpoint is given, that of a *concordia* [concordance] between being-free on the part of the human being and the absolute working of God. The character of the *praescientia* [foreknowledge] and the *praedestinatio* [predestination] of God is bound up with this. All of that worked together to make these factors into the problems of the day at that time. In contrast to the Protestant doctrine of belief (Luther, *De servo arbitrio* [On the Servile Will], 1525[42]), where human freedom is suppressed absolutely, the Jesuits attempted to enhance

42. De servo arbitrio Martini Lutheri ad D. Erasmum Roterodamum (Wittenberg 1525/26).

human freedom. Jesuit theology originated in Spain. The actual founder of this doctrine of indifference is the Spanish Jesuit, Petrus Fonseca. The doctrine was further developed by Bellarmine, who played a major role at the Council of Trent.[43] Among the Spanish Jesuits, Molina's work, *De concordia gratiae et liberi arbitrii* [On the concordance of grace and free will] (1588)[44] stands out with its tendency to determine human freedom positively without restricting the working of divine grace. Against this work and the entire theological direction that was designated "Molinism," the Oratorian Gibieuf wrote *De libertate Dei et creaturae* [On the liberty of God and creature] (1630).[45] Gibieuf's work emphasizes the Augustinian concept of freedom in an extreme way, and says that precisely the presence of a determinatio in summum bonum [determination to the highest good] constitutes being-free in a genuine sense for human beings. Through God becoming present in the human being, the human being first becomes genuinely free. Grace cannot be detrimental to freedom at all since it itself first creates genuine freedom. It has not yet been explained how these connections effected Jansenism. Ten years after *De libertate*, the work *Augustinus* (1640) appeared, causing a stir. The author, Jansen, Bishop of Ypres, had set for himself the task of explicating Augustinian theology in contrast to Scholasticism and Molinism. The more exact title of the book reads: Augustinus sive doctrina S. Augustini de humanae naturae sanitate, aegritudine, medicina contra Pelagianos et Massilienses [Augustine or St. Augustine's doctrine of the health, sickness, and medicine of human nature in opposition to the Pelagians and Massilians].[46] The chief opponent of Augustine was the Irish monk, Pelagius, who instituted a theological orientation, still alive today, albeit not in Pelagius' extreme version, but in a more moderate orientation that is thus designated "Semipelagianism." Semipelagianism took hold especially in the south of France in the region of Massilia. Jansen emphasizes that Gibieuf actually saw what it is all about: the true, the Platonic determination of freedom stands over the Aristotelian deformation. In *De concordia*, Molina writes: illud agens liberum dicitur, quod positis omnibus requisitis ad agendum, potest agere et non agere[47]: The one acting is

43. Cardinal Franz Romulus Robert Bellarmin, S.J. (1542–1621) was a nephew of Cardinal Cervini who, in 1555, during the Council of Trent ascended the Papal Chair under the name of Marcellus II.

44. D. Ludovicus Molina, Liberi arbitrii cum gratiae donis, divina praescientia, providentia, praedestinatione et reprobatione, Concordia. Ad nonnullos primae partis D. Thomae Articulos. [*Concordance of free will with gifts of grace, divine foreknowledge, providence, predestination, and reprobation. To some articles of the first part of Thomas.*] Second edition (Antwerp 1595).

45. G. Gibieuf, De Libertate Dei et creaturae libri duo [*Two books on the liberty of God and creature*] (Paris 1630).

46. Cornelii Iansenii, Episcopi Iprensis, Augustinus seu doctrina S. Augustini de humanae naturae sanitate, aegritudine, medicina adversus Pelagianos et Massilienses. Tribus tomis comprehensa [Collected in three volumes] (Leuven 1640).

47. L. Molina, Concordia, ad nonnullos primae partis D. Thomae Articulos. Ad XIII Articulum Quaestionis XIV, Disputatio II, 8. [To article 13 of question 14, disputatio 2, page 8.]

called free who, insofar as everything necessary for the action is ready, still can act or not, or who, in deciding for a specific direction, still is aware of the possibility of seizing upon another direction. Being placed indifferently before both possibilities is the genuine sense of being-free. In the instant when I have chosen, I am no longer free. Freedom is canceled. Genuinely being-free resides in the status of indifferentia, while Augustine sees human freedom precisely in this determinari [being determined], in placing oneself under a bonum [good]. Now, depending upon how one sets forth being-free, a difficulty presents itself with God's foreknowledge and foregoing action. How do matters stand with God's omniscience? He must, of course, know in advance the specific possibilities that the human being seizes upon. They are there for him, not as futurum [in the future], but as *futurible* [able to be part of a future], that can be seized upon in this way or that way. Molina designates it as *scientia media* [intermediate knowledge]. In a general, theological sense, there is in God a praescientia mere naturalis [purely natural foreknowledge]: God sees in advance everything that could possibly happen. Everything is there in advance in his absolute intellect. [There is also] a prascientia mere libera [purely free foreknowledge]: God sees in advance what happens on the basis of a will. He also sees in advance what is freely set into motion by human beings. That is a praescientia that is neither naturalis nor libera, that has to do neither with what happens universally nor with what is caused by God's will. By contrast, in Augustinian theology freedom is understood in the sense in which "being-free" means not to submit to the world's demands and the devil's temptations, but instead to place one's will under the will of God. Each action of the human being as a human being stands under a finis [an end], and this *finis as bonum* [the end as the good] is the constitutivum [constitutive factor] of freedom. To be sure, indifference occurs in the human will. This occurrence was the basis that Aristotle discovered in his analysis and upon which he set up his concept of freedom. But indifferentia does not occur as a constitutivum of libertas, but instead only qua creatura [insofar as it is part of a creature]; the indifferentia is to be conceived as deficiens [a deficiency]. Indifference is not inherent in freedom, although it occurs in acting.

Descartes takes over this conception for his interpretation of error.

Indifferentia autem illa quam experior, cum nulla me ratio in unam partem magis quam in alteram impellit, est infimus gradus libertatis.[48]

[That indifference, however, which I experience when no reason impels me more to one side than to the other is the lowest grade of freedom.]

The indifferentia is the infimus gradus libertatis [lowest grade of freedom].

48. Descartes, Meditatio IV, 67 [*AT* VII, 58].

[Q]uo magis in unam propendeo, sive quia rationem veri et boni in ea evidenter intelligo, sive quia Deus intima cogitationis meae ita disponit, tanto liberius illam eligo.[49]

[The more I am inclined to one side, either because I understand clearly the proportion of truth and goodness in it or because God thus disposes my innermost thinking, the more freely I choose it.]

The more weight I have to one side, in my willful behavior, the more freely I live. [N]ec sane divina gratia, nec naturalis cognitio unquam imminuunt libertatem, sed potius augent, et corroborant [Surely, neither divine grace nor natural cognition ever diminish freedom but rather augment and strengthen it].[50] Divine grace does not, therefore, reduce human freedom; instead grace increases and fortifies it. Descartes transposes what is theologically designated as the working of God's grace to the relation of the intellect working on the will. *The clara et distincta perceptio takes over the role of grace.* This perception is what makes the judicium's *specific bonum* present to it. The voluntas is thus in its own being determined in the direction of the intellect which provides the voluntas itself with something. The *genuine* simul esse voluntatis et intellectus [simultaneous being of the will and intellect] is to be understood, then, in this way. Just as a determinatio to a bonum is inherent in the will's being, so the intellectus is what provides the voluntas with the perceptum as prosequendum [so the intellect is what provides the will with something perceived as something to be pursued]. The more intrinsically the voluntas holds itself to what is grasped clearly and distinctly, the more genuinely is the human being what he is.[51] Willfully seizing upon the clare et distincte perceptum [what is perceived clearly and distinctly] is for Descartes a human being's supreme possibility of being. As soon as one looks to the origin of Descartes' propositions, one sees that the only basis on which they can be demonstrated has nothing to do with a purely rational knowledge.

§ 28. The sense of being of error: error as res and as privatio, as detrimental to the genuine being of the created human being (creatum esse). Perceptum esse and creatum esse as basic determinations of the esse of the res cogitans

Let us try to establish *the character of res cogitans' being*. It becomes evident that, within the res cogitans, there is a reduction such that, by means of the clara et distincta perceptio, the cogitare et cogitatum [the thinking and the

49. Ibid.
50. Ibid.
51. See the Appendix, Supplement 21 (p. 235).

thought] are placed in a *one-dimensional region* of possible comprehension. That is the *one* direction in which a reduction of the concept of being presents itself within the Cartesian point of departure, a reduction oriented to being in the sense of *perceptum esse*.

We get a *second* determination of the character of the res cogitans' being by way of coming to an understanding of the *sense of being of the cogitare itself*. What kind of an *esse* is the esse of the *error*, the *esse falsum*? The falsum is the cogitatum of the error. Hence, here, too, the *reduction* of the *percipere* and *perceptum*, determined above, is evident. It is no accident that the determination of the esse error is also a determination of esse falsum and that both terms are used by Descartes in the same sense. What type of "being" is the esse erroris [being of the error], and by what means does Descartes determine this being itself? Insofar as errare [to err] is *something*, it cannot be a sheer nihil. On the other hand, the falsum, in relation to the verum, is a not-being, a being that is a not-being and not a sheer nothing. Such a being is a *privatio*.

What is the *genuine factor in the cogitare's positive being that can be breached* (for the falsum esse as a determination of the cogitare is a privatio, defectus), that can be affected by the *defectus* in such a way that the *errare* itself can be a *privatio*? In general, Descartes specifies the character of error's esse as: simul esse voluntatis et intellectus [being simultaneously of the will and the intellect]. What is this *simul esse*? The intellectus and the voluntas are, taken by themselves, complete; they have nothing like a deficient factor. Closer examination of both the intellectus and the voluntas leads Descartes to determine the *voluntas*. Voluntas is *libertas* and libertas is a basic determination of humanitas. In this determination of human freedom, the theological context sets the standard for Descartes. The determination of human freedom is read off from an idea of God's freedom as *actus purus* [pure act]. The factors that he takes up from the contemporary discussion are Augustinian. Augustine's determination of freedom as determinatio in bonum goes back, by a peculiar path, to Greek ontology. It goes back to Greek ontology insofar as the determination of being-free on the part of human beings is determined by the Neo-Platonic doctrine of the twofold movement. According to this doctrine, all created being gets its being from the ἕν, insofar as it is released from this one but at the same time has a tendency to recursus [return to it]. It is inherent in the soul's being to return to the place from which it comes. This formal determination entered into Augustine's concrete explication of human existence. In the nineteenth century within the *Oratorium*, the orientation of Augustinianism in the Catholic Church, reinforced by Jansen, experienced a peculiar revival again. The genuine philosophical foundations set out by Scheler in his ethics are taken from this context.

In Descartes' case, these contexts are present but distinctively *de-*

theologized. It is the *verum* that motivates the inclinatio voluntatis in judicium [the true that motivates the inclination of the will to the judgment]. Insofar as it is supposed to be possible as a motivation, the verum must be given simul cum voluntate [simultaneously with the will], that is to say, as *bonum* for the voluntas or, better, assensio [as a good for the will or, better, for the assent]. The form of the enactment [*Vollzugsform*] in which the verum is given is the *clara et distincta perceptio*. "Being-free" means maintaining the inclinatio to the clare et distincte perceptum in the judgment. Given with this inclinatio is a prefiguring that constitutes the willing being and inheres in the natura of the human being. Insofar as this *being-free*, this *determinari a clare et distincte percepto* [this being determined by what is perceived clearly and distinctly], makes up the nature of the human being, a nature that precisely constitutes the genuine relation to the intellectus, being-determined is something that allows for a *defectus*. According to this, then, the *regula generalis* [general rule] for *freedom* is the clara et distincta perceptio. To adhere in this way to the perceptum is to be-free in a genuine sense and is, insofar as it is carried out, the *usus rectus libertatis* [correct use of freedom]. Insofar as being determined in this way is a proper being, it allows for a defectus. The defectus consists in the fact that the specific manner of enactment [of freedom] does not pay attention to being determined in this way in view of the perceptum and, therefore, errs. The errare is a *usus libertatis non rectus* [incorrect use of freedom].[52] The rectitudo can be violated and, insofar as it is violated, the errare is constituted.

It becomes obvious that *two characteristic factors* are inherent in *error's being*. 1. Insofar as error is a *being*, it is a *res*. 2. Insofar as it is a *defectio*, it is a *privatio*. Descartes sees quite clearly that God is still a genuine cause even for an error, insofar as it is in general a cogitare. Insofar as error is a res, God is responsible for it. But insofar as errare is a non rectus usus [to err is an incorrect use], it is not caused by God, but springs instead from the freedom of the will itself. Thomas says (*Summa theologica*, pt. 1, q. 49, art. 2):

> Ad secundum dicendum, quod effectus causae secundae deficientis reducitur in causam primam non deficientem, quantum ad id quod habet entitatis et perfectionis, non autem quantum ad id quod habet de defectu.[53]

> [To the second objection, it should be said that the effect of a second, deficient cause is reduced to the first, nondeficient cause with respect to what it possesses of being and perfection, not, however, with respect to what defect it has.]

52. Descartes, Meditatio IV, 70 [AT VII, 59].
53. Sancti Thomae Aquinatis Summa theologica. Vol. I, complectens partem primam [containing the first part] (Parma 1852). In: *Opera Omnia* (Parma 1852ff.), Tom. I. Quaestio XLIX. Articulus II: Utrum summum bonum, quod est Deus, sit causa mali. [volume 1, question 49, article 2: Whether the highest good, which God is, may be the cause of evil.]

It should be said that the effect of the second cause, the libertas hominis—insofar as it is deficient, that is to say, insofar as it is detrimental to this being that it effects, insofar as the will is not recte [rightly] motivated—is traced back to the first cause, to God, insofar as this behavior has something of God and perfection, but not insofar as this specific being has a defectus.

[S]icut quidquid est motus in claudicatione, causatur a virtute motiva; sed quod est obliquitatis in ea, non est ex virtute motiva, sed ex curvitate cruris:[54]

[Just as any motion in a limp is caused by the motive power, but what is crooked in it is not by virtue of the motive power, but by virtue of the curvature of the leg:]

It is like the manner in which limping is caused by the cause of the movement (that is God); insofar as limping is a movement, the cause of the limping is a capacity to move, a bonum. But what is a defectus in the limping stems not from the capacity to walk but from the curvature of the leg, thus, from a defectus.

In the case of Descartes, the explication of the error is summarized in such a way that the direction is seen. The errare has turned out to be a *deficere a determinatione* [deficiency in its determination]. In the case of errare, a breach occurs in the genuine determinacy of the voluntas to the perceptum. This deficere is *deficere a libertate* [to be deficient in this way is to be deficient in freedom]. The libertas, however, is what makes up the genuine being of a human being. Therefore, the deficere a determinatione voluntatis is a *deficere ab esse* in the sense of the *esse perceptum* [to be deficient in the determination of the will is to be deficient in being in the sense of "being perceived"]. Insofar as it is a deficere ab esse perfectum [to be deficient in perfected being], this deficere is at the same time *deficere ab esse creatum* [to be deficient in created being] in such a way that the *falsum* is nothing other than a *non esse* of the *ens creatum* [a nonbeing of the created being]. The esse creatum is the *fundamental determination* in the explication of the errare and the being of libertas. To err is to effect a breach in [to be detrimental to: *Abbruch-tun*] the genuine being of the created human being. Insofar as the *errare* is an *esse* of the *res cogitans*, the result is that, as the res cogitans' esse, it is at the same time a *non esse* of the res cogitans qua *creatum* [a nonbeing of the thinking thing qua created]. We have, accordingly, a further determination of res cogitans' being insofar as it is an *esse creatum*. Hitherto the determination was: the res cogitans is a being that can be grasped in a one-dimensional respect in the clara et distincta perceptio. *Perceptum esse et creatum esse a Deo* [to be perceived and to be created by God] are the fundamental determinations of the *res cogitans' esse*.

54. Ibid.

Chapter Four

Going back to Scholastic ontology:
the verum esse in Thomas Aquinas

What is the *foundation* of the two determinations of res cogitans as esse perceptum and as esse creatum? In order to elucidate this question, we have to *go back before Descartes*, to the extent that we see a connection in *Scholastic ontology*. What needs to be said from the outset is this: the genuine connection between the *esse perceptum* and the *esse creatum* is established by the *esse verum*. The entity, in the manner in which it is grasped, is identical with being in the sense of truly being. The *esse creatum* qua esse creatum is characterized as the *esse bonum et verum*. Nothing is gained by this purely formulaic determination. In order to get a hold on the character of res cogitans' being, we need to become clear about how the *sense of the verum esse* is determined *in Scholasticism* itself.

§ 29. The connection of the verum and the ens: being-true as a mode of being (De veritate, q. 1, art. 1)

The *problem of truth* was handled by the entire Scholastic tradition in various manners in conjunction with *Aristotle*. However, the High Scholastic tradition was the first to provide a comprehensive doctrine of truth. We will interpret Thomas' writing "De veritate" [On Truth] in the *Quaestiones disputatae*.[1] Next to this major question "De veritate," these disputed questions include questions, among others, "De scientia Dei," "De praedestinatione," "De conscientia," "De libero arbitrio," "De gratia," [On God's Knowledge, On Predestination, On Conscience, On Free Will, On Grace], thus questions of an essentially theological character, while "De veritate" is philosophical in the sense of the High Scholastic tradition.

The "Quaestio prima" is divided into twelve questions (articles): 1. Quid sit veritas [What truth is]. 2. Utrum veritas principalius in intellecu quam in rebus reperiatur [Whether truth is found more principally in the intellect than in things]. 3. Utrum in intellectu componente et dividente sit veritas [Whether truth is in the intellect that combines and divides]. 4. Utrum una tantum veritas sit, qua omnia vera sint [Whether there is one truth alone, by which all true

---

1. Thomas Aquinas, *De veritate*. In: Sancti Thomae Aquinatis Quaestiones disputatae, Vol. II, complectens de veritate et quaestiones quolibeticas. ["On Truth," in *The Disputed Questions of St. Thomas Aquinas*, vol. 2, comprising "De Veritate" and "Quodlibetal Questions."] (Parma 1859). In: *Opera omnia* [Complete Works] (Parma 1852ff.), Tomus IX.

things are]. 5. Utrum praeter primam aliqua alia veritas sit aeterna [Whether besides the first truth some other truth is eternal]. 6. Utrum veritas creata sit immutabilis [Whether created truth is immutable]. 7. Utrum veritas in divinis personaliter vel essentialiter dicatur [Whether the truth in regard to divinity is said personally or essentially]. (Whether truth's being in God must be grasped in the sense of belonging to God's being or to God's being-a-person, insofar, namely, as the truth has a genuine connection with the inner divine life.) 8. Utrum omnis veritas sit a prima veritate [Whether every truth is from the first truth]. 9. Utrum veritas sit in sensu [Whether truth is in a sense]. 10. Utrum res aliqua sit falsa [Whether any thing is false]. 11. Utrum falsitas sit in sensu [Whether falsity is in a sense]. 12. Utrum in intellectu sit falsitas [Whether falsity may be in the intellect].

We will take up only a few pieces of the account and attempt to interpret them. For the comprehension of the entire doctrine of being-true and truth in Thomas, it is important to become clear about the connection in which the discussion of being-true and truth is presented. The *first article* provides some information about this. Thomas proceeds from a methodological considera-tion: Unde oportet quod omnes aliae conceptiones intellectus accipiantur ex additione ad ens [Whence it is necessary that all other conceptions of the intellect are taken up by way of an addition to being].[2] Every explanation of what something is must come to the formal determination *ens* in such a way that one acquires the concrete determinations of an object through an addere [adding]. What is *verum* [the true]? It is established that verum is an *ens* [a being]. Accordingly, we have to ask: In what *connection* with the ens does the concrete determinacy of verum stand? Can the connection with the ens be construed in the sense that the verum is a determination of the ens, in the manner of an *affectio* [affection]? No. Thomas: since being-true is no thing and no thing-like property, it needs to be asked: What relation does the verum have to the ens? The verum is a *modus* of the ens. The entire discussion of the being of being-true, with regard to being itself, proceeds in this direction. With relation to the ens, the verum esse [to be true] is to be grasped as a mode.

Thomas distinguishes *two modi* in which being can be determined at all. Quite apart from the verum, he begins the explication completely in the man-ner of formal ontology. It is important to see in what place the verum esse comes up. He first distinguishes two modi: 1. *modus specialis*, 2. *modus ge-neralis*. Modus specialis is linked to the manner in which the Aristotelian categories are connected with οὐσία. Various *modi speciales essendi* [special modes of being] thereby present themselves. The being of the verum cannot fall under this connection, since it will prove to be a relativum.

<hr/>

2. Op. cit., Quaestio I, Articulus I [Question 1, article 1. Hereafter: q. 1, art. 1].

The *modus generalis* can be taken in two directions: 1. considered *in se* [in itself], 2. *in ordine ad aliud* [in relation to another]. Insofar as ens is considered in itself and, indeed, affirmatively, the determination of it as *res* results; insofar as it is considered negatively, the determination of it as *unum* results. Ens is, in a negative respect, the sort of being that is characterized by indivisibility. Omne ens considered per se is res and unum [Every being considered in terms of itself is a thing and one].

Insofar as being is considered in the modus generalis *in ordine ad aliud* [in relation to something else], it is an *aliud quid* [different] or *aliquid* [something else], it is something and not an another. Insofar as an ens is considered secundum convenientiam unius entis ad aliud [in terms of an agreement of one being with another], what results is ens as *bonum* or *verum* [a being as good or true]. The possibility of the verum's being first surfaces at this juncture.

How are the esse creatum [to be created] and the esse perceptum [to be perceived] connected with one another? Is it possible to find a basis of ontological determinations from which these two characters of being sprout? And is it possible to determine the manner of considering being that leads to the elevation of these two characters of being out of the ground [*Boden*] of entities? We will answer the question of the motivational connection between the esse creatum and the esse perceptum by showing that both the esse as esse perceptum and the esse as esse creatum lead us back to an esse verum, an esse verum that presents us with the task of determining its being. In order to orient ourselves more easily, the course of the interpretation of the falsum and error, conducted so far, may be briefly given again. We have set this interpretation in motion in order to get a glimpse of the verum. Both modi essendi with respect to the idea are uniformly conceived as the esse in the sense of the cogitatio or, better, of the realm of the cogitationes, the res cogitans. The esse of the res cogitans is clare et distincte perceptum esse [the "to be of the thinking thing" is "to be perceived clearly and distinctly"], perceptum esse equals verum esse ["to be perceived" equals "to be true"]. The peculiar character that emerged in this consideration is that a peculiar reduction [*Nivellierung*] of being presents itself within the res cogitans, insofar as the perceptum esse pertains not only to the cogitatum [the what is thought], but also to the cogitare [the thinking]. The esse perceptum is the genuine esse verum that pertains to both possibilities of the res cogitans as such. The res cogitans is, therefore, 1. being in the sense of the esse perceptum. 2. Error is a privatio [privation] and, as privation, a non esse [nonbeing], not a non esse as nihil [not a nonbeing as nothing], but a non esse entis [a nonbeing of an entity]. The character of the "non" [not] is the usus voluntatis non rectus [incorrect use of the will]. The "not-character" pertains to a rectitudo [correctness]. Non rectus [not correct] means: deficiens a rectitudine, i.e., a determinatione [deficient in correctness, i.e., in the determination]. The deter-minatio in bonum [determination to the good] is the genuine basic determi-nation of libertas [liberty], consequently, [to be incorrect is to be] deficiens a libertate [deficient in liberty]. Libertas is the natura hominis; hence, deficiens a natura humana [Liberty is the nature of a human being; hence, [[to be incorrect is to be]] deficient in human nature]. Natura humana est qua humana natura creata, deficiens a natura creata, deficiens ab esse qua creatum, that is to say, non esse creatum [Human nature is, qua human, a created nature; [[hence, to be incorrect is to be]] deficient in a created nature, deficient in being qua created, that is to say, [[incorrectness is a]] noncreated being]. The falsum is, in short, a non esse creatum [The false is, in short, a noncreated being]. Esse verum is equivalent to creatum esse [Being true is equivalent to being created]. How, in relation to verum esse, are the perceptum esse and the creatum esse characterized as determinations of being? We will solve this problem by making clear to ourselves how the verum is to be understood. This question is not explicitly handled by Descartes. But the entire manner in which he employs verum and falsum esse shows that the *Scholastic doctrine of veritas and falsitas* lies at the bottom of this doctrine of verum and falsum.

Thomas poses the problem in his "Disputatio de veritate" [Disputation on Truth] in the sense that he inserts the verum into the general inquiry into the sense of ens and esse. He sets forth a methodological reflection first. If I want to get clear about the verum, then it must first be established that the verum is a Something: quid [what]. With every subsequent question I must come finally to something ultimate. For if the process were to run on to infinity, then knowing as determining would be impossible. Thus all basic concepts are reduced in the direction of an ultimate concept. Illud autem quod primo intellectus concipit quasi notissimum, et in quo omnes conceptiones resolvit, est ens [That, however, which intellect first conceives as the most known, as it were, and in which it resolves all conceptions, is being].[3] The universal determination to which every determination is reduced is the ens, being in a completely formal and empty sense. Unde oportet quod omnes aliae concep-tiones intellectus accipiantur ex additione ad ens [Whence it is necessary that all other conceptions of the intellect are grasped by an addition to that of being].[4] Thus, insofar as all basic concepts are traced back to ens, it is nec-essary that, from the outset, one acquires the concrete conceptiones through a determinate additio to this concept [ens]. In a completely general way, that is the methodical orientation that Thomas follows in order to determine the verum esse in some sort of sense.[5]

3. Ibid.
4. Ibid.
5. See the Appendix, Supplement 22 (p. 236).

He orients it to the ens insofar as it is something at all and not a nothing. Although ὄν, the entity as such, is the most universal determination for any possible entity, it does *not* have the character of a genus. The *ens* is not a *genus* that could by any sort of specification yield concrete, existing objects. It is necessary, from the outset, to reject this conception, as though on the basis of the ens it could be specified.

[Q]uod ens non potest esse genus; sed secundum hoc aliqua dicuntur addere supra ens, inquantum exprimunt ipsius modum, qui nomine ipsius entis non exprimitur.[6]

[. . . Being cannot be a genus; but in accordance with this, some things are said to add [[some modification]] beyond the being insofar as they express a mode of it which is not expressed by the name "being" itself.]

Since ens cannot be a genus itself, the directions of the concretion of this ens cannot proceed in the sense of a specification. Instead, in this respect one can say that some things [*einiges*] add something to ens as such insofar as these determinations *exprimunt ipsius modum* [express a mode of it], insofar as an *additio supra ens* [an addition beyond being] occurs, insofar as one can uncover basic categories which are modi of the being itself, lying contained in it, that the being itself does not express. These determinations inhere in the being of the very entity as an entity.

The modal consideration of being as such can be carried out initially in two directions, insofar as one distinguishes the modus specialis and the modus generalis. The latter modi are such as accrue to each ens qua ens, while the modi speciales are the sort of determinations that the entity takes on in view of a definite look, in view of its genuine being. All of these [modi speciales] are the sort of categories that obtain for a concrete entity, while the others obtain for every entity and not only for an entity in its concrete being.

The *verum* belongs to the class of *modi generales*. Attention should be paid to the direction in which the verum is directed in the explication, at what juncture it appears in connection with the determinations of ens qua ens, and what sort of possibility it constitutes as a modus essendi. Within the modus generalis, we distinguish two modi essendi, insofar as the entity is considered: 1. purely in itself (ens in se), 2. as ens in ordine ad aliud.

The first direction in considering ens, insofar as it is taken in itself, insofar as I remain solely with the entity qua entity, separates into two subdivisions: a) Insofar as I take this ens in se affirmatively (we would say: "as objectively here"), I come to the basic determination of ens; that is the essentia or, better, res. b) If I take the ens in se negatively, each ens qua res is, as such, something that is in itself and, in this sense, indivisible. This *indivisio* is nothing else

6. Thomas Aquinas, *De veritate*, q. 1, art. 1.

than the sense of individuality used in formal logic. It is this indivisio that I encounter if I conceive the ens in se negatively, and the categorial expression for this indivisio is unum. Omne ens est unum [Every being is one].

Also in regard to the *ordo ad aliud* there is a twofold possibility: 1. secundum divisionem unius ab altero [according to the division of one from another], insofar as I distinguish the one from the other, et hoc exprimit hoc nomen *aliquid*; dicitur enim aliquid quasi aliud quid,[7] each res qua ens in ordine ad aliud is an aliquid [and the term *something* expresses this, for something is called, as it were, another what, each thing qua being in relation to another is a something]. Each entity qua entity is aliquid, aliud-quid [something, some other what], an other and not the one.

[U]nde sicut ens dicitur unum, inquantum est indivisum in se; ita dicitur aliquid, inquantum est ab aliis divisum.[8]

[Whence just as being is called one insofar as it is undivided in itself, so it is called something insofar as it is divided from others.]

The divisio [division] itself provides these two aspects: indivisum in se: unum; divisum ab altero: aliquid [undivided in itself: one; divided from another: something]. In its scientific niveau this explication even moves beyond *Aristotle*.

2. Alio modo secundum convenientiam unius entis ad aliud [In another way, according to the agreement of one entity with another].[9] The second factor presents itself if I consider an entity *secundum convenientiam ad aliud* [according to agreement with something else]. This *convenientia* [agreement] introduces an entirely new determination. It is formally given, but it brings us into concrete relations. Convenientia is the type and manner of agreeing, of coming together, of coinciding in some sense. This determination non potest esse nisi accipiatur aliquid quod natum sit convenire cum omni ente [This determination is impossible unless something is considered that naturally comes together with every being].[10] There is such an *esse* [to be] in the sense of *convenientia* [coming together] only if there is an entity whose genuine being is inherently such as *convenire cum omni ente* [to come together with every being]. Is there such an entity that agrees with every entity? Hoc autem est anima, quae quodammodo est omnia [This, however, is the soul that, in a way, is all things].[11] This connection of the unum ens [one being] with all entities as a whole can only be made intelligible insofar as the convenire is

7. Ibid.
8. Ibid.
9. Ibid.
10. Ibid.
11. Ibid.

inherent in the being of this aliquid [this something]. The source of this determination lies in Aristotle's *De anima* (III, 8, 431b21f.): ἡ ψυχὴ τὰ ὄντα πώς
ἐστιν. πάντα γὰρ ἢ αἰσθητὰ τὰ ὄντα ἢ νοητά.[12] Every entity is conceivable either
in the sense of being perceived through the senses or in the sense of νοεῖν
[thinking]. Insofar as each entity is perceivable by the soul, the soul is in a
certain sense everything; it is what it is in discovering and possessing, in
having every entity. Thomas affirms this proposition of Aristotle now not only
for the νόησις and αἴσθησις but principally for every virtus [power] of the
anima [soul] itself. In the *anima* there is the grasping capacity (*intellectus*)
and the striving (*voluntas*). *Bonum est quod omnia appetunt* [The good is
what all things desire]. Convenientiam vero entis ad intellectum exprimit hoc
nomen *verum* [The term "true" expresses an entity's truly coming together
with the intellect].[13] Verum is a modus essendi [the true is a mode of being],
indeed, such that the ens that is considered here *ad omnia* [for all] has the
soul's character of being. You notice that in this entire explication we have
yet to encounter anything concretely objective. Now, in the course of the
determination of convenientia as a modus essendi, the introduction of a concrete manner of being appears, a manner of being that on the basis of its φύσις
is suited to convenire cum omni ente [to come together with every being],
the very manner of being that is conceived as the coming together of the
accord unius entis ad aliud [the accord of one being with another]. *Being-true*
is a *manner of being* in the sense of a definite being-together of two entities.
Here it becomes possible to see how the verum is brought into the framework
of fundamental determinations of being and how, on the basis of this place-
ment, the verum is constituted fundamentally in view of the formal dimension
of esse in ordine ad aliud [being in relation to something else].

§ 30. The genuine being of the verum as convenientia in intellectus
(De veritate, q. 1, art. 1–3)

What, then, is the *primordial being of verum* and what constitutes the primordial being of verum? Insofar as verum is *convenientia*, the question arises:
Is the verum the *convenire* [the coming together, the agreeing] or does verum
have its genuine being in the *anima* or in the *res cum qua anima convenit* [in
the soul or in the thing with which the soul agrees]?

The sense of verum is divided up into three basic determinations. 1. The
verum is founded in the *res* with which the soul has an accord; 2. id quod
formaliter rationem veri perficit [that which formally perfects the meaning of

---

12. Aristotle, *De anima*, Gamma 8, 431b21f.
13. Thomas Aquinas, *De veritate*, q. 1, art. 1.

the true],[14] what formaliter constitutes the *perfectio* of being-true, *verum* equals *rectitudo* [correctness]; 3. secundum effectum consequentem [according to the subsequent effect], and sic definit Hilarius, quod *verum est mani-festativum et declarativum esse* [thus Hilary defines the true as being that makes itself manifest and clear].[15] In a third sense being-true means *being-in-the-sense-of-making-visible* (manifestativum esse), declarativum esse: *keeping an entity in the clear.*

The question is: Which of these basic determinations is then the *genuine being* of the *verum*? Aquinas's way of deciding this question is characteristic of the transformation that Aristotle underwent among the Scholastics. We need only attend to the first-mentioned element to see how far the tendency toward the specific determination that gained influence presents itself in these distinctions.

Now within this underlying doctrine of being, the reference to anima, and precisely in regard to intellectus, does not overstep this principal consideration of being. We will understand why it does not if we analyze the ground of this consideration of being. Thus [we have] the question of the extent to which the creatum [the created] is co-posited in the verum. We can only decide this question if we become clear about which being in the *genuine* and *primary* sense verum is the modus of. Only then will we have the answer to the question: In what sense does the determination of verum belong to the character of being of the res [the thing]?

To determine the peculiar *connection* of each being more precisely, Thomas uses many and diverse sorts of expressions which are not simply identical in their meaning-function. *Convenientia* [coming together, agreement] is the most general determination of each being's way of being related to the soul, spirit, and so forth. The expression "convenientia" must accordingly be held fast since it will become apparent that the expression has a *double-meaning* and that the peculiar ambiguity first makes this way of beginning possible. Convenientia is the being-related, the being-referred-to-one-another of one entity relative to another.

1. In one direction convenientia has the *determinatio* for the *intellectus*. Insofar as the convenientia as character of the verum is related to knowing, this itself must be determined with respect to the convenientia. Thomas characterizes this determination as *assimilatio intellectus ad rem* [assimilation of the intellect to a thing].[16] *Proportio* [proportion], being carried forward to the thing itself, is inherent in the natura of the intellectus and it is inherent in the intellect's being to have grasped the res as *cognita* [known].

14. Ibid.
15. Ibid.
16. Ibid.

2. It is necessary, *ut res intellectui correspondeat* [that the thing correspond to the intellect].[17] The intellectus is directed, in its being, to the res, while the res, for its part, corresponds to the intellect. On the basis of their nature, both manners of being-together of this mutual orientation to one another can be summed up quite concisely as *conformitas*.[18] This conformitas was characterized as *adaequatio* [adequation, correspondence] in the Jewish–Arabian philosophy of the Middle Ages or rather in their Latin translations. Hence, the formula: *adaequatio rei et intellectus*.[19] Taken in a completely formal sense, the conformitas that constitutes itself from the side of the anima and from the side of the res is the convenientia.

The verum as convenientia has three factors, determined by way of relation: 1. the relation *ratio formalis*, the *convenire*. 2. The *fundamentum*, that of which a convenire is possible at all: the res. 3. The *cognitio* is at the same time itself an *effectus veritatis* [effect of truth]. The concept of verum: 1. in relation to the *fundamentum*, 2. in relation to the *ratio formalis*, 3. in relation to the *effectus* of knowing,[20] a judging's being-true. In relation to these three orientations the principal question arises: In relation to which being is the verum the *genuine modus* of this being? Where is the verum at home?

We want now to consider this question of *the genuine being of the verum*. Here, too, Thomas presents a formal consideration in advance of this decision. In relation to which of the three parts is verum said *per prius* [in the first place] and *per posterius* [afterwards]?[21] Where is it in its genuine sense true so that the remaining determinations can be designated as true per denominationem [in name]? [To begin] negatively, res is not the being that can be primarily designated as the being of the true [*Wahrsein*]. The modus essendi is not proper to res primarily.

> [N]on semper oportet quod id quod per prius recipit praedicationem communis, sit ut causa aliorum, sed illud in quo primo ratio illius communis completa invenitur.[22]
>
> [It is not always necessary that that which receives the predication in the first place is common as the cause of others; rather, it is that in which the nature of that common feature is first found completely.]

In order to get some thread of a clue, Thomas says, it is necessary to heed the fact that what in the genuine sense bears the *ratio communis* [common meaning] does not need to be conceived as *causa* of the rest, but must be conceived instead as that in which the sense of *verum* as *convenientia* is

17. Ibid.
18. Ibid.
19. Ibid.
20. Ibid.
21. Thomas Aquinas, *De veritate*, q. 1, art. 2.
22. Ibid.

completa [the sense of "true" as "agreement, coming together" is complete]. Sicut sanum per prius dicitur de animali [as "healthy" is said in the first place of animals],[23] "healthy" is said primarily of the living, although we also say that a medicine, as effectiva sanitatis [productive of health],[24] is healthy relative to its aptness to make someone living healthy. That in which the sense of verum is complete is true in the genuine sense.

Now, the connection itself between *res* and *intellectus* is achieved and actual in the *cognoscere*. The cognoscere [knowing] itself, however, is motus cognitivae virtutis [a movement of the cognitive power],[25] that proceeds from *intellectus* in the sense of the *assimilatio ad rem* [assimilation to the thing] and back from there. The genuine fulfillment of a movement is present where is it finished. The movement of knowing proceeds from knowing to known over the *res* [over the thing] and thus terminates in the known, while the motus appetitivae virtutis [movement of the appetitive power][26]—in the sense of being willfully out for something—terminates ad rem [at the thing] insofar as it [what is willed] is done, is finished in some sense. Thomas points to the fact that Aristotle in *De anima* stresses a certain circulus between the diverse acts of the besouled being. The terminus of the convenientia, the convenire, comes to its being in the anima itself, in the intellectus; the genuine being of the *verum est in intellectu* [the genuine being of the true is in the intellect].[27] In the context of this Scholastic interpretation of the verum and knowledge, this is at first a surprising result insofar as—in modern terms—knowledge and the being of the truth are transferred into the "subject." The genuine being of the verum is, to be sure, in intellectu, but in the *intellectus Dei* [intellect of God],[28] and God is Himself the ens perfectissimum [the most perfect entity]. The entire context of the convenientia is regarded in a purely "objective" and ontological manner.

> Sed sciendum, quod res aliter comparatur ad intellectum practicum, aliter ad speculativum. Intellectus enim practicus causat res, unde est mensuratio rerum.[29]
>
> [But it should be understood that a thing is related in one way to the practical intellect, in another way to the speculative intellect. For the practical intellect causes things and hence is the measure of the things.]

In the case of the *intellectus practicus* the connection with the res is such that the res, what must be done, is determined in a certain sense by the intellectus

23. Ibid.
24. Ibid.
25. Ibid.
26. Ibid.
27. Ibid.
28. Ibid.
29. Ibid.

that conceives a plan. In the field of the *speculative intellectus* matters are the reverse: the res movet intellectum [the thing moves the intellect].[30]

As a result, there are proportions of measure as to how intellectus and res can be respectively *mensurans* [measuring] and *mensuratum* [measured]. The res itself is principally related to *two* intellectus. *Secundum intellectum humanum* [according to the human intellect] the *res* is the *mensurans*. Knowledge that grasps something measures itself on the thing to be grasped. Insofar as the same thing is regarded *secundum intellectum divinum* [according to the divine intellect], the res is mensurata [measured], that is to say, artificiata or, better, creata,[31] causata [produced or, better, created, caused]. Res ergo naturalis inter duos intellectus constituta [A natural thing is thus set up between two intellects].[32] Each res as such is split in its being and split into these two possible relations: secundum adaequationem ad utrumque vera dicitur [it is called true according to its conformity to each].[33] The res is vera insofar as it is situated in its ordained-being as it is ordinata [ordained] by God's knowing,[34] and it is this being, so determined, that of itself alone *format aestimationem*[35] or, what it is the same, the *mensura* for *intellectus humanus* [that of itself forms the judgment or, what is the same, the measure for the human intellect].

Prima autem ratio veritatis [secundum intellectum Dei] per prius inest rei quam secunda: quia prior est comparatio ad intellectum divinum quam humanum; unde, etiam si intellectus humanus non esset, adhuc res dicerentur verae in ordine ad intellectum divinum.[36]

[However, the first meaning of truth (that in accordance with the divine intellect) is in the thing prior to the second meaning, because the relation to the divine intellect is prior to that with the human. Hence, even if there were no human intellect, things would still be called true in the order pertaining to the divine intellect.]

For only insofar as the *res* is *qua ordinata ad intellectum divinum* [only insofar as the thing exists as ordained to the divine intellect], can it be a *mensura* at all for a human intellectus. Thus, if there were no intellectus humanus, things would still have to be called true in relation to the divine grasping and thinking. Sed si uterque intellectus, quod est impossibile, intelligeretur auferri; nullo modo veritatis ratio remaneret [But if each intellect could be thought

30. Ibid.
31. Ibid.
32. Ibid.
33. Ibid.
34. Ibid.
35. Ibid.
36. Ibid.

away, which is impossible, then the meaning of truth would in no way re-
main].[37] Thus, if one were to think both intellects, even the divine intellect,
as eliminated, then even the being of truth in the sense of a modus rei [mode
of a thing] would have no sense. Accordingly, the authentic being of the verum
is *proprie in intellectu,* inproprie in re; per prius ad intellectum divinum, per
posterius ad intellectum humanum [properly in the intellect, not properly in
the thing; for it is first related to the divine intellect, then to the human
intellect], to human comprehension.

What is it in thinking that can be genuinely characterized as verum? Thomas proceeds from a fundamental [*grundsätzlich*] reflection. What matters is
where the convenientia has its genuine being. That was answered: in intellectu.
And *in what* does this convenientia in the intellectus consist? There must be
a manner of being-related in which the res as well as the intellectus are, in
their genuine possibilities, relevant. The genuine being of the verum is not in
an intuitus [intuition] directed at the quidditas rei [quiddity of a thing] but,
instead, the intellectus is true insofar as it is a *judging* intellect. Insofar it is
a judging intellect, it is a bearer of the verum. Only as *componens* [combining]
and *dividens* [dividing][38] (σύνθεσις–διαίρεσις) does it have its proper effect of
yielding, of itself, something that is its own, whereas in the case of intuitus
the intellect is given over to the similitudo [similitude]. Only when the res is
brought into relation with the genuine activitas intellectus [active intellect],
can I speak of convenientia [agreement]. Likeness [*Gleichheit*] exists only if
the diversa [diverse things] as such are, in their being, relevant to their likeness
relation.

[U]nde ibi primo invenitur ratio veritatis in intellectu ubi primo intellectus incipit
aliquid proprium habere quod res extra animam non habet.[39]

[Hence, the meaning of truth is first found in the intellect where the intellect first
begins to have something proper to it which the thing outside the soul does not
have.]

Thus, the genuineness of the intellect is present where *theoretical knowing*
begins of itself to have something that is its own quod res extra animam non
habet [which the thing outside the soul does not have]. In the course of grasping something intuitively, theoretical thinking is riveted to the thing itself. In
the course of grasping it intellectually, on the other hand, the intellect is
genuinely active, it is there as actus: quando incipit judicare de re apprehensa,
tunc ipsum judicium intellectus est quoddam proprium [it is there as an act:

37. Ibid.
38. Thomas Aquinas, *De veritate,* q. 1, art. 3.
39. Ibid.

when it begins to judge about the thing apprehended, then that very judgment of the intellect is proper to it].[40] In this way the genuine aequalitas diversorum [equality of diverse things] is first attained and the *genuine convenientia* constituted.

This interpretation of the Aristotelian view that the being of ἀλήθεια is in the διάνοια,[41] shows the tendency, alive in Scholasticism, of justifying quite independently propositions which were simply given for Aristotle and whose justification results from an investigation of the context of the tendencies of the researcher's inquiry. From the entire argumentation, it becomes apparent how Thomas wants to uphold the Aristotelian authority and in this way justify an entire theory of convenientia.

§ 31. In what sense the verum is in the intellectus
(De veritate, q. 1, art. 9)

Far more important, however, is article 9 where Thomas shows that and *how the verum is in the intellectus* insofar as the intellectus itself knows the verum *qua cognitum* [the true as known]. *Brentano* characterized this as inner consciousness: that each cogitatio [thought] is at the same time a knowing of itself. This *reditus* [return] into itself inheres, as the identifying feature, in the specific being of every entity that is a *spiritual* being [*geistiges Sein*]. The *reditus in se ipsum* [return into its very self] has been passed down to the Middle Ages through the pseudo-Aristotelian text *Liber de causis* [Book on Causes]. Insofar as the intellectus is that manner of being that also explicitly grasps what it has conceived as such, the being of the verum receives a peculiar elevated status: it is not only conscious, but *elevated into self-consciousness*. This, however, is merely the continuation of the motus [movement] from the res to the intellectus and of the intellectus to itself.

It is necessary that, with every single step, you keep in mind that the analysis is aimed at the characters of being and, with regard to Descartes, that means: we interrogate the res cogitans about the esse that constitutes the esse of the res as such. We have hit upon the more precise inquiry by way of what we saw from the analysis of error: error is a determinate esse in the sense of non esse creatum. Hence, as being in the sense of esse verum, the res cogitans is identical to esse creatum. At the same time, it is esse perceptum. These are the two principal determinations of being, determinations of the sort that, in themselves, they belong together. We have started from the premise that the foundation out of which the two determinations grew presents us with the

---

40. Ibid.
41. Aristotle, *Metaphysica*, Epsilon 4, 1027b27.

verum. How are the esse creatum and the esse perceptum posited together in the verum? This needs to be shown. All determinations of being go back to the esse creatum. A review of the matter will first make it apparent to us that the ens verum is founded in the esse, the basic determination of which is the esse creatum that points at the same time to the esse increatum. This consideration entered by way of our asking ourselves: In what connection is the question of the verum posited? It is of fundamental significance that *being-true* [Wahr-*Sein*] is not oriented to *knowing* and *validity* of knowledge, but instead that the verum has the basic determination of a modus entis [mode of being]. For the ontological problematic of the Middle Ages, the verum stands on common ground with determinations such as unum, diversum, res, bonum, ens [one, diverse, thing, good, being]. They are determinations that the Middle Ages designates as transcendentia, *transcendentals*, because these determinations lie *beyond* each concrete determinacy of being and, for their part, determine each being. The pulchrum [beautiful] is not central in this sense and is mostly treated with bonum and, indeed, under a Neo-Platonic influence (Pseudo-Dionysios Areopagita). We first established that the verum is a modus generalis entis in ordine ad aliud in the sense of convenientia [a general mode of being in an ordered relation to something else in the sense of an agreement]. Closer consideration of convenientia of correspondentia, of assimilatio and conformitas [the agreement of correspondence, of assimilation and conformity] has yielded that convenientia is related to intellectus, that it has its terminus in being-known. The genuine being of verum is contained in being-known. There is an ontological basis for this way of tracing back convenientia, which as such is still a relatio, such that the weight of the relatio lies to one side. Verum's genuine being is traced back to the being of intellectus. In order to understand the further questions posed by Thomas, it is necessary to come to an understanding of *verum's genuine being in intellectus*.

What, then, is the *primordial being* in which the *genuine being of the true* is grounded? If the verum esse is genuinely in the intellectus, what manner of being of the intellectus is the *primo esse* [being in the primary sense] on the basis of which the primordial being of the verum as well as its ultimately genuine sense can be determined? Let us proceed from proprie esse back to the primo esse. Tracing verum back in this way leads to the being of the intellectus in the sense of *intellectus divinus* [divine intellect]. The divine being in the sense of being-qua-knowing is the *primordial* being of veritas [truth] and, indeed, such that verum's *genuine* being in humans and, further, verum's *nongenuine* being in res are determined by this primordial being. Thus, from the standpoint of verum's primordial and genuine being, it first becomes understandable why and with what right the res [thing] is also designated as vera [true]. This consideration leads us back to the esse Dei [God's being] and, with respect to this fundamental being, the ultimate question then presents itself for us as to how this being of God is determined categorially and how the being of truth is built into this being of God. Thus, our consideration ends with the question: What is God's being and how is it determined within the Scholastic inquiry?

We first have to orient ourselves regarding the sense in which the *verum's genuine being in the intellectus* is to be taken. Insofar as the intellectus is the *terminus cognoscendi* [terminus of knowing], the completion of the movement of knowledge, the genuineness of verum's being is also to be seen in this completed being [*Vollendetsein*].

Article 9 gives the answer more precisely. Its title is:

> Utrum veritas sit in sensu. Nono quaeritur, utrum veritas sit in sensu; et videtur quod non. Anselmus enim dicit (lib. de Veritate, cap. 12), quod veritas est rectitudo sola mente perceptibilis. Sed sensus non est de natura mentis. Ergo veritas non est in sensu.[42]

> [Whether there is truth in the senses or one of the sense-powers. In this ninth article it is asked whether truth is in the senses. It seems that it is not for Anselm says (*lib. de Veritate*, ch. 12) that truth is correctness perceivable by the mind alone. But a sense is not of the nature of the mind. Hence, truth is not in the senses.]

Thomas gives the positive answer by taking the opportunity to say something more precise about the being of verum in the intellectus. First: In intellectu enim est sicut consequens actum intellectus[43] [for something is in the intellect as consequent upon an act of the intellect], the being-true is in the grasping itself. Second:

> sicut cognita [vera] per intellectum; consequitur namque intellectus operationem, secundum quod judicium intellectus est de re secundum quod est; cognoscitur autem ab intellectu secundum quod intellectus reflectitur supra actum suum.[44]

> [something is in the intellect as known (to be true) through the intellect; for it follows upon an operation of the intellect, insofar as a judgment of the intellect is about a thing with respect to what it is; however, it is known by the intellect insofar as the intellect reflects upon its own act.]

The *reflecti* of the intellectus [the intellect's being reflected] is conceived in such a way that it non solum secundum quod cognoscit actum suum [it is not only insofar as it knows its act];[45] grasping the act in the sense of an occurrence would not be the truth. Instead, the reflection on an act is such that the

---

42. Thomas Aquinas, *De veritate*, q. 1, art. 9.
43. Ibid.
44. Ibid. [The square brackets in this Latin text are in the original German edition of the lectures.—D.D.]
45. Ibid.

act is thereby objectified, secundum quod cognoscit proportionem ejus ad rem [insofar as it knows its proportion to the thing],[46] the act is objectified insofar as it refers to what it grasps. In the reflection of the intellectus upon this act itself, this matter grasped by this act as true is also given for it. This reflecti [being reflected] in the grasping can only be achieved if the intellectus is such that it grasps its own nature:

> quae cognosci non potest, nisi cognoscatur natura principii activi, quod est ipse intellectus, in cujus natura est ut rebus conformetur.[47]

> [which cannot be known unless the nature of the active principle is known, which is the intellect itself, whose nature is to conform to things.]

This natura lies in *conformitas*. The character of the soul is not taken as a transition, an historical occurrence, in the sense that the soul goes out to some entity. Instead, *being-directed-at a res* pertains to the nature of the intellectus. This openness for the entity is not something imported, but instead pertains, along with other things, to the being of the intellectus itself. Precisely insofar as the intellectus reflects upon itself and, in relation to itself, brings into view the proportio ad rem [proportion to the thing], the intellect sees the veritas [truth], and insofar as the intellect sees and perceives it, it is lifted up in the intellectus' being.

This determination becomes even clearer:

> Sed veritas est in sensu sicut consequens actum ejus; dum scilicet judicium sensus est de re, secundum quod est; sed tamen non est in sensu sicut cognita a sensu.[48]

> [But truth is in a sense as consequent upon its act; while, namely, a judgment of the sense is about a thing with respect to what it is, it is, nevertheless, not in the sense as something known by the sense.]

To be sure, in sensory perceiving, what is perceived is thus there, namely, as true, insofar as, in the being of perceiving, the perceiving comes to its terminus and is true, as the entity that is perceiving. But in sensory perceiving the perceiving is not such that the being-qua-perceiving, together with the matter perceived, would be the object of a reflection accomplished by the perceiving itself. [S]i enim sensus vere judicat de rebus, non tamen cognoscit veritatem, qua vere judicat[49] [For if a sense truly judges of things, it nevertheless does not know the truth by which it judges truly]. In sensory perceiving, to be sure, a specific joint perceiving of the fact of the matter is jointly performed in

46. Ibid.
47. Ibid.
48. Ibid.
49. Ibid.

such a way that the perceiving takes place in this performance. But it does not take up

naturam suam [. . .] nec naturam sui actus, nec proportionem ejus ad res [. . .] illa quae sunt perfectissima in entibus, ut substantiae intellectuales, redeunt ad essentiam suam reditione completa;[50]

[its nature . . . nor the nature of its act nor its proportion to the things . . . [[as do]] those things that are the most perfect in entities, namely, intellectual substances, which return to their essence in a complete return;]

the intellectual substances have a being that is for itself and goes back to itself such that the being is jointly determined by being in such a way that it knows something. These entities have the peculiar character of going back to their genuine being through a completed return. This *reditio completa* constitutes the perfection of this being insofar as, through this reditio, every entity that is grasped by the intellectus is also taken up and appropriated. Through being-able-to-take-up in this manner what is known and grasped, this entity itself increases in *amplitudo*, in the scope of being. A stone is only in a definite way, but such that it could not even have for itself the entity on which it lies; it is merely with this being, next to it. [I]n hoc enim quod cognoscunt aliquid extra se positum [for in this, that they know something posited outside them-selves],[51] these entities are such that, through knowing, they go beyond themselves. The very moment that an entity is fit to grasp its grasping as well, in cognitum redire [to return to what is known]—in the case of sensus incipit redire res sentiens [in the case of the sense, the thing sensing begins to return to what is known]—it begins to go back to itself (see Aristotle on ἡδονή–disposedness). But the reditio completa [complete return] is lacking, to be sure, because the corpus' [body's] being is functionally also part of the distinctive being that comprises a sensus' [a sense's] manner of going beyond itself. Because these corporeal factors are also part of the fabric of the being who grasps things, they are also what prevent a genuine return to that being. In contrast to this limitation, the substantia sciens [knowing substance] is not bound to materia [matter], but is instead pure *forma* [form]. Under this name, it is necessary to understand a manner of being that least of all contains in itself any coactatio [coercion]. Thus, it bears within itself the totality of pos-sible being and, all the more so, if this forma is the *ens absolutum* [absolute being]. The genuineness of verum's being in the intellect is determined in these two respects, namely, 1. that the knowing being [*Erkennendsein*] is the

50. Ibid.
51. Ibid.

terminus of the *convenientia*, and 2. that the knowing being knows its very self.

§ 32. The grounding of verum's genuine being in the primordial truth of God (De veritate, q. 1, art. 4 and 8)

In what, then, is *verum's genuine being grounded*? Where is the *ens* that shapes the *proprie verum* [properly true] into a *proprie verum primo* [properly true in the primary sense] and thus founds every being of the true?

I proceed with the guiding thread of our inquiry. Thomas treats this question in article 4 and, indeed, here he poses the question: Utrum una tantum veritas sit, qua omnia vera sint, whether there is only one truth by virtue of which everything else is true. This question is answered in the affirmative. It contains in itself quite definite presuppositions. The *verum* is in *intellectus divinus proprie et primo*, in *intellectus humanus proprie*, but *secundario*, in *rebus autem improrie* et *secundario* [The true is in the divine intellect properly and primarily, in the human intellect properly but secondarily, but in things improperly and secondarily].[52] Even being-true [*Wahrsein*], insofar as it is an *esse* in the *intellectus humanus*, is a *derivatum* of the *prima veritas* [first truth] which has its genuine and primordial being in God. Veritas autem quae dicitur de rebus in comparatione ad intellectum humanum, est rebus quodammodo accidentalis [But truth which is said of things in comparison to the human intellect is in a way accidental].[53] The things themselves are also true, to be sure, in relation to the human intellect. But it is not part of a res' [thing's] being that it be grasped by a human intellect. Thus, being-grasped and *verum esse* [being true] are accidental for it. The things would still be even if they were not the object of a knowing concerning them. Sed veritas quae dicitur de eis in comparatione ad intellectum divinum, eis inseparabiliter communicatur [But the truth which is said of them in comparison to the divine intellect is communicated inseparably to them].[54] The res' "being-true" in relation to the divine intellect is part of the thing in itself. [N]on enim subsistere possunt nisi per intellectum divinum eas in esse producentem [For they are not able to subsist except through the divine intellect producing them in being].[55] The being of the divine intellect is a *posse producere* [ability to produce]. If one takes this proposition: omne ens est verum una veritate [every entity is true by virtue of one truth] on the basis of its formal determination, it then means:

52. Thomas Aquinas, *De veritate*, q. 1, art. 4.
53. Ibid.
54. Ibid.
55. Ibid.

each esse, insofar as it is ens creatum, is verum [each being, insofar as it is a created entity, is true]. The foundation for the determination of being that is jointly given in the verum lies in the fact that, from the outset, being qua being is determined as esse creatum [created being]. The question of verum's esse leads back to the esse creatum, such that *verum's being* becomes intelligible on the basis of *ens creatum's being*.

The connection of Thomistic philosophy with Aristotelian ontology cannot be treated here. In relation to the sphere of phenomena that consciousness exhibits, a sphere with a completely different sort of content, it suffices to show that this region is determined by an ontology that has a completely different origin with respect to its categories and the possibilities of determining and inquiring prefigured by those categories.

What connection is it then which determines the verum ens [true entity] as a theme of a principal investigation, the connection which is determined by the label "transcendentia"? What is the genuine being to which verum is to be attributed as a modus? Closer examination of this genuine character yielded the esse *in intellectu componente et dividente* [in the composing and dividing intellect], whose being is such that it is characterized by the *reditio in se ipsum* [return into its self]. This genuine character of verum's being poses the question: How does the verum come to be primordially and concretely? The *primo esse* [primary being] in the sense of the *proprie esse* [proper being] is the *esse in intellectu divino* [the being in the divine intellect]. Thomas treats this question in the context of the inquiry that is decisive for him: Is there a truth by virtue of which all others are determined in their being? He treats it, namely, in article 4, which makes clear that this one truth is present. On the basis of this primordial truth, it must then be determined more precisely that it is in fact this *una veritas* [one truth] from which all truths, including such truths as those of negationes and privationes, are derived. Thomas provides this additional consideration, through which the primordiality of verum's being is first determined, in article 8.

The result of article 4 is quite succinct: the truth which can be attributed to res in the sense that it inseparabiliter [inseparably] accrues to things, to res qua res qua subsisting, is to be traced back to the

> intellectus divinus quasi ad causam, ad humanum autem quodammodo quasi ad effectum, inquantum intellectus a rebus scientiam accipit.[56]
>
> [divine intellect as to the cause but to the human intellect in a certain sense as to the effect, insofar as the intellect gathers knowledge from things.]

The intellectus humanus has a relation to the being of convenientia and of res completely different from that of the intellectus divinus. Yet both relations are

---

56. Ibid.

designated as "convenientia." Convenientia with regard to the divine intellect means that the intellect is the *causa*, while the other is the *effectus*. If, therefore, one takes the truth, seen in the genuine and primordial sense, from verum's esse in God, then omnia [all things] are principally vera [true]. Everything which is, is true in relation to the one being of God. In relation to the human intellect, to verum's esse *secundario et proprie* [verum's secondary and proper being], there are several truths, a multitude of true propositions in relation to a multitude of truths which can be gathered from things.

> Si autem accipiatur veritas proprie dicta, secundum quam res secundario verae dicuntur; sic sunt plurium verorum plures veritates in animabus diversis. Si autem accipiatur veritas improprie dicta, secundum quam omnia dicuntur vera; sic sunt plurium verorum plures veritates; sed unius rei una est tantum veritas.[57]

> [But if truth is taken in the proper sense of the term, according to which things are called true secondarily, there are in different minds several truths for the several true things. But if truth is taken in the improper sense of the term, according to which all things are called true, there are then several truths of the several true things; but one truth of one thing is the sole truth.]

In relation to God everything is true insofar as each res is only a veritas insofar as its being-true is grounded on the fact that it is itself related to the intellectus divinus. The truth, insofar as it is said of the res itself, is, of course, in relation to God, but applies to this res in its *forma*. To say "that it *is so*" is to say that "it *is true*." Insofar as the res is, it has in itself a *qualitas* [quality] on the basis of which the suitability for *adaequatio intellectus ad rem* [the intellect's conformity to the thing] takes place.

Thus Thomas acquires, in relation to everything that is, a principal concept of truth that ultimately falls back on the relation of the *causare* and *causari* [to cause and to be caused] in the sense of *making by way of producing, shaping*. The "what" conceived and fashioned by such an intellect is the true being [*das wahre Sein*] in the primordial sense. The additional consideration, through which it is supposed to be shown that in fact everything that is is true, emphasizes that not only the res, but instead also the intellectus depends, in the sense of *derivatio* [derivation], on the one truth, to which the regio of the res [the region of the thing] is subject.[58] The intellectus has its privileged position only *within* [the realm of] the *creata* [created], but loses it in relation to the *una veritas* [one truth]. The look of each thing, its essence, is nothing else than the imitation of the *ars* [art][59] of the productive consciousness of God. The essence, namely, *per formam* [through the form], through which the

57. Ibid.
58. Thomas Aquinas, *De veritate*, q. 1, art. 8.
59. Ibid.

one res is what it is and as such is true, nata est facere de se veram appre-
hensionem in intellectu humano [naturally makes a true apprehension of itself
in the human intellect],[60] being-so-constituted is the fundamentum for a *vera
perceptio* [true perception]. Each *apprehensio* that follows the *lumen naturale*
[natural light] is in itself, insofar as it is a grasp of something, a grasp of true
being. From this it becomes clear that the veritates rerum [truths of things]
contain in themselves entitatem [beingness]. Things are true only insofar they
include entitatem in sui ratione [beingness in its rationale].[61] To this specific
being of the entitas superaddit [veritas] habitudinem adaequationis [truth adds
the relation of conformity],[62] being-true tacks on this specific aptitudo con-
venientiae [aptitude for agreement]. Insofar as the res is created, it is placed,
on the basis of its being-created and as far as its being is concerned, in a
relation to God and to a possible intellect existing with it itself, to which it
conforms [*sich adaequat*]. In *adaequare* (convenientia, convenire) [to conform
(agreement, to agree)], lies a twofold sense: 1. adaequatio ad intellectum humanum [conformity to the human intellect], 2. adaequatio ad intellectum divinum[63] [comformity to the divine intellect], whereby the sense of "adaequare"
is different in each case.

   It might be asked whether [the same holds for] *negatio* and *privatio* insofar
as these are actually true. For example, insofar as I can actually establish a
crime, it might be asked whether a veritas in relation to a privatio itself is
also the sort of truth that stems from the prima veritas [first truth]. But negationes vel privationes . . . non habent aliquam formam [negations or priva-
tions . . . do not have any form];[64] they are negatively determined and, as such,
they apparently have no direct relation to God. A privatio is not an entitas
[entity]. However, insofar as it is put in relation to an intellectus and thus is
a truth, it is grasped, to be sure, but not posited in the sense of an entitas as
existing. [L]apis verus et caecitas vera,[65] a true stone and a true blindness,
non eodem modo veritas se habet ad utrumque [truth is not related to each in
the same way].[66] The veritas has its fundamentum ex parte ipsius rei,[67] in the
thing itself. In the stone as such, in the content of what it is, lies the fact that
it can be related to an intellectus grasping it. Here motivatio [motivation]
passes over from the content of the matter itself to the intellectus. The *correspondentia* is grounded in the content of what the stone is itself. By contrast,

   60. Ibid.
   61. Ibid.
   62. Ibid. [The term *veritas* in square brackets in the Latin text is given as such in the original
German edition.—D.D.]
   63. Ibid.
   64. Ibid.
   65. Ibid.
   66. Ibid.
   67. Ibid.

one cannot say that the blindness contains a positive content in itself on the basis of which it motivates the grasping of it. If I say "vera caecitas" [true blindness], a factor of the privativum esse [being deprived] does not somehow lie in the makeup of the vera. The verum in relation to a privatio is not itself a privatio. Insofar as the privatio is true, it does not get its specific truth-character from the content of what it is true about. At hand is simply the fact that being-blind is related to the intellectus. The fact of being-true, in the assertion of a blindness' being-actually-on-hand, does not have its fundamen-tum in the privatio as such. Being-true in such a case is not supported by the negative being of the privatio. Hence, the capacity for the privatio to be grasped is motivated in the intellectus; in such a way, to be sure, that the intellect positively grasps as well that in relation to which the privatio is a privatio. The privatio itself, however, does not lie in the verum itself. Insofar, however, as it is correct that no negatio lies in the verum, this verum qua positivum is also caused by God.

> Patet ergo quod veritas in rebus creatis inventa nihil aliud potest comprehendere quam [1.] entitatem rei, et [2.] adaequationem ad intellectum, et [3.] [adaequationem] intellectus ad res vel privationes rerum.[68]

> [It is, therefore, clear that the truth uncovered in created things can comprise nothing other than 1. the beingness of a thing, and 2. a conformity to an intellect, and 3. the conformity of an intellect to things or privations of things.]

The grasp and the "being-true" in regard to privatio have their distinctive being in the intellectus' being. Insofar as the intellectus is grasping what something is, the intellectus is itself true and, as such, oriented to its specific bonum [good]. The bonum intellectus [intellect's good] is the verum. Thus, the in-tellect directed outward to an entity in the manner of grasping it is also at the same time caused by God insofar as the intellectus is a limited *bonum*. An entanglement presents itself here which, however, can be easily made acces-sible by completely eliminating every modern manner of consideration. The intellectus and the res are transported into the unitary region of the ens crea-tum [the created entity] and thus knowing, as an objective relation of being, is taken in the sense of being proper to esse creatum [created being].

This basic conception is foundational for all further understanding of the Scholastics. For those who live within these contexts, it is so self-evident that they reject every modern conception as inadequate. But precisely by means of this positive orientation of potentially being-known, of the convenientia [agreement] in the sense of a modus essendi [mode of being], the interpre-tation of the truth-"relation" gains a certainty unattained in other interpreta-

68. Ibid. [The numerals and the term *adaequationem* in square brackets in this Latin text are in the original German edition of the lectures.—D.D.]

tions of knowing and being-qua-knowing. Of course, being-qua-knowing loses its primordial sense, "being-true" and "being-qua-knowing" are modified to the neutral sense of being [*Seinssinn*] of a movement from one being to another. This reduction to the ens creatum makes it possible to grasp this connection in the sense of a formal classification of convenientia among the modi generales [general modes of being].

§ 33. The ways of being able to determine God's being from the perspective of Aristotelian ontology (Summa theologica, vol. 1, q. 2–3)

How now is the entire *region of the ens creatum*, in which the totality of *res* as well as *intellectus qua res* resides, how is this entire region of esse creatum itself determined? We gain a glimpse into the basic determinations by relating it to an *ens increatum*, to the *esse Dei*. The type and manner of being enjoyed by ens creatum as derived from the primordial being is co-determined by the way the basic character of God's being is posited. The question of God's being is treated in several contexts. Let us take up the context in which what is at stake is the proof of the existence of God Himself. We do not at all want to address the question of the proofs themselves. Instead, we want simply to make clear to ourselves what is posited as God's being from the outset in the course of the task of proving God's existence. From precisely what entity do I take the *basis* for the establishment of God's existence itself?

If we focus on this, it is evident that God's existence is not so much the source from which the being of the ens creatum is determined, but vice versa. The being of God Himself is determined on the basis of a definite preconception of created being, in such a way that we are led in this fundamental consideration to see that the ostensibly primordial being is derived from the esse creatum only by way of a quite definite method. That is the genuine basis for what one would later specify as negative theology: a *remotio* [removal] of those characters of being that are unreconcilable with the idea of an ens absolutum.[69]

For such a remotio even to be carried out, a positive idea of an *ens absolutum* must be in the air in order to have some criterion for the necessity of carrying out a remotio. The idea of God is oriented to the idea of the *simplicitas Dei*. From the outset, God is taken as an *ens simplex* in such a way that it is precisely the task of the remotio to suspend the compositio within the determinations of the world's immediately accessible being. From this determination you already see that the world's accessible being is taken in the

---

69. Thomas Aquinas, *Summa theologica*, pt. 1, q. 3: De Dei simplicitate [On God's simplicity].

sense of *producing, forming.* Compositio est compositio ex materia et forma [composition is composition out of matter and form], such that what counts is to suspend every *materia* since by means of matter each being is limited. As a result, the first article of Quaestio III is concerned with the question whether something like a corporeal being can be posited in God's being (Utrum Deus sit corpus). The very possibility of compositio is lacking; what remains is *actus purus* as *essentia Dei* [pure act as the essence of God].

Once again reference might be made to the fact that, in the determination of the verum esse as a modus essendi, the esse is conceived as esse creatum and that the modus essendi of the verum is prefigured by the fact that this esse creatum as creatum is an object of the intellectus divinus. Insofar as every entity, as an entity, is measured on this intellectus, each esse is a verum. Only through the formalization of this concrete connection-of-being in relation to the verum is the inquiry, as Thomas presents it, possible at all. It should be noted that there is, of course, also talk of this in Greek philosophy, that ἕν, καλόν, ἀγαθόν, are determinations that apply to being as such, with the result that a convertible relation obtains and the one can be taken for the other; it should also be noted, however, that Aristotle does not conduct a deductio.

We are led back to *God's being.* If we take a closer look at this being, then we do so not in the sense of a theological consideration. Instead we take the determinations of God's existence and His being into consideration only insofar as we want to read off the *basis* from which God's being is determined, insofar as God is conceived as a *causa efficiens*, as *ens creans* [as an efficient cause, as an entity who creates]. Insofar, that is, as God's being is to be identified, this identification requires a basis. That in relation to which the proof is carried out, *the entity of the world*, must be tilled and articulated. It must be asked: What is the *background of being* that ontologically bears the *being of God* and the *being of the world* and the *being of God towards the world* "in common"?

Thomas elaborates what is concisely designated "proof of God" in various passages: in the first part of his *Commentary on the Sentences*, quite transparently in the *Summa contra Gentiles*, extensively in the *Summa theologica*, pt. 1, q. 2, art. 3: Utrum Deus sit [Whether God is].[70] It is important to examine, in regard to the being that is the point of departure for the task of comprehending God's being, what characters of being step into the function of the fundamentum. In this passage Thomas presents five proofs. That is to say, he considers the *being of the world* in five different respects and, through remotio, in view of each such determinate manner of being of this world respectively, he considers God's being.

First Proof: God's being as the *primum ens immobile movens* [first being,

---

70. Thomas Aquinas, *Summa theologica*, pt. 1, q. 2, art. 3.

unmovable mover] (compare Aristotle, *Physics*, Book VIII: πρῶτον κινοῦν ἀκίνητον,[71] in a different context, to be sure). This *primum ens immobile movens* is accessible by virtue of the fact that the world is taken as we find it in the sense of a res in which something like a *moveri* [being moved] presents itself. The world is viewed as finding itself in motion, motion in the broad sense of μεταβολή. The course of the proof is conducted in a completely formal manner, so that there is no talk of a religious relation of a human's being to God's. Each movement demands a mover and, since this process cannot proceed to infinity, there is need of a *primum movens*, and that is God. We are interested, not in the proof itself, but solely in its basis, the *res in the character of moveri*.

The *Second Proof* is directed at God as the *causa efficiens prima* [first efficient cause]. The existing state of the world is given as a connection of *causae efficientes* (ποιεῖν—πάσκειν). The world consists of connections of effects, being in the sense of effecting. This being demands, as its final explanation, the causa efficiens prima; the entity that brings this about must itself have the character of the causa efficiens prima.

The *Third Proof* aims at the esse Dei as *esse necessarium per se, non ab alio* [God's being as being necessary of itself, not by virtue of another]. It takes aim at God's being in this sense insofar the world is considered as the sort of entity that in many different respects can be *thus* and can also be *otherwise* by virtue of a potential to be in different directions. An ultimate necessity must correspond to these different directions of this potential for being. Beginning with the first determination, these remotiones support one another reciprocally.[72]

In the *Fourth Proof* God's being is determined as a *maxime ens*, as *summum ens* [a maximal being, as supreme being], insofar as the world presents itself in *gradations of being*. Each entity encountered in the world is always what it is within a specific *appropinquatio ad aliquid quod maxime est* [approximation to something which is maximally]. Being-colored or having this and that shape has within itself the orientation of an appropinquatio to a maximum, to a limit value. This appropinquatio, that is apparent in every entity, accordingly demands the being of this maximum itself.

Fifth Proof: Next to this determination, a certain *gubernatio rerum propter finem* [governance of things for the sake of an end] presents itself among entities. On the basis of their character of being and their determination, things are respectively oriented to a certain end, an end by means of which they

71. Aristotelis Physica. Recensuit C. Prantl. Lipsiae in aedibus B.G. Teubneri 1879 [Aristotle, *Physics*, ed. C. Prantl (Leipzig: Teubner, 1879)], Theta 5, 256a9; Theta 7, 260a25.
72. [These *remotiones* probably refer to removals of determinations of composition in being moved, being efficiently caused, or being potentially otherwise, i.e., removals of the determinations underlying the first three proofs respectively.—D.D.]

attain their genuineness. Co-determining is a *finis*, an end in the sense of the genuineness of being, towards which each entity tends.

This being, insofar as it is the basis for the demonstration of God, is in Greek: κινούμενον, ποιούμενον, μεταβλητικόν, καλόν, τέλειον. In these characters it is possible to grasp clearly the essential categories in which Greek ontology sees the πράγματα, the things dealt with most closely, as they are at hand.

Being, thus viewed in the sense of the fundamental categories of Greek ontology, is the basis from which God's being is determined. That this is in fact the case is clearly evident in the following Quaestio,[73] the theme of which is the question: Now what, then, is God actually, how is this being of God determined? Thomas is oriented to the notion that God's being is an *ens simplex* [simple being] of the sort that excludes *compositio* in any sense at all. We do not want to go through this Quaestio in its entirety, although it is precisely the most important for the question and the connections in which we find ourselves. It can be shown how the question of the demonstration of God's existence, the question of the determination of His being, is constantly oriented back to the world's being as the basis. What is peculiar to the determination of Quaestio III is that it constantly hearkens back to the previous Quaestio in the sense that God's being is, indeed, already fixed in the five characters provided. The question (article 1), Utrum Deus sit corpus [whether God is a body], whether there is something like materia in God's being, is answered in the negative through an appeal to the Church Fathers, for whom these questions played an important role in the struggle with Gnostics and Manicheans. For the Middle Ages, these questions became more or less devoid of an object.

Article 2: Utrum in Deo sit compositio formae et materiae [Whether there is a composition of form and matter in God]. As the primum movens, God is actus purus [as the prime mover, God is pure act]; as maxime ens primum bonum [as the supreme entity and first good], there cannot be anything like materia in Him and any compositio is lacking. Herein lies an essential transformation of the Aristotelian ontology, namely, in the fact that the forma itself is secured (returning to Plato) as a manner of being, as being and constituting being. The question becomes clear from one of the objections (the third): materia est principium individuationis [matter is the principle of individuation]. Things receive this specific appearance insofar as the *forma* is limited and restricted by the *materia*.

Sed Deus videtur esse individuum; non enim de multis praedicatur. Ergo est compositus ex materia et forma.[74]

73. Thomas Aquinas, *Summa theologica*, pt. 1, q. 3: De Dei simplicitate.
74. Thomas Aquinas, *Summa theologica*, pt. 1, q. 3, art. 2.

[But God seems to be an individual; for He is not predicated of many. Hence, He is composed of matter and form.]

The basic sense of the category of the individuum in the Middle Ages reveals itself in this characteristic objection: non de multis praedicatur [He is not predicated of many]. The *esse individui* [individual's being] is seen in the predication. The concept of the individuum emerged in the context of the formal-ontological orientation and leads back to Greek ontology. Thomas' proof (even if only one be drawn on) rests upon the conclusions of the previous Quaestio, that *Deus* is the *summum bonum non per participationem* [that God is the supreme good not through participation] and thus can contain no materia. The principle of individuation is not the materia, but rather its specific being as forma that is grounded in the fact that this form is such that it cannot be taken up into a materia. The principium individuationis here is the materia, to be sure, but in a negative sense; insofar as it is that principle, it cannot be relevant for the determination of the being of God Himself.

The third article contains the essential determination that *essentia* and *esse* (essence and existence) are identical for God's being. That has to be the case since it is, indeed, impossible to make any real distinctions in God at all. This proof that God's *esse* is contained in Him rests completely on the orientation of essentia towards ὁρισμός. Not all the determinations of a human's concrete being are taken up in the essentia of a human being, the humanitas: non est totaliter idem homo, et humanitas [a human being and humanity are not totally the same]. The humanitas is the pars formalis hominis [formal part of the human being], whereby another part is also determining. In God, then, homo and humanitas, that is to say, *Deus* and *Deitas* are *identical*. The being of the divinity as such is the being of God. Oportet quod Deus sit sua Deitas, sua vita [it is necessary that God be His Deity, His life]: in His very being, God is His life. Precisely because it was of great significance in the Middle Ages to determine how the essentia and the esse concide, these problems have been treated extensively, such that a whole number of tractates have been handed down to us under the title: *De ente et essentia* [On being and essence].

The fourth article shows us this question of the *identitas* of *essentia* and *esse* from a new side insofar as now the weight of the interpretation is not placed on God's being as a possible compositum [composite], but rather insofar as God's being is conceived as a direct determination of the essentia. Whether God's being is posited in any sort of *genus* (article 5)—the orientation of this question is not formal-logical, but essentially ontological. A summary is found in articles 7 and 8: Deus nullo modo compositus sed omnino simplex [God is in no way composite but altogether simple].

The result for us is that the *verum*, in term of its being, is oriented to the *esse creatum* and that the esse creatum is itself viewed categorially in the basic categories that Greek ontology in Aristotle has developed. Consequently, from the outset, no primordial question is posed. Instead, God is viewed from the outset in the perspective and in the possible ways of determining being, as they have been provided by traditional ontology and as they are given in a specific interpretation of the world's being. These basic determinations are the very ones that accordingly determine the ens creatum in the widest sense. Within the being determined in this way, a human's being must also be focused on this being of the ens creatum, and the natura hominis [nature of the human being] and the perfectio of this natura must be regarded from its standpoint [namely, the standpoint of *ens creatum*, being created]. Thus knowing's specific manner of being, the being of the care involved in knowing, is predetermined from the vantage point of this ontology as is at the same time— insofar as the verum is precisely what matters in knowledge—the object of the care.

Chapter Five

The care of knowledge in Descartes

We now have to see how, in the case of Descartes, the *care of knowledge* is prefigured and determined in a completely determinate manner, *what* it discloses as actually being [*wirklich Seiendes*] in terms of which characters of being, and how it does so.

§ 34. Descartes' determination of knowing's manner of being as judging, against the horizon of being as creatum esse

How Greek ontology and the specific questions given with it were reshaped by the Middle Ages cannot be shown here. For this, the entire sphere of theological inquiry's influence and its influence on philosophy would have to be considered.

With our interpretation we have fashioned the foundation for further discussion with the qualification that, for a radical investigation, the interpretation of Aristotelian philosophy becomes decisive. It becomes decisive in order to step up to the task that concerns us, the *question of knowing's manner of being*, and to do so by working from concrete contexts. We have taken knowing's being to be a *care about acquiring what is true*. The thematic field "consciousness" is given to us in advance by *present-day phenomenology*. We have critically inquired into the manner of being that characterizes this thematic field of consciousness. What motivates this inquiry will become clear in the course of carrying out the investigation.

We have gathered two things so far: 1. what the care of knowing in general is concerned with was determined by establishing the *sense of verum's being*. Care has placed *the true* in its care, the comprehension of truth, the observance of truth [*Wahrheitsbefolgung*]. Insofar as the verum is discussed with respect to its esse, the object of care, what it is concerned about is fixed as to its sense of being. 2. Insofar as [i.] knowing's being is a cogitatio [thought] and the cogitationes [thoughts] fall into the realm of what is determined as a res cogitans [thinking thing], and [ii.] the res cogitans is determined as an esse perceptum [perceived being] and the perceptum [the perceived] as such as a res percepta [perceived thing] which is grasped as verum, and [iii.] the verum is viewed with respect to its foundation, the *character of the cogitatio's being* is foundationally determined as *creatum esse* [created being] and, as this creatum esse, is inherent in the res cogitans. The res cogitans constitutes a human's being [*Sein des Menschen*] and, with the determination of the res cogitans' being, a human's being is pre-determined.

We will have to ask how, against this *horizon*, Descartes determines the *being of cognitio*, of knowing, more exactly. We will have to make intelligible why, precisely in the case of Descartes, knowledge is conceived with the emphasis on it as judgment, as *judicare*. How is this determination and emphasis in the basic approach to knowing's and a human's being motivated at all? To what extent, by means of this fundamental determination of the human being, is the specific path prefigured, upon which, through performance [or exercise: *Vollzug*] of the judicare, the *perfectio hominis* [the perfection of the human being] is attained, the perfection that lies in the *assecutio veritatis* [pursuit of truth]? Insofar as a human's being is, to be sure, a perfectum esse [a perfected being], but such that errare [to err] is given in it, the verum is only a medium esse [intermediary being] and the formation of a being's perfection requires the *overturning of error*. Human being must become error-free. In order to be perfect, knowing must place itself under a definite *regimen*. Given with this regimen is a *regimentation*, a set of rules. In knowing's being as judicare and the regimentation given with it, the *care-character of knowing* is expressed distinctly for the first time. This caring manner of being as observance of truth in the sense of adhering to this definite rule has thus prefigured for itself definite paths of its formation. The manner of the performance itself—insofar as it is about acquiring a basis for knowing, conceived in this way, a basis that corresponds to the sense of the regula [rule]—must be such that the knowing is performed as *continere* and *abstinere*. This "adhering to" and "refraining from" is the specific manner of being of *dubitare* [doubt]. This manner of performing the act of knowing at the same time also pre-determines the path insofar as it is a matter of acquiring the knowing. The dubitare takes the path through the possible *paths of grasping* [things]. On this path the dubitare and intelligere are performed in such a way that they ultimately hit upon something indubitable, on something that, in its being, satisfies the sense of the regula.

The question arises for us: With regard to the cogitare's thus disclosed being, in what sense is the care of knowing in the manner of performing the *judicare disclosive*? Does the judicare diclose something at all or does it only make visible what is already secured? Insofar as it is shown that the care of knowing is only *seemingly* disclosive, *only making explicit something secured from the outset*, what is revealed is the decisive breakthrough to the specific being of care in the sense of a *comforting assurance*, a *tranquilizing [Beruhigung]*. All of the characters of care are drawn back into this basic phenomenon. By this means, the being of the care of knowing, being in this way, opens up at the same time a view to *life's manner of being*. The established characters of being, peculiar to the care of knowing, are definite manners of being of what exists. It must now be established *what existence itself means*, what a basic character of existence or being-here is that expresses itself in the *here* [of being-here: *Dasein*]. One phenomenon of being-here or existence that presents itself is *uncoveredness* [*Entdecktheit*]. Uncoveredness is a basic character of the here and determines the distinctive being of existence or being-here as *being in a world*. In view of these basic phenomena, we are then put in a position to discuss concretely the peculiar sense of the phenomenon that constantly accompanies us, the verum, and to see how, thanks to the determinate historical being that we ourselves are and bear, this explication of being with respect to the ἀληθές has been deferred and deferred by virtue of the fact that it has utterly concealed itself and dissolved into a universal, objective [state of] produced-being [*Hergestelltsein*]. On this path we will acquire what has been the task of these lectures from the outset: not to criticize, but to disclose positive phenomena from concrete considerations. The question is what character of being consciousness has and from what care it springs and whether this care of knowing has a claim to radicality or *whether it is not much more the return to the theme of "existence" that first attempts to make the possibilities of phenomenological research effective.* At this juncture the methodological reflection presents itself regarding the legitimacy of interrogating phenomenology with respect to its theme's character of being. That is the course that we have to take on the basis of the completed interpretation, with the reservation that the correspondingly radical examination of the discussion of the foundation of being cannot be conducted since Greek ontology cannot be interpreted.

I stress that, through the two interpretations of Descartes and of Thomas, we have gained the determination of being of the *creatum esse* [created being] and, with the latter, the *verum* [the true], that is to say, what the care is about. With the creatum esse, the being of the cogitatio and thereby the intelligere, the being of knowing itself, presents itself. We will *now* come to some understanding of *how* Descartes determines a human's being-qua-knowing against the background of the being that has been established as creatum esse.

With a view to creare as the established foundation of being, Descartes says: animadverto [ideam] non tantum Dei, sive entis summe perfecti realem et positivam [I turn my attention not only to the real and positive idea of God or the supremely perfect being].[1] I see at the same time [ideam] nihili, sive ejus quod ab omni perfectione summe abest [the idea of nothing or of that which is most removed from all perfection].[2] I see this twofold being: the ens

---

1. Descartes, Meditatio IV, 61 [*AT* VII, 54. The term *ideam* in square brackets in the Latin text is given as such in the original German edition.—D.D.]
2. Ibid. [The term *ideam* in square brackets here is given as such in the original German edition.—D.D.]

summe perfectum [the supremely perfect being] and the nihil [nihility], insofar as I grasp myself as something. That is the naked and specific fundamental experience itself; as something it is not nothing. I have co-yielded the nihil that I am not. I experience myself as something, but not as God, summe perfectum, and I grasp myself as an ens medium [an intermediate entity], placed between God and nothing and, indeed, this being-placed that is my being is just as determinate as the being between which I am placed. I am also a perfectum [something perfected or complete], but a medium perfectum [intermediate perfection], I am ens creatum and, as such, perfectum, although not necessarily a summe perfectum [something supremely perfect]. A factum that is made per [through something else], up to a determinate end of itself, and made in such a way that it has such a look. Descartes determines this ens medium more precisely by investigating himself in a more exact way with respect to his possibilities, this res that is something and not nothing and not God. He thereby finds that the cogitatio in the sense of *voluntas* [will] is that very possibility of being in which the genuine possibility of being breaks through: that very determination of the being of the ens medium, ratione cujus imaginem quandam, et similitudinem Dei me referre intelligo [the intermediate entity, by reason of which I understand myself to bear a certain image and similitude of God],[3] in relation to which I see that I may in the highest measure attain God's being. The medium ens determines itself in view of the fact that the manner of being in the sense of voluntas is genuinely perfect. What the will in its genuine being constitutes is the determinatio and the determinatio as such is the *determinatio in bonum* [determination to the good]. The genuine medium ens is, therefore, voluntas. This ens is, to be sure, perfectum [something perfected], but as medium perfectum not summe perfectum, so that this determinate being thus has a possibility with a view to absolute perfection. This being is thus seen as the being of the voluntas. Insofar as Descartes in his entire investigation has his eyes on knowledge and views a human's being accordingly, he must determine *knowing's being*, hence, a human's being, fundamentally as *judicium* [judgment]. For only then is a human's being, in keeping with the way it is, related to the summa perfectio [supreme perfection] insofar as the *judicium* exhibits a *modus volendi* [mode of willing]. Judicium is equivalent to assensionem praebere [giving assent].

The reason why the sense of the observance of truth is directed at the assecutio veritatis [pursuit of truth] lies in the same feature as the determination of a human's being through its genuineness in the voluntas. By this means, all manners of exercise [*Vollzugsweisen*] of knowing are determined as abstinere [refraining from] and continere [adhering to] in the same character

3. Op. cit., 66 [*AT* VII, 57].

of being and, with this, the possibility is prefigured in what manner the *non errare* [not to err] is attained through the exercise of a properly conducted being-qua-knowing. The acquisition and formation of a habitus non errandi [habit of not erring] must thus itself be exercised in constant view of what is given in advance by the rule as the course to be observed.

We will have to show further how, on the same foundation of being as esse creatum and the determination of intelligere as judicium given along with it, the conception of the regimentation is also prefigured. You see the place to which the verum moves through Descartes' interpretation of knowing as judicium and how it approaches what is today conceived in the sense of validating as the sense of a being that is certain. By this means the first step away from the actual sense of ἀληθές was taken.

This sort of advance work and process of working oneself into the research itself cannot be carried out on the path of general argumentation, but instead by taking steps on the basis of an understanding of the matters themselves, in such a way that an actual appropriation of them is assured.

§ 35. The regimentation of judging: clara et distincta perceptio as a universal rule of knowing

The interpretation of *knowing's being* runs through specific steps: from what point of view Descartes is led to a particular construal of knowing as *judicium* and how this determination is led over into the basic determinations of a human's being. This knowing, so determined, has prefigured for itself a determinate possibility of its exercise. By means of this basic determination of knowing's being as judicare, this judicare must *place itself under a rule that it posits itself.* The *interpretation of the rule* yields a far-reaching insight into knowing's character of being as a care. This knowing is exercised in the manner of the *dubitare* with the aim of *securing* a ground that satisfies the claim of knowing. The knowing, so secured, opens up a definite domain of being that has become thematic as *consciousness.*

Carrying out the interpretation of the *regimentation*: what the rule is, where it springs from, what it contains in itself.[4] Descartes counts the idea of freedom and being-free among the experiences that are given with the sum res cogitans [I am a thinking thing].

> [L]ibertatis autem et indifferentiae, quae in nobis est, nos ita conscios esse, ut nihil sit quod evidentius et perfectius comprehendamus.[5]

4. For this, compare Appendix, Supplement 23 (p. 236).
5. Descartes, *Principia Philosophiae*, Pars prima, § 41, 20 [*AT* VIII, 20].

[However, we are so conscious of the liberty and indifference which is in us that there is nothing that we grasp more evidently and perfectly].

There is nothing that would be grasped evidentius and perfectius [more evidently and perfectly] than the basic condition of being-free. Here, in the determination of libertas, Descartes again brings in the concept of being-free that he actually rejected: libertas et *indifferentia*. (What mattered to Descartes was solely to introduce his philosophy to the Jesuit colleges. He took the trouble to find a suitable textbook that he needed simply to ape, in order to smuggle himself into the Jesuits' curriculum. The *Principles* is a text guided by specific tendencies, yet it is constructed quite clearly and scholastically [*schulmäßig*] for its purpose of scholastic applicability.) Thus, knowing must be so construed that it is determinable as the sort of cogitatio that is a *modus volendi* and this determinability of knowing compels the characterization of knowing as *judicium*. The judicium is characterized by the *assensus*, through the agreement with what is held up to the *voluntas* by *perceptio*. This knowing, so conceived, is a manner of being within a human's being, one that is at the same time capable of erring. If a human is to achieve his [or her] *genuine* being, then it is incumbent upon him [or her] to accomplish what it is to know and to do so in such a way that he [or she] avoids error. That means: there must be such an inclination and certainty that where a non liquet (the same as "it is not clear") is given, judgment withholds assensus. Thus the habitus must determine itself more immediately as a *continere* and *abstinere* in the manner of withholding assent. In the idea of *perfectio*, the necessity is prefigured that what is to be given from the outset for judgment is given in a quite definite manner. Thus, the question arises: In what way must the being, grasped in the perceptio, present itself so that the judgment can be made as a justified judgment? In what way must the *verum* show itself so that the assensus is such that it represents a determinatio in bonum? The grasp and presentation of what is true must be specifically *guided* in the sense that the guidance shows the true as such, which should be assented to. The true must show itself in such a way that it becomes decidable in itself whether assent can be legitimately reached or not. The guidance in the sense of a *regimen* must at the same time be a *criterion* in terms of which the exercise or nonexercise of assent can be decided. The rule that guides the assent in the manner of a criterion must contain within itself the prefiguring of *how* the truth should and must be encountered, so that it should be able to experience assent. We now have to consider more exactly this *rule*, this way that leads to the presentation of the verum and, by this means, becomes at the same time the measure for the assensus.

1. Let us consider this manner of encountering the verum itself: a) in regard to its *origin*. From what is the supposition that the verum should be encoun-

tered in such and such a manner acquired and drawn? b) From what idea of grasping the truth does the rule get its legitimacy? How is the requisite manner of encountering the verum posited in the rule itself? 2. Let us consider how the rule itself is taken as a rule, how a quite definite care expresses itself in it, and what matter, to be governed by the rule, is posited as in the regimentation itself. 3. How the verum is encountered in the regimentation.

The rule under which Descartes places knowing is the *clara et distincta perceptio* [clear and distinct perception]. As a result, it is necessary for us first to consider what *perceptio* means and what is meant by *clare et distincte*. Descartes employs perceptio in various ways to mean the same as apprehendo, deprehendo, animadverto: to perceive or take up something as it is in itself [*etwas an ihm selbst vernehmen*]. In the *Principles* Descartes distinguishes *two modi*: modus *percipiendi*, modus *volendi* [a mode of perceiving, a mode of willing].[6] Under the first mode he counts sentire, imaginari, intelligere, perceptio (here in a wider sense), such that it encompasses in itself αἴσθησις and the pure νοεῖν. The latter is that very sort of perceptio that is meant in the regula generalis [general rule]. More broadly, the meaning of "percipere" encompasses those very modi that do not have the character of volitio, even if it serves above all to designate what can be grasped in the sense of specific evidence: to take each something up as it is in itself, pure intelligere [purely to understand]. The *modi volitionis*: cupere, adversari, affirmare, negare, dubitare [The modes of volition: to desire, to oppose, to affirm, to negate, to doubt]. In the case of a perceptio so certain that a judgment can be legitimately based upon it, it is not only required that it be a *clara* perceptio but at the same time a *distincta* one. These two aspects thus prefigure in what sense verum is to be encountered.

How does Descartes determine *claritas*? Through the factors that come into question as characteristics of encountering the verum.[7] 1. The perceptum is such that it is grasped by a manner of *grasping explicitly* aimed at it, by a mens attendens [mind attending] to the sort of grasping that is at work where the aim is to get a hold of what is to be grasped in itself. There are also perceptiones that show a certain presence, that present a manner of existing, yet where the explicit focus on grasping what is given in the perceptio need not be present. But if the perceptio is to be clear, it must explicitly take what is to be grasped in the course of accomplishing its aim. 2. The perceptum must be *praesent* [present] for the grasping thus characterized. The being to be grasped may not be given in the manner of being remembered. I can remember something, the remembered can be given clearly and even distinctly in memory itself. Although memory can give the entity itself, it is still not

6. Op. cit., § 32, 17 [*AT* VIII, 17].
7. Op. cit., § 45, 21f. [*AT* VIII, 21f.].

suited for giving the entity as a *praesens* [something presently presenting itself]. Equally unsuited for doing so is a straightforward presenting [*Vorstellen*] of something in the sense of an object having such an effect that no feature of it is thereby left out. 3. The perceptum must be there as a *res aperta* [thing exposed]. By this, Descartes means in any case (that is not precisely apparent) *lying there in the open*, the entity existing there in itself, such that it is in no way concealed, is not indirectly given itself. 4. What is presently and openly at hand in this way must be so perceived that it has the possibility *satis fortiter movere* [to move with sufficient strength] the grasping directed at it. The grasped must be so "praesent" and open that it rivets onto itself the percipere [perceiving] reaching out to it.

These four factors characterize the perceptio as clara [clear]. In order to be able to be a *distincta* [distinct perception],[8] the perceptio must itself be clear. The factor of the distinctum consists in the fact that the perceptio is a sejuncta and praecisa [separate and precise perception], so separate and cut off from other perceptiones that the entire sphere of the perceptio's being-clear is secured. The distinctum is the specific factor of the correspondingly clear delimitation of the clear itself. There are clear perceptiones that are not necessarily also distinct, but there are no distinct perceptions that would not be clear since distinctness is a factor founded on the clarity. Descartes illustrates this with an example that provides an indication of the specific narrowness that is grounded in this criterion.[9] If someone feels a great pain, then he has the pain as existing and has it in an absolutely clear but not always distinct way. Mostly it happens that humans confound what is grasped in the clear sensation of pain with an obscure judgment about what is given in a certain way along with the clear sensation of pain, as when we say that a pain in a tooth is piercing or there is a throbbing in my leg. Here, to be sure, the pain is given in an absolutely clear way, but it is not given distinctly. I localize the pain in the tooth, even while it concerns the res cogitans; even though it is precisely given phenomenally only in the tooth.

Knowledge's way of being as judicium is a human being's manner of being-free insofar as he [or she] is as knower. Being-free is propensio in bonum [a propensity for the good], it is a being capable of errare [erring]. But it needs guidance to keep to itself wherever it has no legitimacy. This guidance must be so given to knowing's way of being, that it accomplishes what is fundamental, providing for the assent the ground to which it assents and, indeed, providing it in such a way that the assent, in assenting, is clear to itself that it assents correctly. The rule that is supposed to regulate the provision of the fundamentum in advance for the judicare must consist in the fact that it se-

8. Ibid.
9. Op. cit., § 46, 22 [*AT* VIII, 22].

cures for the judicare the manner of encountering the verum and secures it with such assurance that it can be decided whether the judicare ought to assent or to withhold its assent.

§ 36. The origin of clarity and distinctness. Descartes' idea of science and the rules for the direction of the mind

What is the *origin* of these determining characteristics of *clarity* and *distinctness*? Where does Descartes get the right to pre-judge, according to what is set forth in the regula generalis [general rule], *every* possible knowledge that might surface? If one looks upon the rule purely in terms of its content, it is not at all immediately apparent in what sense this rule and what it says are supposed to be related to a particular domain of objects. Nothing is said in the rule about the specific object-character of what is supposed to be grasped in the rule. Nor can any more be determined from the rule's contents as to what specific grasping-relation is meant here, whether this percipere is oriented to a definite type of access and interaction with the entity, insofar as the entity is objectively [i.e., as an object: *gegenständlich*] in the knowing. The sense of being-related of the percipere is a purely formal, indeterminately general sense. The rule is a rule for knowledge and, to be sure, for *scientific* knowledge. We take as our guide the *idea of science* supposed by Descartes, such that we inquire back to the source from which it is drawn. Where does Descartes take his specific concept of science from? Are specific experiences of the history of knowledge exemplary for him, such that he draws the specific idea of science from this experience? To expose this origin in a quite rigorous way would require an interpretation of the *Regulae ad directionem ingenii* in its entirety.[10] Only what is most necessary for such an interpretation may be cited here.

Descartes defines science as a knowledge characterized in a determinate manner: Omnis scientia est cognitio certa et evidens [All science is certain and evident cognition].[11] *Certa* et *evidens* are the two factors that make knowing scientific. From this definition arises the specific concept of science and what counts as scientific, as it was understood under the title "science" in France, especially in the sense of mathematics and natural science. [Descartes accordingly advises us] omnes probabiles cognitiones rejicere [to reject all probable cognitions], as not scientific.[12] In view of this idea of science, we

10. René Descartes, *Regulae ad directionem ingenii*. Nach der Originalausgabe v. 1701, hrsg. v. A. Buchenau. [Rules for the Direction of the Mind, according to the original edition of 1701, ed. A. Buchenau (Leipzig: Dürr, 1907).]
11. Descartes, Regula II, 2 [*AT* X, 362].
12. Op. cit., 3 [*AT* X, 362].

place ourselves under the rule that comes from us, with the help of which we may reach the genuine summit of scientific and human existence. Descartes says here: if we take it upon ourselves to prescribe rules for research in the sense of the idea of science, then the first thing is to keep the rules in view. Circa illa tantum obiecta oportet versari, ad quorum certam et indubitatam cognitionem nostra ingenia videntur sufficere [It is essential to meditate only on those objects, of which our minds seem capable of certain and indubitable cognition].[13] Hence, what is characteristic is that a *completely determinate region of objects* is prefigured on the basis of the sense of the idea of science, objects that alone are such as to come into consideration at all as possible objects of scientific research. Prefigured are completely determined domains-of-objects that come into question for scientific research and those that fall out from the outset. Although the rule contains nothing about objects in terms of content, it nonetheless passes a judgment on the entire realm of possible experience in such a way that it prefigures definite objects, those corresponding to the sense of the rule.

Descartes determines this idea of science as cognitio certa et evidens more closely in its structure. The constitutive factors of science as science are: 1. the *intuitus* [intuition], 2. the *deductio* [deduction].[14] Instead of intuitus, also *experientia* [experience]: notandum est, nos duplici via ad cognitionem rerum devenire, per experientiam scilicet, vel deductionem [it should be noted that we have two ways of coming to know things, namely, through experience or deduction].[15] The concept of experientia is the Aristotelian concept of ἐπαγωγή, leading to a matter itself, not ἐμπειρία, "experience" in the sense of the "empirical." These two factors constitute the structure of intelligere [understanding], insofar as it is a scientific knowing. Seen with regard to the scientific character, intelligere can accordingly be exercised as intuitus and deductio or *illatio* [inference].

The *intuitus* is that side in knowing, taken as a whole, that has the basic function of first yielding the object at all, so that all the diverse functions of knowing with respect to its actual exercise are again and again to be taken as judicia [judgments]. Viewed in terms of its genuine being-qua-knowing, each intuitus is a *judicare* [to judge]. What fundamental significance Descartes attributes to intuitus is to be seen from the following observation:

Omnis quippe deceptio, quae potest accidere hominibus, dico, non belluis,

[In fact, every deception which can befall human beings, I say, not animals,]

every deception in the field of genuine, rational knowing,

13. Op. cit., 2 [*AT* X, 362].
14. Descartes, Regula III, 5 [*AT* X, 368].
15. Descartes, Regula II, 4 [*AT* X, 365].

nunquam ex mala illatione contingit, sed ex eo tantum, quod experimenta quaedam parum intellecta supponantur.[16]

[never happens by some bad inference, but solely from the fact that some poorly understood experiences are taken for granted.]

The objective correlate of intuitus are the experimenta: what is grasped as such in the straightforward grasping. The ground of deception lies in the fact that, in judicium [judgment], we have non satis intellecta experimenta [things experienced but not sufficiently understood] as fundamenta [foundations], vel iudicia temere et absque fundamento statuantur [or judgments are made rashly and without foundation].[17] Through the intuitus that has been genuinely executed, the experimenta [things experienced] are to be yielded as the fundamentum for every judicare [judging]. As far as the structure of intuitus is concerned, Descartes shows that intuitus is not a particular faculty, but instead nascitur a sola rationis luce [proceeds by the sole light of reason],[18] emerging and having its being in lumen naturale [the natural light], in human reason. Thus, intuitus is something given with the natural light of knowledge itself and nothing that could first be formed through a specific method of knowledge, insofar as intuitus generally has the function of providing the object, νοῦς. Hence, the weight first shifts to the intuitus as providing the fundamentum.

From this look at the idea of science and its structure, so construed, the question arises: Is there knowledge and are there types of knowledge known to us, of the sort that yield objects in such a manner that they satisfy the requisite sort of exercise of the intuitus?

Ex quibus evidenter colligitur, quare Arithmetica et Geometria caeteris disciplinis longe certiores existant, quia scilicet hae solae circa obiectum ita purum et simplex versantur, ut nihil plane supponant, quod experientia reddiderit incertum.[19]

[From which it may be evidently gathered why arithmetic and geometry are far more certain than other disciplines, since, namely, these alone meditate on an object so pure and simple that they plainly suppose nothing which experience might render uncertain.]

The objects of *arithmetic* and *geometry* are characterized as purum [pure] and simplex [simple] so that they cannot give back anything uncertain to a grasping directed at them. The objects of arithmetic and geometry have in fact an objective character that makes them suitable to be possible objects of rigorous

16. Ibid. [*AT* X, 365].
17. Ibid.
18. Descartes, Regula III, 6 [*AT* X. 368].
19. Descartes, Regula II, 4 [*AT* X, 365].

science. Sunt igitur omnium maxime faciles et perspicuae, habentque obiectum quale requirimus [Of all disciplines, therefore, they are the most easy and
perspicuous, and have an object such as we require],[20] and require on the basis
of starting from this completely determined idea of science. [S]olae supersint
Arithmetica et Geometria ex scientiis iam inventis, ad quas huius regulae
observatio nos reducit [Of the sciences already invented, only arithmetic and
geometry remain as those to which observation of this rule reduces us].[21] The
observation of the rule which says "take into view only objects such as can
be grasped in a certa et evidens perceptio" leads us to the sciences of arithmetic and geometry, the only scientific disciplines that have been elaborated
up to this point. The direction of the supposed idea of science thus provides
in advance that they [the possible objects of the science] are referred to these
specific disciplines, arithmetic and geometry. Descartes concludes the exposition of his second rule:

> Iam vero ex his omnibus est concludendum, non quidem solas Arithmeticam et
> Geometriam esse addiscendas, sed tantummodo rectum veritatis iter quaerentes circa
> nullum obiectum debere occupari, de quo non possint habere certitudinem Arith-
> meticis et Geometricis demonstrationibus aequalem.[22]

It follows from this second rule, not that one should limit oneself solely to
arithmetic and geometry, but instead that those seeking the right path to truth
should not occupy themselves with any objects other than those that have a
certitudo equal to these objects. Here it is articulated, distinctly and unmis-
takably, that the idea of what counts as scientific and at the same time the
idea of the constitution of the possible objects of a science are prefigured by
geometry and arithmetic.

Descartes conceived his idea of science in relation to the history of knowledge and the disciplines given in that history. In the Middle Ages, in part in
connection with Aristotle, the mathematical disciplines also counted as the
most rigorous, but not as the supreme sciences. The supreme science is theology, in view of its object: God.

How did Descartes *draw his idea of science from this basic experience of
mathematical science*? What is the genuinely mathematical character of arithmetic and geometry? By way of reflecting on the history of the sciences,
Descartes posed this question to himself in a completely original manner, such
that the idea of the *mathesis universalis* springs from this reflection. In the
fourth rule, he shows how a more incisive reflection on the course of the
history of science and on the structures of the disciplines counting as sciences

---

20. Ibid.
21. Op. cit., 3 [*AT* X, 363].
22. Op. cit., 5 [*AT* X, 366].

permits one to take away [the notion of] an underlying *primordial mathematics* [*Urmathematik*] that has a completely determinate field of objects, that is actually the place from which Descartes has his idea of science. A peculiar amalgam of ontological and mathematical considerations is revealed, an amalgam still alive today in a completely fundamental manner in Husserl's logic, which is supposed to be a mathesis universalis. Descartes gives a brief exposition of the history of his own preoccupation with mathematical disciplines and their history. He shows that he noticed, early on, that the ancients had, of course, made a series of discoveries in the domain of mathematics, but that they could not rightly justify them. Sed in neutra Scriptores, qui mihi abunde satisfecerint, tunc forte incidebant in manus [But in neither arithmetic nor geometry did writers happen then to fall into my hands who fully satisfied me].[23] None of the authors satisfied him in such a manner that the scientific disciplines [on which they wrote] would have corresponded to an idea of rigorous science. Descartes then proceeds in such a way that he shows, with the orientation towards the lumen naturale, how in it the principles of all human knowing are laid out.

> Et quamvis multa de figuris et numeris hic sim dicturus, quoniam ex nullis disciplinis tam evidentia nec tam certa peti possunt exempla, quicumque tamen attente respexerit ad meum sensum, facile percipiet, me nihil minus quam de vulgari Mathematica hic cogitare:[24]

Although I also occupy myself here with figures and numbers, because the evident objects are to be taken from these domains, it is easy for someone who sees correctly to perceive that I am not at all setting forth reflections on the mathesis vulgaris [ordinary mathematics] in the sense of the traditional disciplines, but instead that I exposit a certain discipline of another sort, a more original discipline in relation to which these latter [traditional] disciplines are derived: quamdam aliam me exponere disciplinam, cuius integumentum sint potius quam partes [that I expound a quite different discipline of which they [[these examples]] are the outer shell rather than its parts].[25] The mathesis universalis is the fons [fount][26] of all others.[27]

The task remains for us of establishing the origin of the two characters that are supposed to regulate the manner of encountering the verum as the fundamentum of affirmation. To this end, let us look to the Cartesian determination of science as certa et evidens cognitio. Attention should be paid from the outset to the fact that the talk here is not about science's object but instead that this interpretation of scientific knowing is oriented to the idea of *certainty*

23. Descartes, Regula IV, 10 [*AT* X, 375].
24. Op. cit., 9 [*AT* X, 374].
25. Ibid. [*AT* X, 374].
26. Op. cit., 10 [*AT* X, 374].
27. See the Appendix, Supplement 24 (p. 237).

and *evidentness.* In its function as a rule, the rule is related to knowledge thus construed as scientific knowledge. The entire reflection is conducted from the outset in such a way that no orientation to a specific realm of being is operative; instead it is a reflection of a completely formal sort. Descartes thereby comes to the conclusion that experientia pertains to the basic function of a scientia to the extent that the ground for its subsequent course is readied. The deductio accomplishes the subsequent course itself. We have to ask, in the sense of this idea of science and in the sense of the idea of scientific structure prefigured through this idea of science, whether any entity might possibly come into question as a possible fundamentum of scientific comprehension. The objects must be such that, insofar as they are comprehended, they can yield nothing uncertain. Of themselves, in terms of the content of their being, they must be purum et simplex. The tendency is accordingly prefigured for every science that seeks to lay claim to a certa et evidens cognitio. [The goal is] the comprehension of objects that are simplicissima [the most simple]. For, the simpler the objects, the less the danger that something obscure remains in the comprehension of them. The idea of the science prefigures the basic constitution of its possible objects. The disciplines that yield objects of this sort are arithmetic and geometry. It is apparent from this that Descartes has oriented his idea of science and scientific knowing to the fact of the matter of mathematical disciplines and, indeed, not to an arbitrary form that it might have been given already, but instead—and this is decisive—to a conception that he himself has developed and, indeed, precisely on the idea, initiated by him, of science as clara et distincta perceptio. And, indeed, this tendency of going back past the already given mathematical disciplines to the mathesis universalis has the sense for him of establishing how, in this science, the idea of a scientific method can be developed in general. Not only is the *idea of the possible objects of science* prefigured from the standpoint of mathematics, but at the same time the *idea of method* is acquired in a definite radicalization as is the idea of the *development of the method.* Reflection on this development of method is connected to a general reflection on the possibility of science. Descartes is obliged to articulate how, with respect to the idea of science that stirs in him, matters stand with the learned tradition and the preoccupation with traditional opinions. In this regard he has his eyes on the Scholastics who worked by drawing upon and discussing authorities for the diverse theories, not, to be sure, in the way that Descartes has in mind. Over against them, he says in Regula III:

Circa obiecta proposita, non quid alii senserint, vel quid ipsi suspicemur, sed quid clare et evidenter possimus intueri, vel certo deducere, quaerendum est, non aliter enim scientia acquiritur.[28]

28. Descartes, Regula III, 5 [*AT* X, 366].

[Concerning the objects proposed, what is to be sought is not what others have thought or what we ourselves suspect, but what we are able to intuit clearly and evidently or deduce with certainty; for in no other way is science acquired.]

It is not necessary to deal with how others have dealt with specific domains of matters; instead what needs to be established is what we are able to grasp clearly and evidently. A science cannot be acquired in any other way.

From this it is apparent how, not directly but indirectly, Descartes already prepares the impossibility of understanding at all what a *science of history* is, as we are familiar with it today. Evident at the same time is the positive turn away from the possibility of coming to a science in this field. It is no accident that in *present-day phenomenology* this same impossibility is given, precisely in this principal inability to understand knowledge within the humanities [*Geisteswissenschaften*] at all. Thus, to a certain extent it appears grotesque that within these sciences today one is busy helping oneself out of their predicament with phenomenology. The ground for this specific tendency inimical to history lies here with Descartes and yet it is motivated in Descartes' case within horizons completely different from what is the case today.

He says that study of the ancients only makes sense in that we are able to establish what has already been discovered and see at the same time quaenam [. . .] supersint excogitanda,[29] what still has to be done. History can accomplish this search. As for the discussion of authorities among the Scholastics he stresses that this is mistaken because what is tenable in each science is not found by many but by a few:

> et nihil prodesset suffragia numerare, ut illam sequeremur opinionem, quae plures habet Auctores. Nam si agatur de quaestione difficili, magis credibile est eius veritatem a paucis inveniri potuisse, quam a multis.[30]

> [and it would not be useful to count votes so that we might follow the opinion that more authors share. For if it is a matter of a difficult question, it is more credible that its truth could have been discovered by a few than by many].

And even if I acquire all the proofs that have been found, I would still not be in a position to conduct a mathematical investigation. This shows that Descartes argues from a particular view of science. Here the contrast between science and history is acute. Si omnia Platonis et Aristotelis argumenta legerimus, de propositis autem rebus stabile iudicium ferre nequeamus:[31] Even if I had become acquainted with all the arguments of the ancient philosophers [Plato and Aristotle], I would still not be able by this means to pass a *stabile*

---

29. Ibid. [The ellipsis in square brackets is given as such in the original German edition.—D.D.]
30. Ibid. [*AT* X, 367].
31. Op. cit., 6 [*AT* X, 367].

iudicium [stable judgment] on the matter itself. From the standpoint of the scientific situation, the position taken here towards history and the history of science itself is understandable. The history of science is construed solely in the sense of a learnedness that is a secondary aim. In the present day, however, the state of things is the reverse and for those who survey the situation today, it is only by way of a *radical historical critique* that any philosophical research can get to the bottom of things at all. Whether that is philosophy is then an unimportant question.

In keeping with the rejection of the importance of historical knowledge as such, Descartes distinguishes two questions. 1. The method must be such that it puts me in the position of never taking a *falsum pro vero* [something false for something true]. 2. It must be such that it makes it possible for me to come to knowledge of all the objects that come in question.

Relative to these two determinations you see without further ado the orientation to the two basic elements of scientific knowledge, the *intuitus* and the *deductio*. The *intuitus* must be correct so that it presents the *deductio* with no false *fundamentum*. The method must be such that the *deductio* proceeds step-by-step from the *fundamentum*. There is no science unless both features are carried out in a manner that corresponds to the sense of science.

With the idea of method, so construed, as his guide, Descartes then considers the history of mathematics. In the course of the consideration, he finds that the history of mathematics increasingly strove to take the domains of objects that it considers, in an ever-more rigorous sense. Et iam viget Arithmeticae genus quoddam, quod Algebram vocant, ad id praestandum circa numeros, quod veteres circa figuras faciebant[32] [and already a certain kind of arithmetic called "algebra" flourishes to accomplish for numbers what the ancients did for figures], so that the fruits are yielded by the methodological principles that are innate in us: fruges ex ingenitis huius methodi principiis natae.[33] The development of these principles is a spontaneous process of maturation of the basic possibilities of knowing that lie within us: nescio quid divini[34] [something of the divine, though I do not know what]. Although mathematical disciplines bear this fruit right now, they still have not achieved complete maturity (perfecta maturitas[35]). I want to radicalize what mathematical knowledge strives for. I do not want to restrict myself thereby to specific domains of objects of mathematics itself; instead I want [to move] beyond the content-specific determination of mathematics to the method as such, to the first components of that around which all mathematical knowledge moves. He

32. Descartes, Regula IV, 9 [*AT* X, 373].
33. Ibid.
34. Ibid.
35. Ibid.

designates this idea "mathesis universalis." Even for this idea there are definite explanations for its development in history itself.

> Cum vero postea cogitarem, unde ergo fieret, ut primi olim Philosophiae inventores neminem Matheseos imperitum ad studium sapientiae vellent admittere [μηδεὶς ἀγεωμέτρητος εἰσίτω³⁶] [. . .], plane suspicatus sum, quamdam eos Mathesim agnovisse valde diversam a vulgari nostrae aetatis.³⁷

> [Afterwards, however, when I would ponder how it thus happened that the first founders of philosophy would admit no one to the study of wisdom who was not in command of mathematics . . . I came to suspect that they knew of a mathematics quite different from the ordinary mathematics of our age.]

What matters is to take this up and develop it fully, to go behind these connections and ask what the common feature is that all these disciplines have in view.³⁸ To this end, he first takes his orientation from the name itself and determines that mathesis has the completely formal meaning of *disciplina* (teaching, learning, learnability, intersubjective communicability), taking something in a definite manner in experience. *Mathesis* is distinguished by the fact that the mathematical method is carried out in such a way that one does not explicitly represent to oneself what is to be experienced respectively, but instead that one comes, on the basis of the validity of an inference, to definite results that thereby show themselves to be valid. That which is common extends to the ordo vel mensura [order or measure].³⁹ Whether mensura quaerenda sit [the measure is to be sought] in the domain with a definite content, e.g., numbers, sounds, shapes, is of no help; ac proinde generalem quamdam esse debere scientiam, quae id omne explicet [and finally it became clear to me that there ought to be some general science which explains everything] that can be explained at all about order and measure, if no definite content is attributed to it at all.⁴⁰ Thus the mathesis universalis is the formal science of the pure connections as such of order and measure. The possibility of the mathesis shows that mathematical disciplines, although they themselves already provide clarity and simplicity of objects, can go back to the simplest objects. A science must be brought back to the simplest factors.

---

36. Eliae in Porphyrii Isagogen et Aristotelis Categorias commentaria, ed. A. Busse. *Commentaria in Aristotelem Graeca*, Vol. XVIII, pars I (Berlin 1900), 118, 18ff. Joannis Philoponi in Aristotelis de anima libros commentaria, ed. M. Hayduck. *Commentaria in Aristotelem Graeca*, Vol. XV (Berlin 1897), 117, 27: "Admit no one not versed in geometry." [This phrase and the ellipsis are given in square brackets in the original German edition.—D.D.]
37. Descartes, Regula IV, 10 [*AT* X, 375f.].
38. Op. cit., 11.
39. Ibid. [*AT* X, 377f.].
40. Op. cit., 11f. [*AT* X, 378].

At ego tenuitatis meae conscius talem ordinem in cognitione rerum quaerenda per-
tinaciter observare statui, ut semper a simplicissimis et facillimis exorsus, nunquam
ad alia pergam, donec in istis nihil ulterius optandum superesse videatur.[41]

[And, conscious of my limitation, I resolved to observe tenaciously such an order
in the pursuit of knowledge of things that, starting out from the simplest and easiest
things, I would never move on to others until it seemed that there was nothing
further to be found in them.]

Ordinary mathematics [*Vulgärmathematik*] provides Descartes with a certain
order which he then construes absolutely, for every science as such. What is
essential is that one opens up and adheres to this order (or these orders, as
the case may be) in conducting research. For, indeed, only then does the
possibility exist of inferring from foundations that have been actually secured.
For the deductio is the path on which all the objects of a scientific domain
can be comprehended. The idea of method contains within itself the idea of
a *series*. The idea of a series is the clue for the methodical development since
it proceeds from the simplest objects to the composite ones.

In the *sixth* investigation (*rule*) the question is discussed: What must a series
contain within itself in order that it be able to take over the guidance of all
scientific knowledge? [R]es omnes per quasdam series posse disponi,[42] all
objects can be ordered by means of certain series,

non quidem in quantum ad aliquod genus entis referuntur, sicut illas Philosophi in
categorias suas diviserunt, sed in quantum unae ex aliis cognosci possunt.[43]

[not indeed insofar as they are referred to some genus of being, such as the categories
into which philosophers have divided them, but insofar as some things can be known
on the basis of others.]

As the clue to all methodical research, serializing is not drawn from the subject matters, from a determinacy of being that accords with a genus. Instead
the differentiation of a possible serializing within a domain of objects must
be oriented by the fact that the series prefigures the path by which one can
be known from the others, in such a way that the series determines utrum
profuturum sit aliquas alias prius, et quasnam, et quo ordine perlustrare
[whether it will be advantageous to examine some things before others and
which ones and in what order].[44] The idea of the series is not gathered with
a view to the objects in terms of their content but, insofar as they are consid-

41. Op. cit., 12 [*AT* X, 379].
42. Descartes, Regula VI, 14 [*AT* X, 381].
43. Ibid.
44. Ibid.

ered among themselves, with a view to their knowability in the sense of deductio.

With this tendency, two determinations present themselves for Descartes. The things are *res absolutae* and *res respectivae*[45] [absolute things and relative things]. You see in these two categories without further ado the reflection of intuitus and deductio. The intuitus always has an absolutum, the deductio a respectivum. The respectivum has within itself an *involutum* [entanglement], something to which it relates back and which is quite frequently an *obscurum* [obscurity] that must be unraveled. Closer consideration shows without further ado that things as diverse as possible from one another in terms of the content of their being are conceived under these two formal categories. The entire tendency of the development of the idea of method is nothing else than a consistently executed mathematization in the sense of the mathematical itself, whereby no value is placed on whether definite categories themselves display contents of a certain sort or not. Falling under the *absolutum* are independens, causa, simplex, universale, unum, aequale, simile, rectum [independence, cause, simple, universal, one, equal, similar, straight]; falling under the *respectivum* are dependens, effectus, compositum, particulare, multa, inaequale, dissimile, obliquum [dependence, effect, composite, particular, many, unequal, dissimilar, oblique].[46]

We are in the process of investigating Descartes' regula generalis [general rule] for its origin and, to be sure, in order to see how, in the manner in which the rule itself is taken, the knowing that places itself under this rule reveals its specific character of being. Mathematics is from the outset the discipline, the objects of which correspond to what he demands of certa et evidens cognitio [certain and evident cognition]. Descartes seeks the categories of the series insofar as it is the path for grasping what itself has the character of an object [*Gegenständliche*]; not insofar as the contents of the objects are taken into view, but insofar as what matters is to acquire a knowledge-connection as such. The development of the series-categories is oriented to this purely methodical consideration. Descartes explicitly remarks that he takes the causa up into the class of res absolutae [absolute things], although, as a correlate concept, the causa is actually related in itself to the effectus.[47] But in regard to the order of knowing with a view to what should be settled first in knowing, the causa is something absolute because the possibility of proceeding further in the deductio depends upon a clarification of the cause itself. The secret of the entire method is to acquire the respective absolutum in the various knowledge-series, not the absolute as far as content is concerned, but the

45. Ibid.
46. Ibid. [*AT* X, 381f.].
47. Op. cit., 15 [*AT* X, 383].

methodical absolute. Now, in regard to the order of the conceptual structure, many things can be absolute in one respect, relative in another. The universale is an absolutum, quia naturam habet magis simplicem [the universal is an absolute because it has a simpler nature],[48] but in regard to its origin in the individual, it is a *respectivum bonum* [relative good].[49] In this way, the import of this development lies in grasping what has the character of an object [*das Gegenständliche*] in accord with the rule.

Given this aim, Descartes also took it upon himself to procure a certain ordering of objects that in themselves correspond to the character of simplicitas. This outline of simple objects is important insofar as, for various domains of being, Descartes sets forth a uniform dimension of commensurate simplicity with respect to what is objective. These are res pure intellectuales, res pure materiales, res communes [purely intellectual things, purely material things, common things].[50] The diversity in content does not interest him at all.

Pure intellectuales illae sunt, quae per lumen quoddam ingenitum et absque ullius imaginis corporeae adiumento ab intellectu cognoscuntur: tales enim nonnullas esse certum est, nec ulla fingi potest idea corporea, quae nobis repraesentet, quid sit cognitio, quid dubium, quid ignorantia, item quid sit voluntatis actio, quam volitionem liceat appellare, et similia, quae tamen omnia revera cognoscimus.[51]

[Purely intellectual things are those which are known by the intellect through a certain inborn light and without the help of any image of a body; for it is certain that there are some things of this sort and no corporeal idea whatever can be imagined which represents to us what cognition is, what doubt is, what ignorance is, what the act of the will is that may be called volition, and similar things, all of which we, nevertheless, know.]

Here we have, to put it modern terms, the essential comprehension of the determinate acts of consciousness. Descartes sets forth the res intellectuales as comprehensible through the *lumen ingenitum* [inborn light] without further ado.

Pure materiales illae sunt, quae non nisi in corporibus esse cognoscuntur, ut sunt figura, extensio, motus, etc. Denique communes dicendae sunt, quae modo rebus corporeis, modo spiritibus sine discrimine tribuuntur, ut existentia, unitas, duratio, et similia.[52]

[Purely material things are those that are only known to be in bodies as are figure, extension, motion, and so forth. Finally, things are to be called "common" which

48. Ibid. [*AT* X, 382].
49. Ibid.
50. Descartes, Regula XII, 37 [*AT* X, 419].
51. Ibid. [*AT* X, 419].
52. Ibid.

are attributed in a way to corporeal things, in a way to spiritual things indiscrimi-
nately, such as existence, unity, duration, and the like.]

(Scheler has simply taken over this position in that he extends the essential
comprehension from consciousness to the universal context-of-being. The basis for this lies in the ancient ontology which, by various channels, has penetrated into the present.)

> Caeterum inter has naturas simplices placet etiam numerare earumdem privationes
> et negationes, quatenus a nobis intelliguntur, quia non minus vera cognitio est, per
> quam intueor quid sit nihil, vel instans, vel quies, quam illa, per quam intelligo quid
> sit existentia, vel duratio, vel motus.[53]

> [For the rest, it is also desirable to number among these simple natures their pri-
> vations and negations, insofar they are known by us, since the knowledge, through
> which I intuit what nothing or instantaneous or rest is, is no less true knowledge
> than that through which I understand what existence or duration or motion is.]

This outline of the simplest things that, viewed with respect to the idea of
scientia, provide the possible fundamentum for the corresponding science,
shows that it is not obtained by inquiring into the various domains of being.

§ 37. The care of knowing as care about certainty, as mistaking oneself

If we briefly summarize, then it must be said that the origin of the content
of the *regula* presents itself in two respects: 1. in relation to *what* the rule has
to regulate; 2. *how* it regulates. *What* it regulates is the *scientia*, read off of
mathematical sciences given in advance. *How* it regulates is carried out on
the path of the *method* that is read off mathematics. These sciences are given
in advance in a definite manner and, indeed, such that this science from the
outset is not viewed with respect to the sort of content the objects have. Instead
the science is taken with a view to the manner of the assenting knowing's
encounter with the objects, that is to say, with a view to the care that interprets
itself in terms of the rule's makeup and places itself under the rule so conceived. The experience of the sciences given in this way in advance thus
reveals itself to be the specific *care about certainty*. It shows that the care of
knowing does not reside [*sich aufhält*] with entities qua entities and does not
approach objects with respect to their factual content but instead approaches
them in terms of their comprehensibility, and this comprehensibility seen with
a view to assent. Thus, the place that the care of knowing as the care about

53. Op. cit., 38 [*AT* X, 420].

certainty resides is a quite distinctive one. Science is experienced here in its distinctiveness as something completely specific and one must make this clear to oneself in order to understand the sort of treatment of objects, content-wise, that is conducted from this vantage point. To put it briefly, care's way of residing in determinate sciences in this fully determined respect shows that the *esse* is placed as *verum* and the *verum* as *certum* primarily in [this know-ing's] care, so that the *ens* reaches its task only through the *detour over the certum*.

This care about certainty with its characteristic residence is then character-ized by the fact that it makes a quite definite claim for the rule developed by it. The care that gives itself the regula does not restrict this rule to the specific domain in which it originated. Instead the rule presents itself as regula *ge-neralis*. Along with the rule itself, the care develops a fundamental claim, of the sort that the rule normatively determining it says at the same time: the only sort of knowledge that is science at all is that which satisfies the rule. The original basis is given up in the development itself.

This claim of the regula as regula generalis leads to the fact that Descartes excludes definite possibilities of knowledge from the domains of science al-together or, in line with the sense of the rule, transforms the disciplines already given. This shows itself above all in the fact that Descartes shows that his-torical knowledge does not come into question at all as knowledge with a subject matter of its own, but instead has only propaedeutic value.

Descartes transforms all the fundamental sciences—theology, metaphysics, mathematics—in line with the sense of regula generalis. With regard to phys-ics, his procedure is as follows. In contrast to the old physics that aimed at the establishment of *qualitates substantiales*, he presses for regarding the ob-jects of physics only to the extent that they satisfy the regula. I am only permitted to take up *extensio*. In fact, the regula generalis was already there for him quite early. It was only a matter of grasping it explicitly and char-acterizing the mathematical disciplines in its sense.

The fate of the doctrine of *innate ideas*, which Descartes had taken up from the Oratorium movement at the time, shows precisely how he transformed the specifically theological and philosophical doctrines and took them up under the guidance of the rule and the principle that they should satisfy the rule. Human beings have an *idea of God's being*. This emphasis had already been given to the doctrine with the aim of securing an apologetic foundation in opposition to atheism. Descartes picked up this doctrine and built it into his doctrine of clara et distincta perceptio. He had to do this in order to become clear about the doctrine. It was a Scholastic doctrine: the intellect's knowledge is only possible in that a fundamentum is given to the intellectus in advance. [The doctrine can be traced to] an Aristotelian theory: ὀυδέποτε νοεῖ ἄνευ φαντάσματος ἡ ψυχή [The soul does not think without a phantasm].[54] Phan-tasms are the very phenomena that for the Scholastics constitute the transition between specifically sensory knowledge and intellectual knowledge. This problem was difficult for the Scholastics since it concerns how a sensory being passes over into a spiritual being. Sensory knowledge provides intellectual knowledge with the species intentionales in advance and the intellectus tends toward them as its fundamentum. The species intentionales are the basis for the explication of the concept of the intentional. From the outset, Descartes could not accept this entire Thomistic conception of knowing. For Descartes, one thing was certain: in the sense of a clara et distincta perceptio, the cor-poreal was only comprehensible as extensio. All other determinations of cor-poreal being, how they appear if I study the physiological intermediate realm, do not come into consideration. Thus, if Descartes sets for himself the fun-damental task of explaining knowing itself, he cannot allow himself to become involved in this intermediate realm since, as soon as he does so, an obscurum is the only thing that he has to grasp. He built the doctrine of innate ideas into his doctrine. Guided by the rule, he must transfer the interpretation of knowing back into the field that is accessible in the sense of the rule itself. This is one of the most distinct examples of how the transformation of the-ological and philosophical problems is carried out with an astonishingly con-sistent application of the regula generalis.

In this claim made by it, because it passes beyond the domain of its origin, the care involved reveals itself as *mistaking* the possibilities that are most its own. It mistakes itself, that is to say, it does not hold itself to what, in the sense of the rule, it is commensurate to, to what it is suited for. In this self-interpretation care no longer sees its *ownmost* possibilities but instead mistakes itself within itself insofar as it interpretively expands the rule to a regula generalis. And, indeed, this mistaking takes place in such a way that it *exceeds itself* [*sichaufsteigerndes*] and thereby becomes a mistaking that is obscured by the fundamental meaning that it ascribes to itself. Insofar as the regula precisely is a regula generalis and thus presents itself as the only possible way to rigorous knowledge, its mistaking is kept in the background. Examination of the character of the claim made by the rule in regard to its content reveals the care of knowing as *care about certainty* in the sense of an *excessive, mounting mistaking of oneself* [*aufsteigerndes Sichvergreifen*]. In knowing's being in this way, a completely determinate movement of existence is evident, a movement that directs the formation of scientific ideas and the entire inter-pretation of existence.

54. Aristoteles, *De anima*, Gamma 7, 431a16f.

§ 38. The care that tranquilizes. Descartes' interpretation of the verum as certum while retaining Scholastic ontology

In this entire context of the development of the rule, what does knowing's being present itself as? What does knowing show itself to be, relative to the manner in which the rule itself is taken as a whole, in view of the phenomenon that this rule is acquired as a rule at all? What does the regimentation itself reveal about the being of knowing as a determinate sort of *care*? We know that knowing is characterized by Descartes as judicium, as modus volendi, as *propensio in bonum*. The *bonum* for the propensio of the judicium is the *verum* [The good in the case of judgment's propensity is the true]. The regimentation shows that the care of knowing grasps the verum from the outset in the sense of the *certum*. Truth conceived primarily as *certainty*; the propensio of the voluntas is oriented to being disposed to *this* bonum. The bonum is no longer the verum but instead the verum qua certum, so that the care, from its own standpoint, interprets a human being's specific *perfectio* in the sense that the voluntas qua judicium is interpreted as *propensio in certum* [a propensity for certainty].

This certum, thus interpreted as the bonum of the propensio of the judgment, is then immediately transferred to the context of being that obtains from the very outset. The possibility of knowledge, thus conceived, is viewed from the perspective of the basic determination of a human being as an *ens medium* [an intermediate being]. We see more distinctly that the ens medium is no ens medium but instead the weight of this being, conceived as perfectum, is redirected towards God. Insofar as this ens medium is an *ens creatum*, it is determined in its possibilities as an ens creatum and also secured with respect to these possibilities. A propensio in bonum is thereby secured in its possibility. The new interpretation of knowing as propensio is transplanted into this context of the *secured* ens, that is to say, care about certainty thus secures for itself from the outset the basis on which it determines its own being. Care about certainty, which at first glance seems like a radical reflection on the fundamentum of knowledge, is a *tranquilizing* [*Beruhigung*] of knowing as a possibility of human being. Care about certainty as a mounting self-mistaking is one with the *care that tranquilizes*.

This peculiar phenomenon in the movement of knowledge is decisive for Descartes. As such, it will prove to be even more peculiar in the doubt-consideration. It will be evident that the path taken by the consideration of doubt is a mere guise [*Schein*] and that the radical reflection is only a guise, that it is merely a way of making explicit quite determinate, preconceived principles and possibilities. Every attempt to avoid arriving at some foundation, all the time following the lead of the cogito, is of this sort. Indeed, on closer inspection, a peculiar displacement [*Umlegung*] of the sense of the verum presents itself and with it a completely inconspicuous, but fundamental repositioning [*Umstellung*] in the basic determination of a human's being is given. Insofar as care interprets itself in such a way that it provides itself in advance with the characterized rule, it determines the verum as certum. However, the verum, so determined, is reinserted into the *old ontology as a self-evident foundation* of the entire explication. The verum, transformed into a certum, is at the same time retained as a bonum, the very bonum that corresponds to the natura hominis [human being's nature]. By means of this *displacement*, human being is interpreted in such a way that its perfectio is elevated in a peculiar way, such that this elevation is from the outset still kept under the guarantee: being created by God and being determined to attain the bonum qua verum. This displacement characterizes the care about knowing (that carries out this displacement) as care about the tranquilizing but ultimately as a care about certainty that from the start precludes any possibility of a fundamental uncertainty with respect to being. From the outset, knowing's manner of being has tranquilized [comforted, assured, sedated: *beruhigt*] itself by including the interpretation of a human's being as something creatum among its assumptions. One has to make this connection completely evident to oneself in order, on the basis of it, to see how, through Descartes, the *old reserve of Scholastic ontology* is all of a sudden *transformed*, but not as though it were a matter of establishing an epistemology. Epistemology does not matter to him at all. His considerations are *purely ontological*. The phenomenon of knowledge as such plays only a secondary role in the process. By contrast, the peculiar *transformation* lies in the fact that he interpreted the *verum as certum* while *leaving the entire ontological foundation in place*, in such a way that this manner of leaving it intact brought with it a reinterpretation of human being.

   Thomas says: Intellectus enim non potest non assentire principiis naturaliter notis: et similiter voluntas non potest non adhaerere bono:[55] the intellectus cannnot fail to assent to the principles that it naturally knows and, similarly, the will cannot fail to adhere to the good. The determinatum esse in bonum is as much a given for the natura hominis as the determinatum esse in verum is for the intellectus, inquantum est bonum, quia in bonum naturaliter ordinatur [Being determined in relation to the good is as much a given for the nature of a human being as being determined for the true is for the intellect insofar as it is good, since it is naturally ordained to the good].[56] The determinatio in bonum [determination to the good] determines a human's being more precisely than the determination of it as creatum does. [A]pprehensio veri non est in potestate nostra: hoc enim [. . .] alicujus luminis, quantum ad hoc non est in

---

55. Thomas Aquinas, *Summa theologica*, pt. 1, q. 62, art. 8.
56. Ibid.

potestate nostra nec imperari potest.[57] The assentiri in the sense of assensus is not in our potestas ["to assent or not" in the sense of "assent" is not in our power], but instead is naturally necessary. The actus rationis subjacet [the act of reason subjugates] a human being's natural manner of being determined. From these passages that can be multiplied at will, such that one could show a connection among them as a whole, it is evident how Descartes takes up this basis but reinterprets this ordinatio naturalis to verum [natural orientation to what is true] by setting up the verum as certum [the true as the certain]. The certum includes within itself an utterly specific conception of truth, a conception that is originally suited to mathematics alone; but it has leaped beyond the domain of its origin and expanded to enjoy an absolute predominance. [O]mnis clara et distincta perceptio proculdubio est aliquid [every clear and distinct perception is without doubt something],[58] insofar as it is something and not nothing—sed necessario Deum authorem habet [but it necessarily has God as its author].[59] That the regula generalis is true is demonstrated by the fact that it is a res that we find. But each res is an ens verum [true being]. Hence, the perceptio as creatum is a verum, hence it is universally binding, just as mathematical principles and the basic rules of mathematical method are nothing other than the fruges spontaneae of the semina [the seeds' spontaneous fruits],[60] which are gathered together, of course, in the clara et distincta perceptio. These semina are aliquid divini [These seeds are something of the divine].[61] They have their being as deriving from their being created by God. The basic rule is transplanted into a human's being which is determined as a medium ens. This medium ens, however, is such that it has its peculiar weight in the bonum reaching up to the ens perfectissimum [most perfect being] and is, in fact, not an actual medium, but instead lies in its nearness to God. What presents itself here is an extreme pelagianism of theoretical knowing.

---

57. Thomas Aquinas, *Summa theologica*, vol. 2, completing the first part of the second part, q. 17, art. 6: "Alio modo quantum ad objectum, respectu cujus duo actus rationis attenduntur: primo quidem, ut veritatem circa aliquid apprehendat; et hoc non est in potestate nostra; hoc enim contingit per virtutem alicujus luminis vel naturalis vel supernaturalis. Et ideo quantum ad hoc actus rationis non est in potestate nostra, nec imperari potest." [Heidegger cites this text in abbreviated form, the full translation of which is as follows: "In another way, in regard to the object, with respect to which two acts of reason are to be noted: one, indeed, that apprehends the truth about something; and this is not in our power; for this occurs by virtue of some light, natural or supernatural. And, thus, with respect to this act of reason, it is not in our power nor can it be commanded."—D.D.]

58. Descartes, Meditatio IV, 74 [*AT* VII, 62].

59. Ibid.

60. Descartes, Regula IV, 9 [*AT* X, 373].

61. Ibid.

Chapter Six

The character of being of the res cogitans, of consciousness

We are now prepared to answer in a radical way the decisive question, the *question of the character of being of consciousness as the thematic field of phenomenology*. We will decide this question by *specifying res cogitans' character of being*. We will have to examine how, by virtue of the characteristic care of knowing, the cogito is found and what character of being it is necessary for the cogitare to have. We will break down into three aspects this examination of the path on which knowing arrives at the cogito: 1. What is the care of knowing in general out for [*Worauf ist die Sorge . . . aus*] in its effort to achieve what emerges as the cogitatio? What is sought? 2. What is the *manner in which the search is carried out*? 3. What is the *concrete path* taken by the search characterized in this manner?

§ 39. The certum aliquid as what is sought by the care of knowing

The cogito sum emerges for Descartes in a fundamental task that he sets for knowledge: to lay the ground first of all for a fundamental science, to prepare the sort of fundamentum for knowledge that is a *fundamentum indubitabile* and fully satisfies what is demanded in the regula generalis. Thus, the search, oriented in this way, must obviously be pursued from the midst of the *position* in which the effort to achieve such a fundamentum eventuates. It is necessary, from this position, to seek the fundamentum in the sense that it satisfies the rule. The search must be carried out by running through the possibilities of knowing that Descartes' concrete scientific position presents. This process of running through the possibilities as a means of seeking the fundamentum is carried out in keeping with the care of knowing.

The first question, the one concerning what is sought, can be determined by us without further ado. It is now merely a matter of making more precise the sense in which the supposition of what is sought determines the character of being of what is to be found. What is sought is the certum in the sense that what alone matters to Descartes is to find a *certum aliquid* [something certain]. *What* that is, is secondary; its "what" is ultimately irrelevant as long as it satisfies the rule. The sharp emphasis is on what is sought as such:

> pergamque porro donec aliquid certi vel si nihil aliud, saltem hoc ipsum, pro certo, nihil esse certi, cognoscam[1]

---

1. Descartes, Meditatio II, 17 [*AT* VII, 24].

[and I will continue further until I know something certain or if nothing else, at least this, that I know for certain that nothing is certain]

if I only find something certain and if it only be that I see that there is nothing certain. [Great things are to be hoped for] [. . .] quid invenero quod certum sit et inconcussum [if I find something certain and unshakeable].[2] It is to be noted that, from the outset, what comes under consideration is *not* primarily the *specific character of being* of what is sought. Instead the only matter for consideration is that what is to be found is to be questioned solely in regard to whether it satisfies the rule. What it is itself, what being it has of itself, these matters do not come into question. In the examination of the third point about how Descartes brings what is sought into view more sharply, we see, namely, that even the rule must satisfy the principle of the series, with the result that what is sought must not at all be merely a certum but instead a certum qua absolutum and simplex [certain qua absolute and simple]. This requirement is prefigured by the regula generalis.

§ 40. *The caring search as dubitare, remotio and suppositio falsi*

The second factor that we are considering is the *search itself*. What is the *manner in which the search is conducted*? The search is a search by the sort of knowing that keeps a lookout; the care's seeing is bent on getting something into view that satisfies the certum [the criterion of certainty]. Everything that is present as obscurum [obscure] or incertum [uncertain] in the *concrete position* in which the search is conducted, is set aside. It is conducted by knowing as judicare [judging] in the manner of a *dubitatio* [doubt]. The judicare denies its assensus [assent] to something presented as obscurum. The judicare becomes the *abstinere* [abstaining] that becomes the *continere* [containing, i.e., content] in the course of conducting the search. This sort of execution of the search in the sense of dubitare is determined more precisely by the fact that what does not satisfy the dubitare does not come into question as a possible fundamentum. Instead, the dubitatio is conducted in the sense of a *remotio* [removal]. This remotio as not-letting-come-into-question ends ultimately for Descartes in a distinctive *suppositio*. The dubitatio incerti [doubt of something's certainty] becomes a *suppositio falsi* [supposition of its falsity]. The doubting of the uncertain is transformed for Descartes into the assumption that this uncertain something is false. This transition, carried out by the search, contains nothing impossible for Descartes. Precisely in this specific transformation, the specific possibility of knowing shows itself; precisely in this sup-

2. Ibid. [The ellipsis in square brackets is given as such in the original German edition. The phrase in square brackets, "Great things are to be hoped for," is a translation of a part of Descartes' sentence that Heidegger omits.—D.D.]

positio, as it were in this radicalization of doubt, the basic property of knowing as judicare reveals itself: its *libertas*, its freedom of the sort that, the more that the knowing in seeking holds itself to its own determinatio in bonum qua certum, the freer this dubitare is. We have heard, after all, that being-free consists in taking seriously the suppositio falsi. We can only say what this peculiar transformation ultimately means for the cogito's character of being, once we have run through the concrete path. The possibility of this transposition can be shown quite schematically by the fact that, indeed, the incertum, which is the object of the dubitatio for Descartes, is nothing other than the non verum insofar as the certum is the verum. As the non verum, the incertum is already in itself falsum and, as falsum, it is a non ens. For this reason, Descartes comes to say that what is given in advance does not exist. This possibility is grounded in the context explicated above. In the stance of this suppositio that is at the same time the stance of the search for the certum, the examination proceeds further and, in the attempt to go further, the search hits upon something that it must address as genuinely found, as something found that corresponds to the search.

§ 41. The path of the caring dubitatio in the First Meditation subject to the regula generalis: the being of the searcher (ego sum) as the first thing found

The *path itself* then for the thus characterized dubitatio in the *concrete position* in which the investigation itself has been placed runs through the possibilities of grasping objects, the possibilities of encountering entities, just in the way that those possibilities are familiar to Descartes. Descartes runs through this very path in the First Meditation. With regard to the path, we have first to consider two things: *what* he thereby runs through, and *how* he runs through it.

In this meditation in the form of doubting, it is necessary to keep in view from the outset that Descartes holds fast to a *definite connection*. He places value on heeding this *ordo* [order]. For him it is inherent in the sense of the method. [I]deoque non alium ordinem sequi potuisse, quam illum qui est apud Geometras usitatus [Hence, it was not possible to follow any other order than that which is used among geometers].[3] The ordo which he maintains is fundamental for him and it is nothing other than the order that *geometry* maintains, the ordo of going back to something *certum* that is *absolutum* and *simplex*, insofar as the *fundamentum* suffices to provide the point of departure for any deductio. What I am seeking cannot be an ens respectivum [relative being]. It must again be a simplex and not a compositum [a simple and not

3. Descartes, *Meditationes de prima philosophia*, Synopsis, 2 [*AT* VII, 13].

a composite being]. Precisely this last point is of fundamental importance in order to understand the type of progression of the meditation. For otherwise one could ask: "Why does Descartes not immediately say: 'Certain objects are given to me, I grasp, for example, the extensio of the fireplace and this, my grasping, I cannot doubt'? Why not start earlier the process of *going back to the cogitatio*?" One understands this process of running through possibilities only if one keeps in mind what Descartes is seeking: certum, absolutum, simplex. The examination by way of doubting cannot come to a halt until such a certum is acquired.

Descartes conceives the possibilities in which something up to now apparently true is given, he conceives them as the sort that are a sensibus or per sensus [from the senses or through the senses].[4] What I up to now assumed as true either is given to me through sensory perception or comes about with the participation of sensory perception. The latter remark applies to mathematical and geometrical truths insofar as they are related to intuitions. Next to these, there is then also a series of objects that are merely mediated by sensory experience in the narrower sense of the term. The care of knowing must pass through these two paths and examine what it encounters on them. Insofar as I run through these two different paths, I need not subject each individual act of experiencing to critique. Instead I hold myself to the principles of these modes of access to entities.

He then carries out his consideration of these two paths in such a way that he increasingly eliminates more and more and shapes the remotio ever more radically so that finally nothing more can present itself that corresponds to the criterion in the right way. It should be noted what falls prey to this *remotio*: 1. everything given through the *senses*, and 2. at the same time also basic determinations like locus, tempus, duratio [place, time, duration], basic determinations that he later specifies as not being perceived by the senses at all, but instead by the *intellectus*, on which he then erects the possibility of a *rigorous physics* that sees only the corporeum qua extensum [corporeal qua extended]. But here even those basic determinations must fall prey to the remotio. Descartes even eliminates *arithmetic* and *geometry*; what they say is, to be sure, simplex and maxime generale [simple and completely universal], yet in spite of this it is not recognized as sufficient. The entire path of doubt itself shows nothing other than the peculiar influence of the regula generalis. Here, in this field, Descartes shows in fact an admirable radicality of philosophizing. Nevertheless, it cannot be said that the origin of the rule itself is philosophically radical.

For the determination of knowledge as judicare that places itself under the depicted rule, we have to see how this knowing, thus characterized, is forced

4. Descartes, Meditatio I, 9 [*AT* VII, 18].

with the task of finding the fundamentum for every possible sort of knowledge; a task, indeed, that must be accomplished from the specific position of knowledge, from having utterly determinate opinions available, opinions proper to a quite specific orientation toward knowledge, from a life led in terms of definite basic convictions about being itself. Here what is available is to be questioned with a view to how it presents itself, how it satisfies what is required by the rule. What is found to be unsatisfactory, is not merely held to be uncertain. Descartes makes the transition instead from the *dubitatio incerti* [doubt about certainty] to the *suppositio falsi* [supposition of falsity]. And, indeed, this transition is not only justified by the fact that the dubitare thereby attains its freedom. This transition has the task of bringing the search into a completely determinate *end-situation*, from which what is sought is found. For a philosophical understanding of Descartes it is indispensable that one accentuates this *subterranean* connection and makes it perfectly clear. The meditation must be understood in connection with the idea of what is sought, the sense of the rule and the path of the series prefigured by it, the method.

Descartes sets out on the path of the search by submitting diverse *opiniones* to an *eversio generalis* [general overturning][5] and, indeed, in such a way that, in accordance with the sense of what he is searching for—a fundamentum as principium—he confronts only the *principia* of these opinions with the rule. The principia of the opinions are, however, nothing else than the *points of departure* [*Ausgänge*] from which he comes to what he has opinions about, *types of access* [*Zugänge*] to it, *ways of dealing* [or interacting: *Umgänge*] with it, such that they [i.e., the principia] provide an orientation for what they grasp. These diverse types of access and dealings with things on the part of living persons are principles, not propositions.

There are, then, types of access, those *a sensibus* [from the senses] and those that are determined *per sensus* [through the senses], that is to say, through the cooperation of the senses, above all, the *imaginatio*. This division is fixed in connection with the traditional partition of consciousness. These types of access and interactions are to be critically investigated. If, in relation to these types of access and interaction or, better, in relation to what is grasped and given in them, an incertum [something uncertain] in some sense turns up, it is not merely left as it was. Instead it falls prey to the remotio [removal] so that what is given therein is posited as nonbeing. This type of access no longer comes into question for the search. (What Husserl means by the reduction is something totally different.) Insofar as these types of access fall prey to the remotio, they are no longer relevant for the search. The end-situation takes shape by means of the remotio. At the end of the path, the

5. Op. cit., 8 [*AT* VII, 18].

search is so positioned that it is confronted with nothing [*nichts*] and with the void [*das Nichts*] of its own possibilities.

Descartes starts with the type of access of *sensory perceiving*, with how it provides access:

> pleraque tamen alia sunt de quibus dubitari plane non potest, quamvis ab iisdem hauriantur; ut jam me hic esse, foco assidere, hiemali toga esse indutum [. . .], et similia:[6]

> [and yet there are many other things about which it is plainly not possible to doubt, although they be derived from them [[the senses]]; such as that now I am here, that I am sitting before the fireplace, that I am dressed in this winter garment . . . , and the like:]

determinate instances of givenness that occur are co-given in a look at the *concrete surroundings* themselves. This givenness is confronted with the rule and the question is raised whether a fundamentum certum is provided by it. This question is answered negatively and Descartes says: what is given here in this way is at first glance not in any way to be doubted as uncertain.

> [M]anus vero has ipsas, totumque hoc corpus meum esse, qua ratione posset negari? [N]isi me forte comparem nescio quibus insanis, quorum cerebella tam contumax vapor ex atra bile labefactat, ut constanter asseverent vel se esse reges, cum sunt pauperrimi, vel purpura indutos, cum sunt nudi, vel caput habere fictile, vel se totos esse cucurbitas, vel ex vitro conflatos; sed amentes sunt isti, nec minus ipse demens viderer, si quod ab iis exemplum ad me transferrem.[7]

> [But that these very hands and this my entire body exist . . . by what reason could this be denied? Not unless I were perhaps to compare myself to I know not what insane persons whose brains some stubborn vapors of melancholy so corrupted that they resolutely assert themselves to be kings when they are paupers or that they are draped in purple when they are nude or that they have an earthen head or that they are all a pumpkin or fabricated from glass; but these are madmen, nor would I seem less demented myself if I would take some example from them and transfer it to myself.]

If I wanted [to doubt] this, I would have to count myself among those insane people who have peculiar opinions even in regard to themselves.

But how, then, do matters stand:

> Praeclare sane, tanquam non sim homo qui soleam noctu dormire, et eadem omnia in somnis pati, vel etiam interdum minus verisimilia, quam quae isti vigilantes: quam

---

6. Op. cit., 9 [*AT* VII, 18. The ellipsis in square brackets is given as such in the original German edition.—D.D.].

7. Op. cit., 9f. [*AT* VII, 18f.].

frequenter vero usitata ista, me hic esse, toga vestiri, foco assidere, quies nocturna persuadet, cum tamen positis vestibus jaceo inter strata![8]

[How perfectly clear, as though I were not a man who is accustomed to sleep at night and to experience in dreams all the same things or sometimes even less probable things than those [[madmen]] do awake; how frequently, indeed, asleep at night, am I persuaded of these customary things, that I am here, wearing this cloak, sitting before the fireplace when I am, nevertheless, lying undressed under the sheets!]

Is it not the case that in a *dream* my existence thus often presents itself to me in a surrounding world that mirrors down to the last hair the one that I find myself in?

[Q]uae dum cogito attentius, tam plane video numquam certis indiciis vigiliam a somno posse distingui.[9]

[Yet when I consider the matter more attentively, I plainly see that the waking state can never be distinguished from a sleeping state by indications that are certain.]

That shows that in fact what is thus given to me is not a certum [something certain] without further ado, but instead an *obscurum* [something obscure] since *being awake* determines the specific type of access proper to having my surrounding world here. Insofar, however, as being awake cannot be distinguished by an absolutely clear criterion from the other sort of interactions in a *dream*, these two types of access cannot come into question as types of access to a possible fundamentum. They belong to a realm of being that comes into question for Descartes from the outset as obscurum, the *intermediate realm* between the res extensae and the res cogitans. It is irrelevant what further is given to me in this manner; I do not inquire any more in its direction since these two basic determinations (being awake and dreaming) are irrelevant.

Ideoque saltem generalia haec, oculos, caput, manus, totumque corpus res quasdam non imaginarias, sed veras existere [And, therefore, at least these general things, the eyes, the head, the hands, and the entire body are not imaginary, but true things that exist].[10] To be sure, it is possible that the fireplace given to me in its specific concreteness does not exist. But how, then, do matters stand with the idea of *something in general*? Does not this givenness in the end have a legitimate sense of being? (It must be noted that the entire discussion is conducted on the basis of the concept of res, a concept that is extended in a completely formal manner.) Perhaps even these *generalia*

8. Op. cit., 10 [*AT* VII, 19].
9. Ibid.
10. Op. cit., 11 [*AT* VII, 19].

are not something that I can say exists. Perhaps they still contain something of a specifically sensory character: imaginaria esse possent [they can be imaginary things],[11] insofar as the idea of coloredness is given along with the generic fireplace. Although they are more general, these generalia are not, relative to their type of origin, to be addressed as being.

And in fact I find in the fireplace the extensio (something more simplex et universale[12]),

figura rerum extensarum, item quantitas, sive earumdem magnitudo et numerus: item locus in quo existant, tempusque per quod durent, et similia,[13]

[extension, the figure of extended things, likewise the quantity, or the magnitude and number of them; so, too, the place in which they exist, and the time through which they endure, and similar sorts of things,]

thus I also find *universalia*, over and against the generalia, and, indeed, such that are no longer related to specifically sensory instances of givenness. These basic determinations of the given are, so to speak, the colors with which each actual thing as such is painted (ex quibus tanquam coloribus veris omnes istae seu verae seu falsae, quae in cogitatione nostra sunt, rerum imagines effinguntur [from which, as it were, true colors, all those images of things in our thinking, whether true or false, are formed]).[14] The transition from the generalia to the universalia shows what Descartes is, as it were, under way to: there is still something more simplex. The elimination is always achieved under the idea of the rule of setting aside each and every compositum insofar as a compositum, as such, always continues to bear in itself a possibility of an obscurum.

Quapropter ex his forsan non male concludemus Physicam, Astronomiam, Medicinam, disciplinasque alias omnes, quae a rerum compositarum consideratione dependent, dubias quidem esse, atqui Arithmeticam, Geometriam, aliasque ejusmodi, quae non nisi de simplicissimis et maxime generalibus rebus tractant, atque utrum eae sint in rerum natura nec ne, parum curant, aliquid certi atque indubitati continere.[15]

[Hence, from these considerations we might quite properly infer that physics, astronomy, medicine, and all other disciplines which depend upon consideration of composite things are dubious; and that arithmetic, geometry, and other disciplines of this sort, which treat only of the most simple and maximally general things and

11. Ibid.
12. Ibid. [*AT* VII, 20].
13. Op. cit., 12 [*AT* VII, 20].
14. Op. cit., 11 [*AT* VII, 20].
15. Op. cit., 12 [*AT* VII, 20].

care little whether they be in the nature of things or not, contain something certain and indubitable.]

The maxime simplices [maximally simple] sorts of givenness are apparently those of mathematics, such that one can say that it has the simplicissima et maxime generalia [the most simple and maximally general things] as its object.

[N]am sive vigilem, sive dormiam, duo et tria simul juncta sunt quinque, quadratumque non plura habet latera quam quatuor.[16]

[For, whether I am awake or asleep, two and three joined at the same time are five, and a rectangle has no more than four sides.]

Here, now, he has the sorts of givenness, for which the conditions of access, made uncertain from the outset, are no longer relevant. We know, indeed, that the regula [rule] was drawn from these objects. And, in spite of this, Descartes does not stop here. Why not stick with the objects of which he himself says that they are given in an absolutely clear and distinct way? Because they can provide no fundamentum absolutum for the fundamental science [*Grundwissenschaft*] since that is the *prima philosophia* [first philosophy], ontology in the old sense. He wants to articulate, according to the sense of the rule, propositions about being, about the caused being, about the being of God. He cannot do this with mathematical propositions. The sense of the entire meditation moves in the direction of prima philosophia in the sense of the old metaphysics and has nothing to do with epistemology.

Hence, this givenness, too, must be shaken:

Verumtamen infixa quaedam est meae menti vetus opinio, Deum esse qui potest omnia, et a quo talis, qualis existo, sum creatus: unde autem scio illum non fecisse ut nulla plane sit terra, nullum caelum, nulla res extensa, nulla figura, nulla magnitudo, nullus locus, et tamen haec omnia non aliter quam nunc mihi videantur existere?[17]

[Nevertheless, fixed in my mind is the traditional opinion that God exists who can do all things and by Whom I am created such as I exist. However, how do I know that He has not brought it about that there is no earth at all, no heaven, no extended thing, no figure, no magnitude, no place, and yet that all these things seem to me to exist just as they do now?]

It should be noted that the conviction of God's existence co-determines the concrete situation, a conviction reflected in the quite specific preconception

16. Ibid.
17. Op. cit., 12f. [*AT* VII, 21].

of the sense of being in general as the same as esse creatum, and that, therefore, in every context where he is concerned with being, the conviction of the esse Dei [God's existence] is co-present therein. As a result, this question, whether or not a *deceiver* has created me, is not a strange one but instead is given without further ado for Descartes on the basis of his meditation and must also be taken into consideration.

> Ideoque etiam ab iisdem, non minus quam ab aperte falsis accurate deinceps assensionem esse cohibendam, si quid certi velim invenire.[18]

> [And, therefore, I should withhold assent in the future from these opinions no less carefully than from those obviously false if I want to find something certain].

It could be the case that my special way of grasping these objects would still be uncertain in spite of this. In order to be certain even up against this uncertainty, I once again take a step from the dubitatio to the suppositio:

> Quapropter, ut opinor, non male agam, si voluntate plane in contrarium versa me ipsum fallam, illasque aliquamdiu omnino falsas imaginariasque esse fingam.[19]

> [On account of this, as I see it, I would do well if, turning my will in an opposite direction, I would deceive myself and pretend for a while that those things [[that I believed]] are altogether false and imaginary.]

In this way Descartes has worked himself up to what I call the *end-situation*:

> putabo caelum, aerem, terram, colores, figuras, sonos, cunctaque externa nihil aliud esse quam ludificationes somniorum [. . .]: considerabo me ipsum tanquam manus non habentem [. . .]: manebo obstinate in hac meditatione defixus.[20]

> [I will think the heaven, the air, the earth, colors, figures, sounds and all external things to be nothing other than delusions of dreams . . . ; I will consider myself as not having hands . . . ; I will remain stubbornly fixed in this meditation.]

He places himself face to face with the void [*das Nichts*] and seeks to maintain himself in this situation. That means, however, in relation to the end-situation itself, that he is not only placed *before the void*, but also inserted *into the void*, devoid of *any possibility* of still encountering something. Characterized, to be sure, as out for something certain, my search is confronted with the void and is itself inserted into the void. Thus, it is placed before the void and into the void.

---

18. Op. cit., 14 [*AT* VII, 21f.].
19. Ibid. [*AT* VII, 22].
20. Op. cit., 15 [*AT* VII, 22f. The ellipses in square brackets are given as such in the original German edition.—D.D.].

But *it itself* still *is*, although the path of access to something is denied it. It still stands in the expectation of something. All the search can encounter now is the *being of the one searching itself* and, indeed, what is found that satisfies the sense of the regula is not somehow the dubitare as such. Instead what is found is the *being of the one searching*, that contains *its being* in itself. I still find the dubitare as an esse and the dubitare is *cogitare*. To this extent, the esse is a *sum* [the "to be" is an "I am"]. The esse of the very res that I come upon is the sort of being that must be expressed by the "sum." Not somehow the presence of the dubitare as a thing is what is found, but instead the fact that an *esse* is also given in the dubitare.

§ *42. The caring search in the Second Meditation for what the ego sum is under the guidance of the regula generalis: the ego cogito*

First let us pursue the further course of the meditation:

Nondum vero satis intelligo, quisnam sim ego ille, qui jam necessario sum, deincepsque cavendum est, ne forte quid aliud imprudenter assumam in locum mei.[21]

[In truth, I do not yet understand satisfactorily who I am, that "I" which I necessarily now am, and from now on care must be taken lest I imprudently assume something else in place of myself.]

We have now to consider how Descartes answers the question of the *whatness* [*Wascharakter*] of what he finds. For the determination of the ego, Descartes allows only what satisfies the rule, what is so given that it is given in the sense of the rule and thus identifies itself as an entity. On what path do I come to determine *what* this ego is? Should I hold myself to a definitio?

Hominem scilicet, sed quid est homo? dicamne animal rationale? non, quia postea quaerendum foret quidnam animal sit, et quid rationale, atque ita ex una quaestione in plures difficilioresque delaberer.[22]

[A human being, namely, but what is a human being? May I not say a "rational animal"? No, because it would be necessary to inquire what an animal might be and what rational and, thus, from one question I would slip down into many and more difficult questions.]

I want to see how I was given to myself in my *opiniones*. I want to discuss my existence in view of what has the sort of determination that satisfies the rule. He does not hold himself to any sort of definitiones, but holds himself

---

21. Descartes, Meditatio II, 18 [*AT* VII, 25].
22. Op. cit., 19 [*AT* VII, 25].

instead to what was given of itself in the natural consideration of existence: Sed hic potius attendam quid sponte, et natura duce cogitationi meae antehac occurrebat quoties quid essem considerabam [But here I will attend rather to what occurred spontaneously and naturally to my thought before, whenever I considered what I was].²³ Thus, he begins his meditation anew in the same sense:

nempe occurrebat primo, me habere vultum, manus, brachia, totamque hanc membrorum machinam, qualis etiam in cadavere cernitur, et quam corporis nomine designabam.²⁴

[it occurred namely first that I have a face, hands, arms, and this entire machine of members which can also be discerned in a corpse and which I have designated with the name "body."]

It should be noted how Descartes sees his own existence as a thing with determinate properties, how he sees it in the categorial determinations of a given thing with properties. He pares it down in the sense that he excludes what is not given in the sense of the rule: everything that is determined in any sort of way by the senses, everything that contains something obscurum. For the determination of *what* the ego is, the only sorts of givenness that come into question are such as came into question for the determination *that* it is. The question: quid sum? [what am I?] is settled by the fact that Descartes says: sum res *cogitans*; quid est hoc? nempe dubitans, intelligens, affirmans, negans, volens, nolens, imaginans quoque, et sentiens [I am a *thinking* thing: what is this? Namely, a doubting, understanding, affirming, negating, willing, refusing, also imagining and sensing being].²⁵ Now even the sentire [to sense] is taken up into the determination of what the ego is, because Descartes has pressed ahead to a more acute determination of sentire, in such a way that he determines it as an animadvertere [to turn attention to] as such, whereby the mediation by the senses becomes irrelevant.

[L]ucem video, strepitum audio, calorem sentio; falsa haec sunt, dormio enim. At certe videre videor, audire, calescere.²⁶

[I see light, I hear a noise, I feel heat; these things are false, for I am sleeping. Yet I certainly seem to see, to hear, to feel warmth.]

[S]ed fieri plane non potest cum videam, sive (quod jam non distinguo) cum cogitem me videre, ut ego ipse cogitans non aliquid sim.²⁷

23. Ibid. [*AT* VII, 25f.].
24. Ibid. [*AT* VII, 26].
25. Op. cit., 23 [*AT* VII, 28].
26. Op. cit., 24 [*AT* VII, 29].
27. Op. cit., 30 [*AT* VII, 33].

[But if I see or (which I am not now distinguishing) if I think that I see, it plainly cannot happen that I, this very thinking thing, am not something].

Seeing, hearing, smelling are now reinterpreted into a cogito me videre, videor videre [I think that I see, I seem to see], and so forth. I have myself along when I see, I am co-given to myself. That means, the sentire is ultimately also a cogitatio that is, to be sure, subsequently co-determined by the organs. Thus, only what has the character of the res cogitans falls into the determination of the ego.

§ 43. What is found by the care about certainty: a valid, universally binding proposition

But we have to pose the decisive question of how, on the basis of the way it is *determined that and what the res cogitans is*, it becomes apparent what Descartes *genuinely sought* and *found*. With the help of the interpretation of the formulas for the cogito sum, let us try to see how Descartes formulates his "find" and what he lays claim to it as.

In accordance with the orientation of the mediations pertaining to the search, Descartes enacts dubitationes, suppositiones, remotiones [doubts, suppositions, removals]. The search for the res cogitans itself and the determination of its being are oriented to this *horizon of givenness of its own existence*, to this horizon: in front of the fireplace, with paper in hand, dressed. The critical consideration is always directed at the principles. That means: the principles, the manners of access to the entities familiar to Descartes, are affected by the remotio. These principles fall prey to the remotio and, indeed, first what is given in this way and then, in a return to this knowing's conditions of being, to the types of comprehension. The type of comprehension when I am awake, insofar as it is co-determined by my physiological being, remains irrelevant. Descartes brings the meditation to a close with a sweeping: fallam me ipsum [I will deceive myself]:[28] I want to deceive myself. Descartes characterizes the end-situation in this way: manebo obstinate in hac meditatione [I will remain steadfast in this meditation],[29] I remain stubbornly standing where I am brought by this search;

pergamque porro donec aliquid certi vel si nihil aliud, saltem hoc ipsum, pro certo, nihil esse certi, cognoscam.[30]

28. Descartes, Meditatio I, 14 [*AT* VII, 22].
29. Op. cit., 15 [*AT* VII, 23].
30. Descartes, Meditatio II, 17 [*AT* VII, 24].

[and I will continue further until I know something certain or if nothing else, at least this, that I know for certain that nothing is certain.]

It is important now that one envisions for oneself the *end-situation* in its *structure*. 1. Being placed before the *void of "givennesses"* is characteristic of it; as is 2. being placed into the *void of possibilities of access*; he is no longer able to be out for something, in the manner of searching for it. 3. That the search is placed into and before the void is characterized in a twofold way: a) insofar as it is characterized in its being out for [bent on, set on: *Aussein*] something; it is out for a fundamentum absolutum and simplex and, qua searching, it has this completely determinate character of "being out" [*Aussein*]; b) it is determined by a definite horizon against which something like a certum can be encountered in general. This horizon is likewise determined by the path; the horizon of my own existence now falls prey more and more to the remotio. The direction of expectation remained in force and, indeed, it is directed at me myself. That must be kept in view in order to understand that there is nothing violent in the way that the dubitare *turns around* to itself; instead this *turnaround* [*Umschlag*] lies in the very tendency of the search. The search is pressed to make the *leap* to see itself.

Enitar tamen et tentabo rursus eandem viam quam heri fueram ingressus, removendo scilicet illud omne quod vel minimum dubitationis admittit, nihilo secius quam si omnino falsum esse comperissem; pergamque porro donec aliquid certi vel si nihil aliud, saltem hoc ipsum, pro certo, nihil esse certi, cognoscam.[31]

[Nevertheless, I will make an attempt and I will try again the same path that I had pursued yesterday, removing, namely, all that which admits the least doubt, no less than if I had discovered it to be altogether false. And I will continue further until I know something certain or if nothing else, at least this, that I know for certain that nothing is certain.]

In remaining steadfastly at this point, I want to make every effort to go further into the possibilities that I still have. The next step that is sought *leads the search up against itself.* The dubitare confronts the dubitare and so the question arises: What is it, then, that this thus characterized searching finds? The dubitare is placed before itself and, to be sure, in a manner of searching of the sort that the search now interrogates what it confronts, the dubitare: "Are you a certum [something certain]?" What do I actually confront in the dubitare? In the dubitare, the *me dubitare* [that I doubt] confronts me and the me dubitare shows me as *me esse* [that I am]. Is that, therefore, a *certum*? Indeed, *cogito sum* [I think, I am]. What that which is found actually is, we will have

31. Ibid.

to establish more precisely in a moment. For now, it is necessary to hold fast to the fact that the dubitare is found as me dubitare, me esse [that I doubt, that I am].

In the same sense Descartes takes the further step of determining what was found with regard to *what* it is. Into the determination of that "what" he only takes up what satisfies the rule itself: me velle, me affirmare, me dubitare [that I want, that I affirm, that I doubt], so that he says: Quis sum? Res cogitans [What am I? A thinking thing]. Hence, in the course of the determination of the "what" of that which he has found in his search to be indubitable, his concern is to delimit and determine *what remains standing in this region of being of the cogitatio* [thought]. But it cannot be part of Descartes' purpose to show, in the course of the determination of what the ego is, that it is the unity of a manifold. (This view guides Buchenau's entire translation.) The question of the unity of a manifold is not a problem for Descartes at all. He asks: What belongs to the regional context of the res cogitans? He determines the "what" of what has been found and he does so on the basis of what belongs to the regional context of the cogito. *That the res cogitans is* and *what it is* are thus determined in this way.

We have to ask more precisely: *What* is it *actually* [*eigentlich*] that Descartes has *found*, and what is it that he himself actually means to have found with the *cogito ergo sum*? Is what is found a certum and [if so,] in what sense? What is found is an aliquid [something] not qua res; not the dubitare as such is what is found and not the esse of the dubitare. Instead what is found is: me dubitare, me esse, that for me to doubt is my being. Not found is aliquid qua res, but instead *aliquid qua state of affairs* [*Sachverhalt*]. The basic finding of the search is a *veritas*, a *proposition* articulated in relation to what is objectively the case [*Gegenständliche*]; an object as such, the dubitare or the ego, is not found but instead a *standing* is found, the standing of a state of affairs, that the me dubitare is in the me esse, the co-givenness of the esse in the dubitare. This standing is taken up in the *proposition*: *cogito ergo sum*. Thus, one can say, in short, that what satisfies the certum sought is not a res, but a *proposition*, a *validity*. The care about certainty seeks and finds a validity with the character of being *universally binding*. Insofar as Descartes abruptly turns the care of knowledge around into the interpretation of verum as certum, the basic finding is correspondingly not a res, but instead a veritas, a *proposition that is certain*.

What now needs to be proven is that this is in fact what Descartes deliberately sought and that the veritas as veritas satisfies what is sought. We will attempt this by recapitulating the *various formulations of the finding* and seeing what is itself expressed in them. In order to understand the transition from searching to finding and to understand it in a truly unitary way, it is necessary to keep in mind that the searching itself has an utterly specific *determinatio*. The search gets its determinatio by bringing itself into the end-situation.

Exempli causa, cum examinarem hisce diebus an aliquid in mundo existeret, atque adverterem, ex hoc ipso quod illud examinarem, evidenter sequi me existere, non potui quidem non judicare illud quod tam clare intelligebam verum esse, non quod ab aliqua vi externa fuerim ad id coactus, sed quia ex magna luce in intellectu magna consequuta est propensio in voluntate.[32]

[For example, I examined during these days whether something exists in the world and I noticed, from this very fact that I examined it, that it evidently follows that I exist, that I was unable not to judge that which I understood so clearly to be true, not that I was compelled by some external force but because a great propensity in the will followed from a great light in the intellect.]

From this end-situation, where every possibility of an obscurum had disappeared, there followed the propensity in the judicare to assent to the given. This assent to what now presents itself to me was not a forced assent and it was also not the sort of assent that arises from an indeterminate situation: atque ita tanto magis sponte et libere illud credidi, quanto minus fui ad istud ipsum indifferens [and thus, the less indifferent I was toward that very thing, the more spontaneously and freely I believed it].[33] My situation was one of tense expectation. The less indifferent it was, the more my propensio [propensity] was determined. By means of the process of the remotio, that propensity brought to fruition in itself the definite determination of the certum as fundamentum absolutum [the certain as the absolute foundation]. One must picture for himself this specific determinatio in order to see the search catching the searching being itself.[34]

---

32. Descartes, Meditatio IV, 68 [*AT* VII, 58f.].
33. Op. cit., 68f. [*AT* VII, 59].
34. See the Appendix, Supplement 25 (p. 237).

PART THREE

Demonstrating the Neglect of the Question of Being
as a Way of Pointing to Existence

Chapter One

Misplacing the question of the res cogitans' specific being
through care about certainty

§ 44. *Descartes' perversion of "having-oneself-with" into a
formally-ontological proposition*

Contemporary epistemology, in connection with a peculiar opposition to Aristotle, at the same time subscribes to the idea of truth in the sense of validity.
The reason for this lies in the uniform origin of this philosophical discipline
in Descartes. This orientation has led at once to the impossibility of understanding at all what Aristotle understood by truth, and then to a modification
of this being into the certum. The roots of these connections lie in Descartes
and, for this reason, the examination of the *shift over* from *verum* into *certum*
is important not only for our *question of the character of consciousness' being*,
but also for the fact that contemporary philosophy's orientation to consciousness is forced into impossibilities of a fundamental [*grundsätzlich*] sort, the
impossibilities of grasping such phenomena as spirit, life (phenomena that are
constantly lined up with consciousness), insofar as one approaches these phenomena with specific categories.

For us, the question of this shift means seeing how it indicates nothing
other than *transferring consciousness into the categorial sphere of the formally
ontological*. This transfer has the peculiar character that one believes oneself
assured of a sphere that is certain, but in such a way that, on the other hand,
one is not in a position to interrogate the sphere as to its own *character of
being*. This transfer has found precise expression in Descartes *not* insofar as
he himself takes the *cogitare* in the sense of a *matter* [*Sache*] that has been
found, but insofar, instead, as what concerns him is to have found a *proposition that is certain*. This proposition involving the cogito has for Descartes
the character of a formal-logical proposition that holds for this thing that we
can characterize, in short, as a *thing-of-thought* [*Denkding*]. A mathematical

formalization is attached to a specific condition; for the rest, the cogitatio, in terms of its structural character, is irrelevant. It is enough that the thing-of-thought yields the possibility of this proposition.

For us the further question arises: If what is found in the end-situation [of the doubt] is a proposition, a state of affairs [*Sachverhalt*] that is transferred into a proposition, how do things then stand at all with the *matter or affair itself* [*Sache selbst*] that yields this state of affairs? The state of affairs, after all, cannot be invented. If the result found is a state [*Verhalt*], then the matter that yields the state must still be visible. A motive rooted in the matter must in some sense be given for drawing this state from the matter itself. The matter itself must be seen in some sense. The positive question arises: How does Descartes come to the formulation of this state of affairs in the sense of a formal ontology? What did he find that gives him the right to set the state off in this way? We will ask ourselves: How does Descartes determine the res cogitans itself in the passage where, in the end, he takes the imaginari [imagining] and sentire [sensing] up into the res cogitans? Here what is characteristic of the res cogitans must come to the fore, what condition sentire and imaginari must satisfy in order to be taken up into the res cogitans. What is the *regional character* of the *cogitatio in general*, that justifies taking sentire and imaginari up into the realm of the res cogitans? He also encounters sentire and imaginari on the path of doubt. But he suspended both because they were encountered under the condition of being awake and dreaming. Yet, towards the end of the Meditation he takes both up again into the res cogitans. What is the peculiar feature that also transfers to sentire and imaginari the suitability of being, ultimately, "cogito"?

Descartes makes the decision at the conclusion of the Second Meditation:

Fieri enim potest ut hoc quod video non vere sit cera, fieri potest ut ne quidem oculos habeam, quibus quidquam videatur; sed fieri plane non potest cum videam, sive (quod jam non distinguo) cum cogitem me videre, ut ego ipse cogitans non aliquid sim.[1]

[For it can happen that what I see is not truly wax, it can happen that I do not have eyes to see anything; but if I see or (which I am not now distinguishing) if I think that I see, it plainly cannot happen that I, this very thinking thing, am not something.]

Equated here are *cum videam* [if I see] and *cum me videre cogitem* [if I think that I see]. Descartes sees the connection in this way: "jam non," not now [is the distinction relevant, namely,] when transferring the videre into the res cogitans is what matters to me. [In this context] sentire [to sense] is the same as cogitare me sentire [to think that I sense], cogitare [to think] is the same

1. Descartes, Meditatio II, 30 [*AT* VII, 33].

as *cogitare me cogitare* [to think that I think]. Hence, it is apparent that Descartes conceives the cogitare from the outset in this way: [it is] a peculiar being whose manner of being is in *how it has itself along with* [*Wie des Sich-mit-habens*] [i.e., along with seeing, thinking, imagining, etc.], a being that, in the course of being of a certain sort, has itself along at the same time. A phenomenon that Descartes does not explicitly fix upon is also included in this basic determination. "Cogito" does not simply mean: "I ascertain something that thinks"; instead it is a cogitare, indeed, such that I myself have this entity along with [thinking]. This determination is later designated "*self-consciousness*" or "inner consciousness" that accompanies every act of consciousness. But you see without further ado that no talk of accompanying gets at the actual fact of the matter. The being of the cogitare is a having-oneself-with [*Sich-mit-haben*]. Precisely because it is inherent in the cogitare's being to have itself in a peculiar way along with [thinking, sensing, etc.], Descartes can say: Is qui cogitat, non potest non existere dum cogitat [He who thinks is not able not to exist while he thinks].[2] Yet as long as one conceives the inner consciousness as an accompanying phenomenon that can be lacking and also not be lacking, one has not seen the factor that is decisive for Descartes. Since, however, he takes this phenomenon in the res cogitans at the same time as the basis for making out of this relation a formal-ontological, absolute relation since such a proposition is what concerns him from the beginning, he takes this connection as an opportunity for extracting and setting off a formal-ontological proposition. But the moment that one takes the content of this proposition in a formal-ontological sense, this proposition is no longer suited to its object. Rather, precisely by taking the state of affairs as the opportunity for a formal proposition, Descartes *perverts* the *specific being* of what he had earlier seen: the phenomenon of *having-oneself-with*.

If, by contrast, one takes this proposition in the sense of a *formal indication*, in such a way that it is not taken directly (where it says nothing), but is related to the respective, concrete instance of what it precisely means, then it has its legitimacy. The character of the *respectiveness* [*Jeweiligkeit*] is inherent in the cogitatio's being. Each being in the sense of existence is characterized by its respectiveness and further determined by its *temporality*, and even further by the specific type of being of this ego sum in what it has. Descartes leaves out of consideration the entire fact of the matter of the cogitatum. It is important that you see this one thing: that Descartes takes this proposition from a *specific, phenomenal reserve*, the res is set into a state of affairs in such a way that what matters is the being of the certum as veritas. With the [concern for] validity, he no longer gets at the res; it only comes into consideration in a more secondary fashion with respect to its respective manifoldness. *The sense of the "sum" is emptied into the formal-ontological sense of being-something.*

2. Descartes, *Principia philosophiae*. Pars prima, § 49, 24 [*AT* VIII, 24].

For this reason, too, Descartes' formulation "I am a thinking thing (sum res cogitans)" is appropriate for him. He says himself that he can and wants to say nothing about the "I" and "am" since the question of being in regard to the specific being of the res cogitans is from the beginning only a secondary concern of his. He has secured this attitude toward the cogito by placing the search under a specific assortment of conditions. One must keep in view that this searching doubt is not something indeterminate, something general, but rests instead upon a quite definite conception of the cogito itself, one that is placed under quite definite conditions in such a way that, from the realm of what can be found, only something quite definite is fit to be encountered by this search. Everything else that does not correspond to it [this search] falls prey to the remotio [removal].

An example of how important this peculiar structure is for Descartes can be drawn from how, along with the first thing found, he simultaneously finds the criterion for finding it:

> Sum certus me esse rem cogitantem, nunquid ergo etiam scio quid requiratur ut de aliqua re sim certus? [N]empe in hac prima cognitione nihil aliud est, quam clara quaedam et distincta perceptio ejus quod affirmo.[3]

> [I am certain that I am a thinking thing, do I not then also know what is required that I may be certain of any thing? For in this first thought there is nothing other than a specific clear and distinct perception of what I affirm.]

This cogitare [thinking] that first finds something is not only a "having-something-present," but at the same time a cognitio [knowing] in the sense of the clear and distinct illumination of the "having-present" itself, in such a way that it sees itself along with [what is seen]. It is the same phenomenon that we already saw in Thomas,[4] where Thomas clarifies the distinction between intellectus and sensus, that a different possibility of a reditio, of going back to itself, presents in the different facultates animae [faculties of the soul] and that in the case of sensus this possibility is only limited, but in the case of the intellectus becomes complete (from *Liber de causis*, going back to Aristotle).

§ 45. Summary characterization of the res cogitans found by Descartes: misplacing the possibility of access to the res cogitans' genuine being

If we now summarize: How does what Descartes found through the search that places itself under the specific rule appear, and what does it say with respect to the res cogitans' character of being?

3. Descartes, Meditatio III, 33 [*AT* VII, 35].
4. Thomas Aquinas, *De veritate*, q. 1, art. 9.

1. The being that is predicated of the res cogitans is the *esse certum* and this alone. 2. From the outset, it is not part of the tendency of searching for and determining the cogitare to question it as to its *specific* being at all. Posing this question of being is in no way part of the task of Descartes' research, although he later lays claim to this *formal being* as the absolute being. 3. Not only has the tendency of the research not posited this task, but it is precisely this search that from the beginning *blocks* the *possible path* to determining this being at all; it displaces and disguises [verstellt] the possibility that the matter is given to itself with respect to its specific being. It is instead the case that precisely this being of the res cogitans must, as it were, set aside its specific being in order to become formal and enter, as a mere something, into the proposition.

4. As to the determinations of the res cogitans' being, what is taken into consideration stems from *traditional ontology* and, indeed, the sort of ontology that was primarily not oriented at all to this context of the res cogitans' being as such. 5. What this traditional ontology takes principally as a foundation, it *no longer* has in the *original sense*; instead it has the foundation in a way that has been transformed in a quite definite way, a transformation that is most distinctly apparent in the supposition that esse means nothing other than *esse creatum*. Contained in this supposition is the notion that God's being, just like the being of the created, is conceived categorially in the same sense as esse creatum. God is merely the causa prima and absoluta of the esse creatum [the first and absolute cause of created being]. If, by contrast, one looks upon this basic ontological determination with a view to its origin, one comes to see that the ὄν ultimately says ὄν ποιούμενον, not created being in the sense of creatum esse [being created] by God, but created being instead as a phenomenon of concrete existence. The esse creatum oversteps its limits insofar as it is taken beyond the world's being. Because God's being is also taken up as actus purus into this indifferent being as esse creatum, there is from the outset nothing to keep Descartes from laying claim without further ado to this being for the res cogitans.

6. Thus, one can say that this type of determination of the res cogitans as esse creatum not only does not pose the question and, further, not only *misplaces* [verstellt] *the possibility of access to the res cogitans' genuine being*, but that this searching and finding brings to fruition in itself a quite definite *lack of a need* to inquire into the res cogitans' being. The certum esse [being certain] has priority when it comes to the predication of being. Every further question of being is determined and guided by it.

Chapter Two

Descartes' inquiry into res cogitans' being-certain and the lack
of specification of the character of being of consciousness as
the thematic field of Husserl's phenomenology

From here we are confronted with the final task of looking into how the entire
inquiry into the res cogitans' being and the answer to it hang together with
the *specification or lack of specification of the character of consciousness'*
being as the *thematic field of phenomenology.*

§ 46. *Descartes and Husserl: fundamental differences*

In considering the relationship of Husserl's work to Descartes, it is imperative
not to cling to external analogies. Doing so would give away the genuine
means of understanding what Husserl intends. It would be a mistake to identify the Husserlian doctrine with Descartes. From the outset it must be emphasized that a *fundamental difference* obtains in how Husserl grasps *consciousness content-wise,* but that, on the other hand, precisely with respect to
settling the question of consciousness' being and in regard to the *sense of the*
esse certum, Husserl moves *completely in the orbit of Descartes' sense* of it.
Indeed, today more than ever before he intends to go beyond Descartes in
order to grasp this sense in an utterly absolute manner.

We can go into the fundamental difference between Husserl and Descartes
only briefly here. We shall focus predominantly on the connection initially in
regard to something negative: 1. the region of being of *consciousness* is set
up as *absolute* without inquiry into being itself in any other sense than in the
question of *being absolutely certain;* 2. we must come to some understanding
of the *sense* of *being certain,* of the phenomenon of *evidence,* as Husserl
conceives it and conceives it much more acutely than anyone before him does.
We will have to consider briefly these two factors: setting the being of consciousness up as an absolute region of being and the idea of evidence. We
will have to consider them in order to decide to what extent the thematic field
is determined in view of its assigned role of providing the basis for all further
philosophical problems, of ultimately deciding the basic problem of reason.

It was shown what comes into consideration for Descartes in setting consciousness' being up as the point of departure that satisfies the demand of the
regula generalis; it was shown what is positively considered with respect to
its inherent content [*sachhaltiger Bestand*]. The question of what Descartes
saw in this res, what was (without a justifiable motive) [pivotal] for the for-

mation of the fundamental proposition, yielded the following: Descartes grasped the factor that each cogitare is at the same time a cogitare me cogitare [thinking myself thinking]. That Descartes sees therein a constitutive factor is apparent from the fact that precisely this basic determination is a regulative factor in terms of which it is decided whether such characters as sentire [sensing] and imaginari [imagining] are taken up into the realm of the res cogitans. From this fact it becomes clear: the res cogitans' being is the sort of being that in its being consists in having-itself-with. This givenness in the cogitare is for Descartes the fundamentum for the elevation of this specific state [*Verhalt*] in the subject matter [*Sache*] seen in this way. The state of affairs [*Sachverhalt*] that enters into the proposition: is qui cogitat, non potest non existere dum cogitat [he who thinks is not able not to exist while he thinks] is determined with respect to its being, not by the res, but by the sense of "certum." The proposition itself, the standing of the state of affairs expressed therein, is subject to the rule of the principle of contradiction, which is a rule about the compatibility of propositions. Moreover, viewed in regard to its state of affairs, it is the sort of norm that has only limited validity. The principle of contradiction is not valid absolutely, but for a quite specific regional context; it is not valid even for the formal-ontological [realm] of the pure "relations-of-something" [*Etwas-Beziehungen*]. Instead it holds only for such as are purely posited [*reine Gesetztheiten*], in the sense that they are even more formal than the "something's" [*Etwasse*].[1] I touch on this point in order to indicate that even this orientation of absolute evidence does not suffice for a radical examination of matters. The proposition "cogito sum" is the finding, having the character of the fundamentum absolutum simplex, with which Descartes reassures himself [*sich beruhigt*]. The sense of the res cogitans' being is determined by this character of being, namely, a proposition with an inherent content. The question of the res cogitans' being is settled once and for all. It no longer comes into question for Descartes because what matters much more for him is merely to proceed from this fundamentum by way of various possible classifications and to arrive on the path of the deductio at further propositions about contexts of being. In relation to the character of being of the finding into which the res cogitans is taken up, we can thus say that the foundation of being is the esse certum [to be certain]. The research tendency is formed from the outset *in such a way that it is not part of its purpose at all to pose a question of being,* to pose it in the sense that the research presents the subject of its inquiry so freely that the subject speaks from the standpoint of its own character of being. What is sought can only come into question insofar as it satisfies the sense of being that is held up to it as its standard by the search: being in the sense of esse certum. What categories of being come

1. See the Appendix, Supplement 26 (p. 239).

into question within this examination and the entire organization of sciences are categories that have been traditionally taken over and that are considered not in need of questioning. They have been taken over in a form that already distanced itself from their origin, such that the experiences from which they were drawn are no longer present. Instead they are oriented to and interpreted in other contexts of being (Christendom). The vital tendency in Descartes' case is the tendency towards justification of the sciences, towards formation of ever-new disciplines, a tendency that becomes a particularly characteristic factor in the history of the human spirit [*Geistesgeschichte*] precisely since the time of Descartes. Earlier this tendency was not known as a basic tendency, whereas today it has intensified to the point of being grotesque. What is *primarily* in question is *science* and the possibility of its establishment; *secondarily* it is the *being* of what is treated, so that the concept of being in fact comes to be determined in the following way: being is equated with being a possible domain for treatment by a science—a concept of being that is in fact decisive for Husserl.

Our inquiry into the determinations that we have given in this summary is not complete. We have to investigate the extent to which they hold for that domain of objects whose interrogation was our point of departure, namely, consciousness as the thematic field of phenomenology. We also have to investigate how this connection between Descartes and Husserl is actually to be conceived, whether it is of the sort that makes it legitimate to say in the same or even a magnified sense of "consciousness" as Husserl's thematic field what was said with regard to the res cogitans' character of being in the case of Descartes. I must insist that you keep present before you the entire inventory of what I have said in the lecture. It is supposed to be nothing less than a *proper preparation for the critical encounter* with what is set forth as the *thematic field* in *present-day phenomenology*.

Let us orient our comparative considerations on five focal points. 1. The first to be considered is the relation of the *way of doubt* to what Husserl designates as *reduction*. 2. The second is the relation between the *cogito* (Descartes) as the thematic point of departure, on the one side, and *consciousness* (Husserl) in that role, on the other. 3. The third point is the question of the character of the *absolute* with respect to the *res cogitans* and the question of the sense of the *absoluteness* of *pure consciousness*. 4. The fourth point is the connection of the *res cogitans'* character of being as an *esse creatum* with the fundamental determination of the being of *pure consciousness* as the being of an *ens regionale* [regional entity]. 5. The fifth point concerns the *ultimate, motivating context of research* in Descartes' case and the *ultimate, decisive tendencies* of the *fundamental science* as the *phenomenology* of *consciousness*.

We will orient the consideration in such a way that we first become clear about the *fundamental difference* of both positions respectively, in order to see from this vantage point how a *common* character obtains in spite of the difference in decisive connections, a common character such that it becomes apparent how Husserl, in spite of the difference, stands within the uniform, basic tendency of Cartesian research, in such a way that in him the care of knowledge is ultimately at work as *care about certainty*.

a) Descartes' way of doubt (remotio) and Husserl's reduction

Ad 1. With regard to the first point, at first glance both paths have something common, indeed, so much so that one could almost say: "The *reduction* is at bottom the same as the *remotio*." For with respect to the point of departure, both are at home in the same domain. Just like Descartes, Husserl proceeds from the "I in my surroundings." So, too, the aim of these two paths seems to be the same insofar as it is a matter of pressing forward to the cogito as absolutum. And, ultimately, the way of proceeding is the same insofar as both are carried out in the sense of a suspension: Descartes in the manner of the remotio, Husserl in the manner of the reduction. This coinciding is supported by the fact that Husserl himself explicitly refers to the Cartesian examination of doubt.

On closer look, *fundamental differences* are evident, at first merely with regard to the *aim*. Descartes wants to arrive at an absolutum in the sense that, on the basis of it, all further sciences can be justified and erected, hence, the fundamentum as the point of departure for specific series of proofs. For Husserl it is not a matter of attaining a fundamentum for all sciences but instead to find a science, a new science that not only takes the fundamentum as the point of departure but makes it the very theme of this science, the fundamentum not as the "from whence" of going further [*das "Von-wo-aus" eines Weitergehens*], but instead as the "about which" of a science [*das Worüber einer Wissenschaft*]. That means, however, that Husserl occupies a position completely different from Descartes, relative to all sciences. That means, the sense of the suspension in Descartes' remotio is fundamentally different. In the case of Descartes, it is a suspending and setting aside of specific contexts of being and the correlative manners of grasping them because they do not satisfy the regula generalis. The sciences are regarded as uncertain and what can be grasped in them is regarded as subject to deception. For Husserl the sciences are not set aside, but instead co-posited [*beigestellt*], taken up into the fundamental theme that is sought. The reduction has the positive sense of bringing the sciences and what is grasped in them into the new science's thematic domain. The reduction has the positive task, not of criticizing entities with respect to certainties and uncertainties, but instead of making them thematically suitable to treatment in the science sought.

Accordingly, the sense of the *point of departure* [*Ausgang*] of the two ways is basically different. In Descartes' case, the orientation to my surrounding world [*Umwelt*] occurs in light of the critical question whether it is a certum [certainty]. In Husserl's case, the opposite tendency is at work, the tendency not to shake up this surrounding world, not to uncover obscurities, but precisely to see the surrounding world itself in its original givenness and, along the way, to see my behavior towards it. Whether Husserl, given the manner that he carries out the observation of the surrounding world, is capable at all of seeing it is secondary. What is positive is the tendency, not to shake up but to co-posit being for the sake of the possibility of inquiring into it anew in the sense of the new science to be constituted. Thus, the reduction does not have the sense of leading to an end-situation as in Descartes' case, in such a way that the search sees itself confronted with nothing and inserted into the void of possibilities of finding. Instead the reduction develops the possibility that every merely possible being comes into view; hence, not nothing but instead the entirety of being, with a specific modification, is supposed to become thematically present.

b) Descartes' cogito and Husserl's consciousness

Ad 2. It becomes abundantly clear, already on the basis of what we have said relative to the diversity of the paths, that the *cogito* is regarded differently by Descartes than it is by Husserl. Descartes interrogates the cogito first in the position of the point of departure as "my being" with a view to whether it is a certum, a res, that satisfies the regula generalis. By contrast, Husserl does not interrogate the cogito with a view to whether it satisfies some norm; instead he sees it positively. In a positive way he seeks a basic structure and sees it in what he designates as *intentionality*. He views *consciousness* positively with respect to this decisive factor of its structure. But for the entire further problematic of consciousness, that has a definitive significance: the intentionality itself of consciousness is not some sort of condition of the ego, but instead in this "directing itself-at" [*"Sichrichten-auf"*], that at which it is directed [*das Worauf des Gerichtetseins*] is also given. Intentionality is not to be construed as a peculiarity of mental processes; instead it is to be given as a manner in which something is encountered, in such a way that what is encountered comes into view along with the encountering: the "directing itself-at" in unison with its specific "at which" [*Worauf*]. That is the fundamental sense of what, from the outset, is meant by intentionality, so that in the [phenomenological] attitude, in one with the cogitare, the cogitatum is thus given as the entity in the manner in which it is respectively encountered for the access to it and dealings with it.

With this discovery of intentionality, for the first time in the entire history of philosophy, the way is explicitly given for a radical ontological research.

Brentano and the Scholastics still proceed in fundamentally diluted and muddled versions of the problems. Husserl has, in a positive sense, seen something fundamentally new. For this reason, too, the research that makes consciousness in terms of this basic character its theme is fundamentally superior to a philosophical direction that one likes to associate with phenomenology, namely, the Austrian theory of object, that has never moved beyond an utterly primitive level of consideration. Brentano never understood what it is all about and he merely clung to the utterly trivial distinction between object and grasp. Today the Austrian school has entirely degenerated into logistics and thus become completely impotent. The fate of the theory of object also shows that it in fact never understood the necessity of an ontology, that it came to be an empty computation of relations and complexes of relations and has become unable to see when it comes to the treatment of concrete contexts of being.

The division between Husserl and Descartes is apparent precisely in what Descartes and Husserl make of the phenomenal find of the cogito me cogitare [I think that I think]. For Descartes this fundamental find becomes solely the basis for the abstraction of a formal-ontological proposition that, given its certainty-character, satisfies the certum and that as such becomes the point of departure for propositions of the same valid character that are not necessarily related to consciousness' being. For Descartes it is not a matter of taking the res cogitans up thematically. For Husserl, by contrast, this distinctive phenomenon of consciously "relating-oneself-to" becomes the point of departure for a principal conception of reflection. The fact of the matter of reflection [here is] not the fundamentum of a formal-ontological proposition but instead the instrument for the formation of the genuine path of considering things: "the phenomenological method proceeds throughout in acts of reflection."[2] One must thereby pay heed to what is reflected upon: consciousness with the basic character of intentionality. The reflection is not on mental processes, but instead on the manner of behaving toward the objective world. It is, accordingly, a fundamental error to characterize Husserlian phenomenology as "act-phenomenology" or as "transcendental psychology," in the manner that Scheler does. If one does this, one must take the concept of act in the manner that Husserl wants to have it understood. Phenomenology is precisely not directed at acts in the old sense, but instead at the entirely new domains, at the manner of "relating-oneself-to," in such a way, that that "towards which" [*Worauf*] one relates oneself is present. As long as I do not have this basis, I am not in a position in any sense to see anything like a character of being in the direct consideration of entities; indeed, I am not in a position to pursue anything like ontology. Thus, I come back to the fact that the basis for an ontological research is in fact set forth here for the first time in the history of

2. E. Husserl, *Ideen I*, § 77, 144.

philosophy, in such a way that one can move forward in the manner of scientific investigation and not in the form of mere reflection.

c) The absolutum of Descartes' res cogitans and the absoluteness of Husserl's pure consciousness

Ad 3. The *absolutum* in Descartes means nothing other than the fundamentum simplex for the beginning of the deduction. "Relative" means for Descartes everything that is deduced, everything that does not occupy the first position in the context of justification. For Husserl, "relative" means being the sort of entity that makes itself known in consciousness, the sort of entity that within consciousness has the possibility of presenting itself in consciousness itself. *Consciousness* as the *absolute being* accordingly means the very being in which every other possible being makes itself known, the sort of being that has the possibility of presenting itself in itself in consciousness. That is the sense of the consciousness towards which Husserl strives. The fact that in the development of phenomenology within the milieu of contemporary philosophy, phenomenology has reshaped itself for him into a science of reason, is a secondary question. This question does not interest us at all in this connection; here what matters to us is *to understand and further cultivate phenomenology as a possibility*. However, one can only further cultivate if one goes back to the vital roots. The determination of intentionality first enables the phenomenological method of research; for this method is possible if along with the reflection the act on which one reflects is present, [including] that at which the reflection is directed, not the natural object, but the object in the manner of its being meant. To use a trivial example, a table is not taken up into phenomenology's field of problems as this specific object, but in such a way that it is placed into consideration in terms of how it is an object [*Wie seines Gegenstandseins*]. That means that not the table (simply with regard to the capacity of experiencing it) would be present but instead that here the character of its being-real becomes present, the character that also belongs to the realm of phenomenological analysis itself.

The third factor that yields a difference is the determination of the *absolute*. We can best make this clear to ourselves through the corresponding characterization of the relativum. The cogito is the fundamentum absolutum simplex insofar as it is the beginning for the further deduction. As the beginning of the proof, the fundamentum is fundamentum for all possible objects in general. For Husserl, consciousness is not the point of departure for a chain of proofs; instead, consciousness itself is absolutum in the sense of an *extraordinary region of being*. In this sense of the absolutum lies the character of the realm of objects that fill this realm on the basis of their unique inherent content [*Sachhaltigkeit*]. For Descartes the cogito is solely the first point of departure for securing and abstracting a formal-ontological proposition. For Husserl, finding something absolutely certain from which something else could be deduced is not what matters; instead, precisely this fundamentum is the theme of a science. Not to look from the fundamentum to something else, but instead the fundamentum is the absolute theme.

d) Descartes' res cogitans as ens creatum and Husserl's pure consciousness as ens regionale

Ad 4. The difference just mentioned becomes even clearer in regard to the fourth point, the inquiry into the *character of being* of the res cogitans and consciousness. The *res cogitans* is determined as *esse creatum*. In the esse creatum, the esse verum is also given and, in Descartes' case, this falls prey to a revamping into esse certum. The res cogitans' being is grounded ultimately in the being with the character of esse creatum. Consciousness as *absolute consciousness* is determined by the fact that it is a possible region for a science or an *ens regionale*. The division between consciousness and entities, that announces itself in consciousness, is the *primordial division in any doctrine of categories*, according to Husserl. Being as consciousness is that in which every transcendent being in any sort of sense is present. What matters is that consciousness, taken in the sense of the fundamental structure of intentionality, is a possible realm of being in which each transcendent being as such makes itself known and can be traced. Husserl lays down this distinction as the ground for all further consideration of being. Being as consciousness is thereby set forth from the outset as the very being that yields a domain of subject matter [*Sachgebiet*] for the fundamental science that underlies all other sciences and in a peculiar way "justifies" them. Later we will get closer to this sense of being, i.e., being in the sense of "possible object of a science," by tracing the sense of this specification of being and its motive to the very care about certainty that led to the specification or lack of specification of the res cogitans' being. Before we do that, however, there remains the characterization of the difference in both positions with respect to their ultimate orientation.

e) The connection that ultimately motivates Descartes' research and the tendencies that are ultimately decisive for Husserl's phenomenology

Ad 5. The horizon for Descartes is the sort of horizon proper to the *Catholic system of belief*. This is not only noticeable in how Descartes lays the old ontology of High Scholasticism down as the basis for his fundamental considerations; it is explicitly evident in his dedicatory letter to the theological faculty of the Sorbonne, with which he prefaces the *Meditations*. His aim is to provide, in a scientific manner, the necessary rational foundation for the Catholic system of belief. This aim springs from an insight into the system of belief that of itself demands such a justification:

> Nam quamvis nobis fidelibus animam humanam cum corpore non interire, Deumque existere, fide credere sufficiat; certe infidelibus nulla religio, nec fere etiam ulla moralis virtus, videtur posse persuaderi, nisi prius illis ista duo ratione naturali probentur: Cumque saepe in hac vita majora vitiis quam virtutibus praemia proponantur, pauci rectum utili praeferrent, si nec Deum timerent, nec aliam vitam expectarent. Et quamvis omnino verum sit, Dei existentiam credendam esse, quoniam in sacris scripturis docetur, et vice versa credendas sacras scripturas, quoniam habentur a Deo: quia nempe, cum fides sit donum Dei, ille idem qui dat gratiam ad reliqua credenda, potest etiam dare, ut ipsum existere credamus; non tamen hoc infidelibus proponi potest, quia circulum esse judicarent.[3]

> [For although it suffices for us believers to accept as true by faith that the human soul does not die with the body and that God exists, for unbelievers they would certainly seem to be unable to be persuaded of any religion and almost any moral virtue until these two claims are proven to them by natural reason. And since in this life greater rewards are often promised to vices than to virtues, few would prefer the right to the useful if they did not fear God and did not expect another life. And although it is altogether true that God's existence should be believed because it is taught in sacred scripture and, conversely, that sacred scripture should be believed because it comes from God (since if faith is God's gift, the same one who gives grace to believe other things can also give it that we may believe him to exist), this can, nevertheless, not be proposed to infidels since they would judge it to be circular.]

The existence of God must be established in accordance with reason so that someone standing outside the faith has motives for subjecting himself to the rule of faith. Descartes undertakes this meditation in the sense of this task and, indeed, with the claim of believing himself to have given in the meditation completely valid proofs of God's existence and the immortality of the soul for the first time. This entire complex of the two basic elements of belief is called the praeambula fidei [the preamble of faith]. Descartes even appeals here to a Council. One cannot make the aim of the meditation clearer than Descartes does here. Of secondary significance thereby is the question of the extent to which Descartes wrote the letter to the Sorbonne out of fear of the stake.

By contrast, Husserl's *more fundamental* examination that is meant to be constitutive in the investigation of consciousness as absolute being is undertaken with the aim of laying the foundation for an absolute *science of reason*, based upon itself, with the absolute justification of reason, [and] of establish-

---

3. Descartes, *Meditationes de prima philosophia*, Dedicatory Letter, 2f. [*AT* VII, 1].

ing the rules for a perfectly free development of humanity. That does not exclude the possibility that remains of the old metaphysics tacitly play along in this undertaking. But the basic orientation of Husserl is fundamentally different [from Descartes'] and, from this vantage point, so, too, is the foundation insofar as it is effective as the ultimate determination of the being of the objects spoken of.

§ 47. Husserl and Descartes: connection and uniform basic tendency in the care about certainty

These differences that on closer examination jump before our eyes do not, however, prevent what has been said about the *specification of res cogitans' being* from being extended to the supposition of *consciousness* as the thematic field of phenomenology; indeed, they even demand it. Moreover, it is all the more required since the *same care of knowledge* is at work in the supposition and development of the thematic field of consciousness. Here, care has taken leave of its origin and stands on a higher level of movement, it has *diverted and obstructed even more radically* the possibilities of encountering the *specific* being of consciousness.

a) Undiscussed appropriation of the cogito sum

Three situations are characteristic: 1. It is necessary to heed the fact that although the reduction, in view of its methodic sense, is fundamentally different from the path of doubt, it presupposes for itself precisely the result of the path of doubt in the sense of something self-evident. The proposition "cogito sum," that emerges from the end-situation of the path of doubt, is now taken simply as a triviality and thus laid claim to at the outset of the reduction. This triviality is mediated by the prevailing psychology and epistemology insofar as they stand under the particular influence of English philosophy (which goes directly back to Descartes), but insofar as this philosophy makes consciousness itself the theme as immediately given. The *cogito sum* is not only *not discussed*, but is *taken over as self-evident* in Husserl's case. Consciousness is the point of departure towards which, without being further questioned at all, the entire reduction is oriented.

b) Explicitly laying claim to the certitudo for the absolute region of being

2. It is not only that the cogito is taken over as a triviality without being discussed. The self-evident character is expanded in a principal sense insofar as [Husserl] now explicitly lays claim to this *certitudo*, not only for a deter-

minate formal-ontological proposition erected on the cogito or for the individual cogitationes, but instead for this particular realm of objects as such in
its entirety. The cogito is now set up as the explicit norm for the comprehension of this *absolute region of being* itself. The self-evident character is thus
expanded at the same time in this principal sense.

c) The uprooting that occurs in taking over the cogito
sum as the certum for the process of setting up consciousness' absolute
self-evidence as the nucleus

3. This process of taking over the cogito sum is carried out in a manner that
explicitly abandons the basis on which the certum esse's sense and legitimacy
rests. It simply falls into forgetfulness, not merely in Husserl's case but already
in the course of the entire philosophy following upon Descartes. There is *no
longer any acquaintance* at all with the entire *ontological, basic framework*
as such. One is explicit about not wanting to know anything more about this.
The cogito sum is free-floating. While Descartes had still tried to prove his
criterion by tracing it back to God's absolute being, one renounces this today
and demands the absolute self-evidence of this criterion itself. This development is expressed most incisively in a remark by Husserl (in a seminar exercise): "If Descartes had remained at the second Meditation, he would have
come to phenomenology." That is to say, if Descartes would have forgotten
the entire basic context of being, in which the cogito is in general justified,
then what phenomenology today wants would have remained. The remark is
not made on the basis of a clear insight into the historical contexts, but on
the basis of a rejection of talk of God and the soul right at the outset of the
philosophy. What *phenomenology* itself wants reveals itself therein: *setting
consciousness up as the nucleus* [*die Ansetzung des Bewußtseins*] in the sense
of *taking up the cogito sum as certum* in the manner of something self-evident
and in the form of a principal expansion and in the manner of an *uprooting*,
determined in such a way that the thus motivated process of setting consciousness up springs from *care about certainty*.

d) Care about certainty as care about the formation of science

The *care about certainty* is here a *care about the formation of science*. [I have
in mind] the transformation and new development of science based on a science held up as a model, the transformation of Cartesian psychology and
epistemology into the fundamental science of the phenomenology of consciousness. At the same time, it becomes obvious that what is primary for
this care in the sense of the formation of science is to acquire a domain of
subject matter [*Sachgebiet*] for possible scientific treatment. From the outset,

every entity is conceived and determined in terms of its suitability as a domain of subject matter for a science concerning it. Thus, in the same sense the possibility of encountering the entity *as an entity* in its *character of being* is misplaced insofar as the entity is encountered as the possible region of a science. In contrast to this, it would, of course, first have to be asked whether the domains of subject matter presented by the traditional scientific disciplines have a genuine origin in the world of being to which they allegedly intend to apply. The thematization has to be undone, it is necessary to inquire into the *specific* being as such. It is necessary to interrogate whether this being is in need of the kind of development for a science applying to it. Only in this way is it possible to speak of a possible constitution of new sciences.[4] But, now, insofar as the remarkable situation obtains for us today that all domains of life and worlds of being are theorized in a peculiar way by virtue of the dominance of the care about the formation of science, the basic task arises of first going back behind this theorizing in order to *gather anew from existence itself the possible basic position.*

---

4. See the Appendix, Supplement 27 (p. 239).

Chapter Three

Husserl's more primordial neglect of the question of being,
opposite the thematic field of phenomenology, and the task of
seeing and explicating existence in its being

§ 48. *Husserl's mangling of phenomenological finds through the care,
derived from Descartes, about certainty*

The tendency at work in Husserl brings with it further fatal determinations
precisely for what was brought to light by him in phenomenological research.
Moreover, they are fatal because this achievement is mangled by an interpretation of the results in terms of the *care about certainty* and what it is concerned about. We will have to consider these *manglings* in three respects: 1.
in regard to *intentionality* itself, 2. in regard to the conception of *evidence*,
and 3. in regard to the determination of phenomenological research as *eidetic*.

These three features show that, in spite of Husserl's accomplishment, the
cogito sum and its certitudo are in fact at work in a much more fundamental
sense in him, such that here it comes *less than ever* to an *explicit inquiry* into
the character of consciousness' being. Instead all interest here is diverted
directly to forming a basic science and to considering the entity from the
outset with a view to its suitability as the theme of this basic science. Being
in the sense of *being a region for science* misplaces more than ever the possibility of letting the entity be encountered in its character of being.

This tendency (grounded in the dominance of today's idea of science) must
be *reversed*, insofar as it is necessary to see that this point of departure is not
an original one. The concept of consciousness has in fact been simply taken
over by Husserl from Cartesian psychology and Kantian epistemology. Taken
over with it is the entire set of the fundamental categories in which consciousness is characterized, categories which, for their part, do not owe their
origin to an analysis of this being in the sense of an inquiry into its specific
character of being.

Accordingly, insofar as the task of making consciousness the theme rightly
obtains, it must first be asked: What is the specific being that is made here
into the domain of a subject matter [*Sachgebiet*]?[1] From this vantage point,
from the correct examination of the tendency of a correct theme, the path thus
also leads back to the necessity of determining a region's inherent content

1. See the Appendix, Supplement 28 (p 239).

through a *return to its pre-regional character*. This tendency springs from the dominance of the care about certainty in a specific type of exercise of care about the development of science.

a) Intentionality as specific, theoretical behavior

The same care about certainty leads, then, to *mangling* in a peculiar way what—in spite of all this bracketing in a traditional respect—was *positively* accomplished in phenomenology. It leads to this: 1. with respect to *intentionality* insofar as this is always construed (less explicitly than implicitly) as *specific theoretical* behavior. Characteristically, intentionality is translated for the most part as meaning, intending something [*Meinen*]; one speaks of willing, loving, hating, and so forth as meaning something. Through this fixing of usage, a definite prefiguration of perspective creeps into every intentional analysis. This is explicitly evident from the fact that it is expressly claimed that for every intentional context of a complicated sort, *theoretically meaning something* forms the *foundation*, that each judgment, each instance of wanting, each instance of loving is founded upon a *presenting* [*Vorstellen*] that provides in advance what can be wanted, what is detestable and loveable. This transformation lies in the fact that the prevailing study of intentionality is itself oriented to the *intentional in knowing*. It is a methodical misunderstanding to make the investigation of emotional experiences simply analogous to knowing. This misunderstanding is characteristic, since it involves taking up structures that are acquired directly from an examination in a completely different direction. Even the entity, insofar as it is to be studied principally in its immediate givenness, is taken in terms of the specific *theoretical conception* of it. The entity is exemplified by a real entity qua thing. As the foundation of all the various possibilities of being, this entity qua thing-of-nature alone becomes the substratum for the determination of culture, history, and so forth, in such a way that being in the sense of nature is accorded the character of a value. Thus, even within the *erection of the regions of being* the predominance of care about certainty is apparent in the attitude toward theoretical knowledge of nature.

b) Evidence as theoretical knowing's evidence in grasping and determining

2. [The second way that care about certainty leads to mangling what is accomplished in phenomenology is] in the interpretation of *evidence*. Within the method of phenomenology, evidence plays a fundamental role, not least on the basis of the connection with Descartes' cogito. It should be said that what Husserl says about evidence is far superior to everything else that has ever

been said about it and that he has placed the matter on a suitable basis for the first time.[2] Evidence is ultimately interpreted in terms of its manner of being accomplished as a coincidence of what is meant and what is grasped in itself. This way of bringing what is meant to where it coincides with something intuitively given constitutes the evidence. The evidence itself is normatively determined by indisputability and disputability, analogous to the way the cogito sum is normatively determined by the principle of contradiction. Evidence is a *specific sort of evidence for grasping and determining*, a specific sort of evidence that is transposed, by way of analogy, to the remaining manners of behavior and their evidence. It is transposed in such a way that Husserl sees that each object-domain, corresponding to its inherent content, has a specific sort of evidence. By contrast, the *genuine* question of evidence in a fundamental sense first begins with the question of the *specific* evidence of the access to a being [*Sein*] and of the disclosing of this entity [*Seiende*], of holding onto and keeping to a being that has become accessible. Only within this phenomenon, so conceived, does the theoretical evidence have its place. Evidence is determined for Husserl by his concept of truth.

c) Eidetic reduction of pure consciousness under the guidance of ontological determinations alien to consciousness

3. [As for the third way that care about certainty leads to mangling what is accomplished in phenomenology,] the predominance of care about certainty is apparent in that the account, in reference to the thematic field of "consciousness," remains with the determinations of *traditional ontology*, indeed, even further, with those of *formal logic*. Insofar as the domain of pure consciousness is gained in the process of going through the transcendental reduction, it is, first as pure consciousness, simply the uniqueness of the stream of consciousness of a definite individual being. But, as such, it is not yet really the possible domain of a science. Acquiring scientific propositions is what matters, not speaking of this or that pure consciousness. Pure consciousness in general needs to be determined. Transcendental consciousness falls prey to a further *reduction*, the *eidetic*. The *generic characters* of various experiences are to be established; consciousness in general is to be determined by the basic character of "intentionality" and then the various *basic genera*. The methodical division is guided by the *ontological determinations*: *genus, species, eidetic singularity, specific difference*—*categories* that have their definite basis and *have nothing to say about such a being as consciousness*. Given this predominance of the care about certainty, it is not surprising that, in the course of the formation of the method of investigation of pure consciousness,

---

2. See the Appendix, Supplement 29 (p. 240).

something like the idea of the mathesis of experiences became possible. This fact alone shows how robustly alive the Cartesian bent of science is. In the *Ideas* Husserl leaves up in the air the question of whether the descriptions of pure consciousness are possible by means of a mathesis of experiences.[3] Today it has become factical and all the intensity of the Husserlian work is concentrated on still finding a much more radical point of departure in the cogito than Descartes was able to, with the aim, beginning from there, of finding the mathesis of experiences and determining the pure possibilities of experiences purely a priori. The phenomenological principle "To the matters themselves!" has undergone a *quite definite interpretation*. "To the matters themselves" means "to them insofar as they come into question as the theme of a science." Thus, it is evident here that he misplaces and distorts for himself [*sich selbst verstellt*] what he wants insofar as the examination is limited to the field of the regional characters of the entity itself.

Accordingly, through the supposition of consciousness as the thematic field of phenomenological research in the genuine sense, what every philosophy is after is misplaced and distorted [*verstellt*]. Consciousness is a region of experiences. Life itself as the entire set of experiences is determined as the region of these individual facts, in the sense of the region of a subject matter. It does not come to understanding *life itself in its genuine being* and answering the *question of its character of being*. Every philosophy of humanity, every philosophy of spirit, life, culture is a singular *lucus a non lucendo* [clearing by not clearing]. One wants to make a philosophy about existence without inquiring into it itself.

§ 49. Investigation of the history of the origin of the categories as a presupposition for seeing and determining existence

It could be said, on the one hand, that the steps taken to gain this insight of ours have been rather roundabout and, on the other hand, that the sum result is rather meager. In regard to this last point it should be said that it would be a misunderstanding if one were to understand the discernment of the demonstrated neglect as a sum result. Simply to acquire a view of Husserl's standpoint would be the most irrelevant matter in the world. What matter are the underlying states of affairs. It is necessary not to let go of one fact of the matter, namely, that the treatments of what one today sets up in a decisive sense as philosophy's theme are subject to the powerful force of a specific tendency and that it hardly suffices, even within phenomenology, to appeal to merely looking at and devoting oneself to the subject matters. It could be that

3. E. Husserl, *Ideen I*, 141.

all that is burdened down by a plethora of prejudices. In order to get *at the matters themselves*, they must be *freed up* and the very process of freeing them up is not one of a momentary exuberance, but of fundamental research. *The seeing must be educated* and this is a task so difficult that it is hard for it to be overemphasized since we are, like no other time, saturated by history and are even aware of the manifoldness of history.

The preparation for gaining insight into the neglect is far from exhausted since we have pursued only *one* thread: knowing and the care of knowing or, better, its correlate: truth. These connections remain the ones most easily accessible to us today. Much more difficult, however, is the connection that obtains between a human's *nontheoretical being* and what one designates as *bonum*. It is not as though one could simply examine these connections in analogous fashion; here completely different connections, Christian theology and the formation of dogma, come into question. It is evident also that, just as the ἀληθές deteriorated [*verfiel*] into the *verum* and *certum*, so the ἀγαθόν undergoes a characteristic process of deterioration [*Verfallsprozeß*] even into the present age, where it is determined as *value*. I will set forth what is most important about these connections in the lectures on Augustine and, indeed, in the analysis of the Augustinian concepts of summum bonum, fides, timor castus, gaudium, peccatum, delectatio [highest good, faith, pious fear, joy, sin, pleasure]. The various possibilities are centered in *Augustine* in such a way that powerful forces proceed from them to the Middle Ages and to modernity.

But even this history of deterioration is not sufficient to get us in the right place to see the connections which we have been talking about. Both basic determinations must be traced back to *Greek ontology* and this itself must be taken into consideration insofar as it forms a definite psychology, a doctrine of life, or however one might designate it. Only research oriented in so fundamental a way, research of the specific *history of the origin of the categories* will put us in the position to see and categorially determine *existence as such* on the basis of *concrete experiences*, free from categorial determinations that emerge in a completely different field. You see yourselves that what we have gained is in fact something slight and it would be a misunderstanding to take what we have gained in the sense of a philosophy. It is not a matter of gaining a philosophy; whoever wants that is to be advised to avoid seriously the paths of this research. The research itself (that sets this task for itself) stands outside what one designates as philosophy in the customary sense. This research sets for itself solely the task of forming the *basis* for something of this sort. In this task, it is in the constant danger of coming to naught and failing.

If what has been worked over is thus negative in a quite definite sense, then it must also be said that, in spite of this, something positive was gained by way of the demonstration of neglect. We have conducted the demonstration of neglect by way of pointing to the specific character of care and care determined as a manner of existing. Even this positive outcome initially comes into consideration only as a contribution to the clarification of the specific situation of the interpretation. The more transparent the situation becomes, on the basis of which the interpretation is made, the more the possibility grows of setting aright and seeing the historical.

§ 50. Retrieval of the characteristics of the care of knowing that have been run through and pointing to existence itself in terms of some fundamental determinations

We want to try to sum up what we have gained in the course of the examination with respect to the *being of care* and to recapitulate what is divulged in the diverse *characters of care* as a manner of being of existing as such. We also want to recapitulate what we have seen in these characters of care, in particular, the *care of knowledge*, with regard to *existence's character of being*. In connection with this summary and broader interpretation of care as a way of existing, we will hit upon a fundamental connection between the being of care itself and what is cared for by this care, what is genuinely under its care: existing as such. By this means we will acquire a more primordial conception of the connection that we already encountered in Descartes, construed in a hasty and formal way, namely, that consciousness is an entity that is in the manner of *having-itself-with*. Husserl takes this fact of the matter as the basis for the elaboration of the path, the method of phenomenological research itself. We see therein a peculiar determination of care's being and, with it, existence itself insofar as care is a manner of existing.

In phenomenology's call "to the matters themselves," "matter" means an entity insofar as it is encountered as characteristic of a possible region for a science. Each entity is seen through science; the aesthetic, for example, through the history of art just as it is capable of being there in the form of an object. Thus, the principle seemingly has a radical tendency. In the way that it is *interpreted*, however, it blocks the path and does not open it up. How one might open existence up is not something self-evident nor is it given without further ado by virtue of the fact that one sets aside easily detectable prejudices. The task correspondingly arises of *explicating existence in its being* but of first developing and securing the standpoint for this task itself. This task is not methodical research but research of a concrete sort. In this introductory examination we have endeavored from the outset to direct our view to a specific phenomenon of existence, namely, *knowing*, and we have specified it as the care of knowing. The characterization of the various concepts of truth (from being in the manner of being-uncovered to being-true in the sense of a value and its explication) is connected to the being, for which truth holds as a proposition and a validity. That is a strand of the basic phenomenon that has remained in focus from the outset and is designated "existence."

A far more important stretch of research refers to the ἀγαθόν. The extent to which these connections are gained by looking at existence needs to be submitted to a critical examination. For their part, these two investigations oriented to ἀγαθόν and ἀληθές are to be brought back into a more primordial context of being, the context of what was treated by Greek ontology. Insofar as all investigations are traced back in this direction and, hence, ultimately to the way human beings are, one can also designate this process as anthropology. However, if one so designates it, then it is not in the sense of Dilthey's analysis through historical expositions, but instead in the sense of an investigation that is principally set on categorial connections. When we attempt *to retrieve what we have run through,* and do so in such a way that we direct our attention explicitly at the care to know as a manner of existing and thereby at existence itself; and when we take heed of the extent to which the characters explicated in regard to caring are determined as characteristic of existence's being; we are retrieving the path in the sense that we take the *demonstration of neglect as a means of pointing to existence itself in terms of its fundamental determinations.* What emerges in the course of this demonstration should not be sought as a sum result and theory. Instead, the genuine and sole way of deliberating on what has been gained consists in rendering it fruitful for the cultivation of the soil in which the concrete research is to be conducted, to sharpen the eye for what stands before it, to interrogate existence with regard to its categories of being. The more primordially the situation develops of itself and becomes transparent to itself, the more apparent and comprehensible it becomes what should be submitted to an interpretation. What we set forth should be taken solely in this methodical sense. That is to say, that we have specified care by way of formally indicating it as a manner of existing. Care is taken in a specific, concrete instance as the care about knowledge. We must now concretely envision these two determinations: *care as a manner of existing in the care of knowing.*

a) Three groups of characters of care about already known knowledge and their determination as a unity

For this purpose let us limit ourselves to *one* character of care's being, a character that we have gained in the course of demonstrating the fundamental character of caring: the being of care about certainty as a *disclosing-being.* We will interpret the established caring-characters as characters of existing, solely in relation to this fundamental character. It may be recalled, that 1. *being-disclosive* was taken as the primary movement of the care about certainty; [and that the other characters included] 2. *holding on to* what was disclosed; 3. *shaping, elaborating* what was held onto; 4. *committing oneself* to what was elaborated; and 5. *losing oneself* in what the care has committed itself to.[4]

We saw earlier how the care about certainty can be characterized as *neglect* and *ensnarement*, that the care about certainty keeps to a peculiar movement and that in the movement existing gets out of the way. We left the interpretation at this level. We did not pass on to seeing the character of neglect and that of ensnarement on the part of existing. What now matters is to highlight care about certainty in its concrete movement as a disclosive-being with respect to its *specific characters of caring* and to understand them as characters of existence's being. The interpretation that is now to be given has a shortcoming in that it is expressed one-sidedly without the concrete connections that must be brought into view from the interpretation of ἀγαθόν.

The characters of care that have emerged from the interpretation of the care about certainty, insofar as it is disclosive, may be recounted as follows. Three of them have already been unpacked, but in the subsequent course of the examination we tabled elaboration of the remaining characteristics.

The *first group* is: the way that the care about certainty in its regimentation *oversteps itself* [its limits], a self-exceeding that *mistakes itself*. Given along with these determinations is a *tranquilizing* [a calming reassurance: *Beruhigung*] insofar as the certum esse as a possibility of being is diverted to the esse creatum as bonum and, with this, is assured through being-created. The fourth character is that of the *masking*.

The *second group* encompasses the characteristics of *misplacing*, of the *rise of the needlessness* of inquiry into being's character, and of the *falling prey* [*Verfallen*].

The *third group* encompasses the characteristics of *obstructing* and *diverting*.

Each of these three groups leads back to *a specific character* of the way that the care about certainty is.

α) Overstepping oneself, mistaking-oneself, tranquilizing,
and masking as remoteness from being

Ad 1. In the first group, the mounting care about certainty shows itself in such a way that it detours into a quite specific way station which we may specify as its *remoteness from being*. What primarily matters to the care about certainty is, namely, *validity* and a *binding character*. But what something is valid of, the entity itself, does not come primarily into view, it is not given

---

4. [This translation departs from the original German "das *Sichverlieren* an das, was der Sorge sich verschrieben hat" for which the literal translation is: "losing oneself in what has committed itself to the care."—D.D.]

its due. Yet at the same time the manner of being of knowing in itself is not interrogated as to its being and is not deeply unsettled in its being. It looks as though that would be the case and precisely the search [for an indubitable first principle] makes it appear so. Yet this eversio [overturning], this appearance of deeply unsettling every possibility of knowledge, is carried out on the basis of its *foregoing tranquilizing*, in that the certum esse is secured as bonum. The eversio and the passage through the path of doubt is the peculiar *masking* that the care about certainty provides itself as though a radical founding in fact mattered to it. By means of this masking, care transports itself wherever it wants. It gives itself the look of being radically scientific, concerned with the formation of science, understood as universal validity and what is universally binding on every entity. The care about certainty thus abides in the manner of the masking, in the binding character of what can be publicly and currently said about an entity, without primarily envisioning the entity as such. Everything is seen in the idea of science, reformation of science in the idea of the certum. I characterize this way station of care as its *remoteness from being*, remote both from the *world's being* and, even more, from *existence's being as such*.

β) Misplacing, rise of needlessness, and falling prey
as the absence of existence's temporality

Ad 2. The *misplacing* and the *rise of needlessness*, which the factor of neglect contains in itself, portray a new factor of care's being. Thanks to the way that the care about certainty resides in the validity and the concern for binding propositions, and thanks to the science that thus comes to renown, the access to being is definitively *misplaced and disguised* [*verstellt*] insofar as it is taken as passing through science. As a result, care, residing in this manner, from the outset becomes *devoid of need* in the sense that it does not interrogate at all what it works with (the entire fundamentum of ancient ontology) as to its suitability and its origin; it does not inquire at all into the suitability of what this care again and again sets as its task. That means, however, that the tradition is not itself seen *as* tradition at all. If *what* a tradition befalls and *how* it does so are kept in view, then the tradition is explicit. Insofar as that is not the case and the traditional is taken over in such a way that the entire work of founding is taken over, it is apparent that the tradition has been lost sight of. Insofar as the tradition comes from the past and the visibility of the past is lacking in the present and does not come to life, the *temporality of existence remains absent* in various respects. This is apparent from the fact that Descartes grasps the cogito solely as a res cogitans, as a multitude of cogitationes, a multitude of matters tied together by the ego, without so much as the slightest talk of a *temporal stretch between birth and death*. The care of certainty as the care about certainty is at the same time a concern that temporality remain absent. That means, however, not encountering existence as such. The care about certainty is a *misplacing* of being.

γ) Obstructing and diverting as leveling being

Ad 3. Next to the remoteness from being and the absence of temporality, the last-named group, the *obstructing* and the *diverting*, provide a third determination of the being of the care about certainty: the *leveling of being*. Insofar as the care about certainty as care about validity and the binding character of a proposition reside in the formation of science, entities are conceived as a definite totality of possible regions, which can be reached through an assortment of sciences. From the outset, all being is set upon as an assortment of regions of being, reachable by valid propositions. In the process existence as such is transported into the same uniform field of being that the entities belong to. By this means, in an explicit sense and, indeed, in the context of scientific care, the care about certainty *obstructs* the possibility that the being of existence could be encountered in its own possibility, in keeping with the way it is, *prior* to this primary classification. Care about certainty *diverts* every question about being into a question about being-an-object for science. Within this direction of the basic question, every question of being is decided. In relation to existence, this means that the very care about certainty pounds every being down to one and the same level.

b) Flight of existence in the face of itself and the uncoveredness
of its being-in-a-world, burying any possibility of encountering it,
distorting as a basic movement of existence

These three characters: the *remoteness from being*, the *absence of temporality*, and the *leveling* are to be viewed together in one as a *basic determination of existence itself*. What needs to be asked is how existence is apparent as such in this determination. 1. These three characters of the care about certainty (certainty itself as a manner of existence) divulge existence as something that *flees in the face of itself*, so that, on the run from itself, it also procures the possibility of concealing existence [takes care to be able to conceal existence: *die Möglichkeit des Verdeckens des Daseins mitbesorgt*]. 2. Existence flees in the face of itself and *buries its possibilities of encountering itself*. In this basic movement of existence, the basic finding, discussed earlier, is now apparent. It is apparent that the care, insofar as it is bent on something that it takes care of, takes care of its own existence as well in the course of taking care of something. And here, of course, in the manner of the flight in the face of existence, it also takes care to bury existence itself, to render an encounter with it impossible. Taking care of care's being in the course of being bent on something by caring, that is the same phenomenon that Descartes took as cogito me cogitare and the occasion for a formal-ontological proposition, that Husserl developed as the reflection, as the particular path of access to consciousness. For us, a peculiar, *basic movement* of existence itself is apparent therein. Yet this movement holds for each concrete care. This basic character that is one of the orientation points for a fundamental interpretation of existence, may be characterized terminologically as *distorting* [*Verdrehen*]. What this is supposed to say is that, from the outset, existence cannot be *primarily* taken in any sense at all through the phenomenon of intentionality. From the outset, the phenomenon of intentionality is directed at seeing something in a direction towards something.

We want now to make clearer to ourselves what it means that the structure of being of existence lies in the structure of distorting. We intend to do this by conceiving more incisively what can be gathered from the specific movement of being as being-on-the-run from [taking flight in the face of: *Auf-der-Flucht-sein*] itself. Insofar as it is a matter here of the care about certainty and certainty is bent on grasping the world, that means that every manner of being bent on something by way of grasping it, every instance of determining what the world is, is always in some sense a way of co-determining the manner of being of knowing as such, whether explicitly or not. Each being qua grasping, each knowing is, when seen in terms of the basic distorting phenomenon, an interpretation of existence itself. That is to say, however, that existence's being (in the sense of the manner of being of care about certainty) flees in the face of itself with respect to being known, with respect to its being interpreted. What care flees is existence inasmuch as it can be known and interpreted. Being in the sense of *being-in-a-world* means *being-uncovered*, standing *visibly* in a world. It is in the face of the *uncoveredness of existence* that care takes flight. An attempt that did not come to fruition is the ἀληθές of Greek ontology. This ἀληθές is the Greeks' glimpse into the uncoveredness, but it was in turn concealed by the Greeks themselves. We want to envision what it means that existence flees in the face of itself and, indeed, with regard to its basic determination of *being-uncovered*, of *visibly being-in-the-world*. At the same time, the phenomenon of uncoveredness will provide an opportunity to conceive even more incisively the extent to which *historicity* is a basic determination of existence itself.

What must be shown is how, on the basis of the established characters of caring, specific factors in the way that existence itself is moved can be determined and, indeed, determined in relation to itself. We have divided the characters of caring as the care about certainty into three groups and have read a *specific movement* off from each of these three groups. Knowing's manner of being as care about certainty resides in a peculiar remoteness from being, that is to say, in a position that does not let this knowing, so characterized, come near its own being, but instead interrogates every entity with respect to its character of possibly being certain. The care to know as the care about certainty tranquilizes [comforts and reassures, sedates: *beruhigt*] itself with this very certainty. The second group [comprises] the misplacing, the development of the characteristics of needlessness, the movement of care as the absence of temporality. The characteristic factor in this connection is this being's relation to tradition. What matters to this care of knowing is finding a foundation and yet it is precisely this care that takes over without any further criticism the entire stock of ontological determinations that provide the ground for the being of this care itself. Thus the entire tradition reveals itself, the tradition out of which the care of knowing has developed this ideal of science as something no longer acquired in a primordial sense. Insofar as the explicit appropriation of the tradition is absent, it means that knowing itself, in being, is not clear about its own possibilities of being. For only where a being sees itself in its setting, can the tradition that befalls it, become explicit. The final group of characteristics then determines the broader factor of the movement, the factor that we characterize as the leveling of being. Every entity is seen in terms of one uniform, basic level of being and the decisive interest is dictated by science, by the system of science. Entities are seen from the perspective of the idea of the system of science. From this vantage point, entities are divided up into an assortment of regions. By this means, every determination of being and, in particular, that of existence already moves on a level that is no longer suitable for a genuine inquiry into being, but instead is bent solely on conceptualities and propositions about them. These characters typify knowing's being, namely, knowing's being as a manner of existing.

Insofar as knowing in the respects mentioned is remote from the entities as such and, in particular, from the being of existence (hence, from itself), this manner of being moved characterizes the movement of existence's flight in the face of itself. This movement of existence's flight in the face of itself is not one that simply moves away from existence into the specific residence of science. Together with this flight in face of itself, existence is concerned with displacing itself. Existence's encounter with itself qua existence is made impossible by this ontology. Concern for the idea of science shapes a specific ontology which is clung to as the sole possibility of interrogating existence. The tendency [is] towards burying existence itself.

With the characterization of this "flight" factor of existence, a basic phenomenon of existence is revealed, one that I designate "the distorting." Inherent in this phenomenon is the fact that being in the sense of existence is not characterized by a [structure like] "something relates to something" [or] I behave towards [or relate to: *mich verhalte*] an object. Rather, this phenomenon says that the entity that one intends to capture with "consciousness" is the sort of thing that, in being positioned towards the world, is also concerned with its own existence. It is not necessary that an explicit reflection on the

"I" appear. A concern for existing itself lies in the matter that one pursues. Where the reflection is lacking, the phenomenon reveals itself in the sense most proper to it. Precisely then it becomes apparent that this distorting is a way in which the genuine being of care is included in the object of concern; it becomes apparent from the fact that it [the object of concern] pervades existence in its being. It is existence itself in the sense of this being. We are fighting here with a particular difficulty in our language since existence *is* the sort of being that, if it is to be determined in an ontologically adequate way, basically cannot be determined as a being that one *has*, but instead as that very being that one *is*. Therein lies already a completely specific interpretation of the entity as the entity existing and, indeed, this character shows a possibility of existence's being. The entity that one *is*, is the entity that bears within itself the possibility of becoming "I am." This possibility, however, does not need to lie explicitly in existence; indeed, existence is bent on blocking this possibility.

This basic phenomenon of distorting, a basic phenomenon that has long been determined as reflection, is seen here concretely and, indeed, in terms of a preview of the structure of existence's being as such. For us this phenomenon has the character of a methodic clue, insofar as, viewed from its vantage point, the basic character of consciousness, the *intentionality*, is cut down to size and led back to its limits, to the *limits of its interpretative function*. At the same time this phenomenon is the structural ground on which such phenomena as joy, terror, sadness, anxiety can be explicated—phenomena that are overlooked if they are determined as intentionality. I cannot grasp the phenomenon of anxiety as a manner of being-related-to-something; it is instead a phenomenon of existence itself.

c) Facticity, threat, eeriness, everydayness

With respect to the concrete basic situation it is important that one keep in view the ground for the *further development* and *characterization* of the movement of the care about certainty as existence's flight in the face of itself by way of concealing. The care about certainty flees in the face of existence insofar as it is possible for existence to be known. The flight of knowing in the face of existence itself is the flight of knowledge in the face of existence with respect to its possibility of being *transparent, interpreted, uncovered*. Existence *is* in this character of being-uncovered, it is being in a world. This phenomenon has the character-of-being of an entity that is in the manner of being-in-a-world as being in the here [*Da*]. We also say of a stone: "it is here," but it is here in the vicinity of my world, in the vicinity of my being that is in the world in the manner of *having the world in view* [*in der Weise des die Welt Sichtig-habens*]. "Having in view" means that *the* entity that is in the world is in view along with it [*Mit-sichtig-sein*]. This *being-in-view-along-with-the-world* is expressed in the *here* [*Da*]. Existence [*Dasein*] is here and now, in its respectiveness [*Jeweiligkeit*], it is *factical*. The *facticity* is not a concrete instance of some universal, but instead the primordial determination of its specific being qua existence.

If we look closer at the phenomenon of existence's flight in the face of itself in the manner of *concealing*, as the sense of existence is interpreted in this flight of being in the face of itself, it is apparent that existence is of the sort that *resists itself*. This manner of defending-itself-against-itself is not a contingency of existence but instead constitutes its being. What it defends itself against, the *threat*, lies in existence itself. The threat against which existence defends itself, lies in the fact that it *is*. *That it is* is the threat of existence itself. We see this phenomenon of the threat, with regard to resisting itself in the manner of the flight and the concealing, in the particular limitation of care about certainty.

If we now pose the question of what it is that existence defends itself against and what the threat actually is in the face of which existence flees, we then take the index for our consideration from the *direction* of the flight and fleeing's manner of being. Care about certainty characterizes existence's being as such and, as far as it is concerned, what needs to be done is to disappear in some *tranquilizing*, some *comforting reassurance*. In this tendency of the care about certainty lies the care one takes to tranquilize the being of knowing itself. To make matters concretely visible, we must draw on the second possibility: the *care of curiosity*, that very care of knowing that has been the guide of Greek knowing in particular. In knowing, what matters is *becoming at home with an entity*, of being at home with it in a manner of existing that has been secured. That is to say, however, that insofar as a familiarity [with entities] in the world is what the flight flees towards [*wohin*], that *in the face of which* [*Wovor*] existence *flees* by way of the *care about certainty*, is an *eeriness* [a state of not being at home: *Unheimlichkeit*]. Eeriness is the genuine threat that existence is subject to. Eeriness is the threat that is in existence of itself. Eeriness displays itself in the *everydayness* of existence. This phenomenon of eeriness has nothing to do with loneliness, with an inability to take part that prevents one from this and that. As soon as existence loses itself in reflection on itself, it becomes invisible. It is obscured if one conceives existence in the sense of a personality. Eeriness is, if one asks what it is, *nothing*; if one asks where it is, *nowhere*. It expresses itself in existence's flight in the face of itself as the flight into familiarity and tranquilization.[5]

_____

5. See the Appendix, Supplement 30 (p. 240).

Appendix

Supplements to the Lectures from the Lecture Notes
of Helene Weiss and Herbert Marcuse

Supplement 1 (to p. 4)

Aristotle's *De anima*. If one translates it "On the soul," then it is misunderstood today in a psychological sense. If we adhere, not to the words, but to what is said in Aristotle's investigation, then we translate it: "About being in the world." What are crudely designated in an easily misunderstood manner as "faculties of the soul," "perception," "thinking," "willing," are for Aristotle not experiences, but ways of existing of someone living in his world.

*

Supplement 2 (to p. 6)

What is visible is the color and yet something else, something that we are able, of course, to characterize in discussion (καὶ ὃ λόγῳ μὲν ἔστιν εἰπεῖν) but for which we have no positive expression (ἀνώνυμον δὲ τυγχάνει ὄν) (418a26ff.). Something of this sort also falls within the sphere of what can be seen along with [the color] and taken up in seeing. Color is what is, as such, extended over something visible: χρῶμα . . .ἐστὶ τὸ ἐπὶ τοῦ καθ᾽ αὑτὸ ὁρατοῦ (418a29f.). The respective coloring of something existing is perceived in each case ἐν φωτί (418b3). Color is not perceivable without light: χρῶμα οὐχ ὁρατὸν ἄνευ φωτός (418b2). The entire explanation of what we have to understand by color, the perceivable, the visible depends upon what we must understand by daylight, light. What is light, the daylight? ἔστι δή τι διαφανές (418b4). It is apparently something of the sort that lets something else be seen through it. Daylight is the presence of fire, presence in the broad sense of the heavens. φῶς δέ ἐστιν ἡ τούτου ἐνέργεια, τοῦ διαφανοῦς ᾗ διαφανές (418b9f.). Light is what actually allows for things to be seen and what makes up the daylight.

*

Supplement 3 (to p. 21)

Hence, in this way the perceiving is, as this speaking in time, a unitary perceiving, but at the same time such as has its own being in being several things
for several things, namely, in perceiving a manifold. It is διαιρετόν and, in
spite of this, ἀδιαίρετον (427a2ff.) and, to be sure, in the manner of perceiving.
Perceiving has in itself the possibility of this *splitting up* [*Aufsplitterung*].
From this it becomes understandable how we grasp the world κατὰ συμβεβηκός. We always see the world in an *as*. If I see something in the distance,
then I do not see something indeterminate there. Instead we take it initially
and mostly *as* something. This determinate, basic character of the world becomes accessible only on the basis of lifting [something] up [or setting it off:
Abheben], on the basis of a definite manner of perceiving [or taking it up:
Vernehmen] (κρίνειν). And because the basic manner of perceiving is such that
it addresses the world *as* this and this, the ground is laid therein for the
possibility that it presents itself as this *and* this. Here lies the basis for the
possibility of deceit. What shows itself (φαινόμενα) is revealed as only presenting itself in that way and not being so.

*

Supplement 4 (to p. 22)

Only as such a δύναμις is the αἴσθησις a definite potential being [*Sein-Können*]
in the middle, a μεσότης; as [in the] middle, perceiving is such that it speaks,
that it is a speaking, λόγος τις; as such a λόγος, as speaking, it distinguishes
(κρίνει); [and] as such it perceives (δέχεσθαι), so that something happens to
the one perceiving, he becomes another (πάσχειν, ἀλλοίωσις).

It is necessary to see clearly the principle on which all these explications
of αἴσθησις rest: designated here as ψυχή. *The ψυχή* is something that *δυνάμει*.
(In the tradition, already in Neo-Platonism, δύναμις is understood as faculty
[*Vermögen*]. One interprets [this], as though some occult forces that one can
determine are at work in the soul; set against this sort of occultism, modern
experimental psychology appears far superior.)

δύναμις does not mean force, faculty, but instead a quite *concrete manner
of being*. ὂν δυνάμει and ὂν ἐνεργείᾳ are the basic manners of being for Aristotle.—That these determinations play such a role in Aristotle's psychology
should not be surprising, since Aristotle characterizes the ψυχή as οὐσία. The
soul is not the same as substance, a little clump of something as it were, but
instead an οὐσία, a manner of being. This character of being in the living is
the soul which is characterized by the fact that it is δύναμις; its being is

characterized by *being-possible* [*Möglichsein*]. Its manner of being is such that for it something *completely determinate* is *possible*. The manifold: nourishing, perceiving, thinking, willing soul, these diverse manners of potential-being of what is alive are not functions that function peacefully with one another such that what would matter would be merely to determine these connections precisely—instead one must recognize the grounding of these diverse possibilities in a definite, layered primordiality of the potential-being. If a specific living thing, e.g., an animal, is characterized as a perceiving-being, then all other possibilities of ψυχή, nourishing, reproducing, are determined, in terms of the way they are, through the perceiving-being.

If, therefore, the human manner of being is ζωὴ πρακτική, characterized by "a concern for something, a concern that goes about through reflection," living in a concerned intercourse [with things and others], then all its other possibilities of being are to be understood in this primordial possibility and only as somehow taken up [*aufgehoben*] in this its genuine being, taken up in this leading possibility of being. Hence, it is fundamentally wrongheaded to assemble together distinctions, perceiving, etc., and center them, after the fact, in the ego-center. Those are all mythologies, when contrasted with what Aristotle saw and explicated. Similarly, to analyze a perception in isolation is from the outset methodically absurd when measured purely on the matter at hand. What matters much more is that the possibility of perceiving in the human being is grounded from the outset in the fact that he *speaks*, in the fact that he *wants something*.

*

Supplement 5 (to p. 30)

We still have to make sure of the extent to which Aristotle was explicitly conscious of the fact that the possibility of deception has its genuine field, where things are taken *as* such and such in some manner, where they are encountered in terms of a definite conception, thus not where they are simply confronted, but instead where the world always stands in some definite regard. *De interpretatione*, chapter one (16a12f.): περὶ γὰρ σύνθεσιν καὶ διαίρεσίν ἐστι τὸ ψεῦδός τε καὶ τὸ ἀληθές. In the sphere where there is something like being-taken-together and being-taken-apart-from-one-another, there is the false *as well as* the true. The καί [the "and"] here is important; where namely σύνθεσις and διαίρεσις are, truth and deception are *both* there, namely, as possibilities. What this means is clearer in *De anima* III, 6 (430b1ff.) where it is said quite precisely: τὸ γὰρ ψεῦδος ἐν συνθέσει ἀεί, the deceiving is always there where there is synthesis. καὶ γὰρ ἂν τὸ λευκὸν μὴ λευκόν, τὸ μὴ λευκὸν συνέθηκεν.

ἐνδέχεται δὲ καὶ διαίρεσιν φάναι πάντα.—Everything that is ἐν συνθέσει can be articulated ἐν διαιρέσει, what is encountered in an unexplicated fashion can break out in definite regards; in ordinary ways of addressing things, there is always σύνθεσις—or—depending upon what one sees, the same is also διαίρεσις. Ἐνδέχεται . . . if I address a white object as not white, the "not white" has already been co-posited (συνέθηκεν) from the outset in the manner of pointing it out. With the "not," I already move, relative to the object, into a definite regard that does not lie in it itself; I place it into the regard of possibly not-being-white. The sentence seemingly signifies no genuine λόγος, but instead a straightforward addressing in the sense of an ὁρισμός [definition]. But the "not" is by no means a mere not; with the "not," the "as" is already posited. *For the ὁρισμός there is no negation.* What is to be negated is taken in a regard *as* something, even if only as a possible "not" of it itself. By this means, the field of possibility of the existence of deception is sharply circumscribed. Only insofar as there is something like σύνθεσις and διαίρεσις, is there something like deception. *De anima* III, 3 (427b11ff.): ἡ μὲν γὰρ αἴσθησις τῶν ἰδίων ἀεὶ ἀληθής, καὶ πᾶσιν ὑπάρχει τοῖς ζῴοις, διανοεῖσθαι δ᾽ ἐνδέχεται καὶ ψευδῶς, καὶ οὐδενὶ ὑπάρχει ᾧ μὴ καὶ λόγος. The perceiving of a component of the matter specifically proper to the manner of perceiving—this perceiving is always such that there is no possibility of deception there. As long as and insofar as I see at all, I see something complete. (To be heeded in the διανοεῖσθαι is the δια: isolating, as in the διαίρεσις.) This perceiving itself, however, can be performed in the manner of deceiving (διανοεῖσθαι δ᾽ ἐνδέχεται καὶ ψευδῶς) (*De anima* III, 3, 427b13) and is only on hand there, in accord with the way it exists, where there is λόγος, ostensive speaking. Thus we see the inner connection between the necessity of addressing being in some regard or another and the possibility of deception. To what extent Aristotle has pressed ahead in this connection: existence = speaking that speaks in some regard or another, [according to] definite preconceptions—that is shown also by *De anima* III. (The central investigation of the human manner of being in the world.) Aristotle speaks of the fact that perceiving, as it in fact takes place, is never *pure* perceiving, e.g., the perceiving of colors as such, but instead we always have an interest in the things to a certain extent. The world is always there in such a way that the speaking speaks in regard to a perceiving that is such that we have an interest in the things. τὸ μὲν οὖν αἰσθάνεσθαι . . . Pure perceiving is like mere naming, a simple confronting, leaving the things simply, inexplicitly standing there. (I see the colored.) That is the αἰσθάνεσθαι in this prepared sense. ὅταν δὲ ἡδὺ ἢ λυπηρὸν αἴσθησις . . . : If, on the other hand, we experience something enjoyable or disturbing, then the perceiving is like a speaking, that is κατάφασις or ἀπόφασις, namely such that something is grasped *as* something. If, in perceiving this way, I all of a sudden encounter something enjoyable, then the perceiving itself *and* the enjoying in seeing are

one in the process. [This perceiving] is there from the same middle or intermediate position, τῇ μεσότητι. And insofar as this unitary perceiving is the
primordial perceiving and the one nearest to us, insofar as the things of the
world are πράγματα, things to be taken care of by us, the natural intercourse
with them is an ἥδεσθαι or λυπεῖσθαι. As long as one is oriented to a theory
of a faculty of the soul, one does not see these connections. But Aristotle
philosophizes on the basis of the matters at hand and not in connection with
a current textbook of psychology.

*

Supplement 6 (to p. 36)

Today we can say that Aristotle, by means of this comment while simply
pointing out the fact of the matter, showed a much more fundamental insight
into the genuine contexts than contemporaries do through their hasty asserting,
their elaboration [of them] in terms of self-consciousness.

*

Supplement 7 (to p. 41)

Thus, three concepts of consciousness present themselves, three concepts that
remain internally connected and were at work at the time without this connection being seen. This connection was first established by Husserl. Consciousness is, accordingly, the regional title for the entire inventory of the
soul's experiences [*seelische Erlebnisse*] that become accessible as such
through consciousness in the sense of inner awareness, so that this [awareness]
pertains to a distinctive class of experiences that are characterized as consciousness of something.

*

Supplement 8 (to p. 52)

That is supposed to mean: the tendencies that lie in the problems should be
made transparent and certain. A problem is not something arbitrary and not
binding. Instead, as a definite question, it is a question to and about something
in a definite regard. The question is thus already a definite decision about how
one inquires into the interrogated subject matter. In the posing of the problem,
a definite sort of access to the subject matter itself is co-posited, and the

method is co-posited and co-decided at the same time. If a critique resolves to conduct itself as a "clarification of the problems," then that means: taking up definite domains of subject matters, with a definite tendency in the treatment of them, and taking up those domains and that tendency as they figure in the problems. Consciousness is taken up as the domain of a subject matter.

*

Supplement 9 (to p. 65)

Then it is assumed that this would be an absolute misfortune for humanity and it is not deemed necessary to question whether or not, in the end, the necessity of skepticism is expressly grounded in existence. Appeal is simply made to the acknowledgment that, since historicism leads to skepticism, one can prove nothing with it. In a negative sense, so to speak, history is rendered innocuous. This threat is nothing other than the care about preserving absolute validity and excluding history as irrelevant for philosophy. [For us] that means making this care's neglect explicit. One does not look at historical being at all. We must understand this concrete neglect in terms of the following: 1. How is history seen here at all? Is it supposed in such a way that, with it as one's point of departure, concrete existence could be made intelligible? 2. On the basis of a history thus supposed, what is said about the connection between the validity of norms and the being subject to those norms?

Thus, consideration of the neglect will provide occasion for orientation about what is also claimed in this care, insofar as the care (the idea of philosophy as rigorous science) in the genuine sense lays claim to the idea of reason as its concern and with it simultaneously lays hold of the chief task of humanity. (For concrete orientation, see Wilhelm Dilthey, *Einleitung in die Geisteswissenschaften* [Introduction to the Humanities]; then *Aufbau der geschichtlichen Welt* [Structure of the Historical World]; *Abhandlungen der Akademie der Wissenschaften* [Essays of the Academy of Sciences], 1910.)

*

Supplement 10 (to p. 69)

Troeltsch has recently treated the problem of historicism with this lack of clarity.[1] As a document of the times, this book is special. It shows how prin-

---

1. E. Troeltsch, *Der Historismus und seine Probleme*. Erstes Buch: *Das logische Problem der Geschichtsphilosophie* [Historicism and Its Problems, First Book: The logical problem of the philosophy of history], (Tübingen 1922).

cipal questions can be treated in an extensive publication without even so much as a question being directed at the matters that are at stake in the case. This sort of study—for those familiar with existence, this is clear—will become the guiding thread for the next twenty years until something else, perhaps again nature, becomes the object of the babble.

*

Supplement 11 (to p. 69)

Dilthey's work concentrates itself on this, that the development of the history of the human spirit [*Geistesgeschichte*] since the eighteenth century becomes so transparent for him that Dilthey himself, in the historical consciousness, has an inkling of an existential possibility [*Existenzmöglichkeit*]. Insofar as he also raises the question traditionally, he also remains in the inquiry passed down [to him]: How is a science of history possible as science? "Critique of Historical Reason." Of course, he still does not consider that other side of the "Globus intellectualis," instead shifting the weight more and more to historical consciousness; but he succumbs again and again to the traditional orientation to science. These positive possibilities of Dilthey's work remain unknown; indeed, they are in the process of being made—through the combination with phenomenology—utterly impossible.—In the criticism of this life-work under the rubric of "historicism," what is positive gets lost and, in the sense of the care [underlying that criticism], the position taken [by Dilthey] is interpreted with respect to [the criterion] of absolute validity. The criticism is made without its foundation being secured. One dispenses with establishing what is actually found here, on the basis of which the distinction between validity and factuality is set up. The facts of the matter are not secured, the facts on which such a distinction is based, unless one intends to take into consideration the small basis of theoretical judgment. Everything is reinterpreted as founded and shaped by the theoretical.

*

Supplement 12 (to p. 74)

The call to the matters themselves, a call springing from care, is *conditioned* in a completely definite sense. The analogue holds for the concept of philosophy, as Scheler has elaborated it (a philosophy of the matters [*Sachphilosophie*]) and which one could much more designate as a philosophy of specific dogmas.

*

Supplement 13 (to p. 74)

Last time we arrived at a certain conclusion to the explication of care, with emphasis on the fact that the peculiarity of care about already known knowledge, ensnaring itself in itself, broke out into the two factors: a concern for objective content and rigor. These two factors, laid claim to in the breakthrough of phenomenological research and still laid claim to today, turn out to be determined by the care that has now been characterized; that is to say, they did not emerge primarily in view of the matters that were to be presented. The care at work in the concern for objective content, regarded in a completely extreme sense, is nothing else than the demand to go along with this care, i.e., positing matters with a view to an ultimate, universally binding character. Only by means of this testing place are matters deemed worthy to be worked on. The call "to the matters" is not a matter of freeing up what is objective such that it could be decided, on the basis of the respective worthiness of the question, what type[s] of matters, in accord with their being, deserve a specific investigation. Insofar as the care is about the validity of the knowledge in question, the rigor is a formal rigor, indeterminate with respect to the matters; it is rigorous, as far as the subject matter is concerned, only in relation to mathematical objects. The specific evidence of mathematical knowledge provides the guiding thread for the idea of philosophy as rigorous science. With this point of departure, it is not asked whether the character of the object, what philosophy of itself has as an object, can be subsumed under such an a priori. This question is not posed even once and, hence, the demand for a philosophy as rigorous science is a dogmatic one. By virtue of the sort of concern for objective content and rigor [that it embodies], the care proves itself to be concerned with remaining entirely with itself. With regard to the problem of what constitutes the character of consciousness' being, we have come as far as care about already known knowledge accounts for it, namely, as it is shown in the reductions.—But it does not stop with this science being treated as an isolated discipline; instead it is set up as the basic discipline of all philosophical and thereby at the same time every possible science. Care about already known knowledge not only forms this field as a specific task, but instead devotes itself to it in such a manner that the alternative (ideal validity—empirical matter-of-factness) is extended to all possible sciences. The science thus enhanced takes over the leading role of elucidating every existence of any sort and with respect to the most diverse aims. Everything is subject to the jurisdiction of reason, which represents itself accordingly.

*

Supplement 14 (to p. 77)

This basic fact of the matter was already constantly providing the measure in the lecture. The point of departure with Aristotle is determined by the theme of the lecture's subject matter. This examination was directed at representing the content of the subject matter and so, too, we are constantly led back to the history in the later analyses. This entire basis of the investigation lies this side of the contrast between a systematic and an historical examination. The explications are immediately misunderstood if one wanted to file them in some free-floating, systematic context. *The theme is the factical existence as such that is, as such, historical [historisch].* The historical [*das Geschichtliche*] determines the character of being of the thematic. This [is said] by way of orientation to how such a return to a definite, historically concrete instance is motivated by the matters themselves. Insofar as the factical disclosing of the designated care is apparent in Descartes' research work, we now have to go back to it.

*

Supplement 15 (to p. 79)

It needs to be determined, 1. that care about already known knowledge is alive in Descartes' work. Only then is it possible to make intelligible how this care discloses consciousness as a specific being.—2. This disclosing [is] to be illuminated on the basis of the being of care. For the first of these points, it must be shown that the designated care is at work in Descartes. We have a source for this in the treatise on method, *Discours de la méthode*, 1637. Then, the first four of the *Meditationes*, particularly the fourth; the first part of the *Principia philosophiae*; and the *Regulae ad directionem ingenii*. I cannot proceed here to a more detailed consideration of Descartes.

Regarding the historical consideration of Descartes today, it must be said that the attitude towards Descartes has enjoyed a certain upswing, in the sense that there is an effort to get closer to Descartes' roots. Suspicious, apologetic interests have, however, guided this way of pushing Descartes back into the Middle Ages. It has already for some time become customary to demonstrate that the well-known "Cogito ergo sum" is already in Augustine. If one wants to demonstrate this, it is in itself indisputable. Still, a difference exists between what Descartes was striving after with this and the context in which it is to be found in Augustine. Zealous people believed that they did a particular service to Augustine with the demonstration mentioned above. The connections are not to be had so cheaply that one should believe oneself to have deciphered a relation simply on the basis of similarly sounding sentences. The work on the illumination of Descartes' connection with the Scholastics is also pursued above all by French scholars. Yet, they lack the necessary, hermeneutical means. Already before them, [there is] Freudenthal on "Spinoza and the Scholastics" (in a *Festschrift* for Zeller).[2] Even today French scholars have not gone beyond registering external data. A genuine understanding of Descartes' connection with the Middle Ages has not been gained. We will not be able to go into these connections any more, apart from the question of the true and the false.—Where is it evident that the designated care is the leading care for Descartes? In the *Discourse on Method* Descartes does not want to give a methodology. Instead, he wants merely to relate the practical application of his method, how he came to his method in his life, what motives for its development were at work in him. He explicitly remarks that he does not want to persuade anyone else of this method, but instead to give them the option of likewise securing and developing the method of knowledge for themselves. He published this discourse in 1637 with three other discourses. The others then appeared once more as *specimina philosophiae*. A brief account of the content of the discourse: Descartes says that he had an interest in science from the beginning. He soon saw how mathematical science had a particular rigor with respect to knowability. In philosophy, however, there was no sentence that was not disputed. This orientation led him to set aside the entire interest in science and to make his inquiries in life. But again and again the wish for knowledge of what is indubitable became vital in him. Giving up interest in all concrete and—in his sense—contingent knowledge, he finally set about forming rules of conduct for the sake of genuine knowledge; he made for himself a principle of developing a path to knowledge that is absolutely certain; even if the path does not lead far, he does not want to chance upon it. Here the interests in making certain of knowledge as such can already be seen. He develops four ground rules of knowing-behavior, regulae perceptionis [rules of perception]: 1. Only what is comprehended in a clara et distincta perceptio exists. 2. Each difficulty that surfaces in knowledge is to be broken down into its component parts. 3. In the investigation of truth, one ought to begin with the simplest and most easily known objects. 4. One should strive for completeness in considering the respective sphere of objects to be known.—The primacy that the validity of knowledge has for Descartes reveals itself already in this specific interest in the development of such formal rules, prior to any effort to free up access to an entity. Regardless of what the indubitable is, insofar as the care prefigures a specific realm of being for it,

---

2. J. Freudenthal, "Spinoza und die Scholastik." In: *Philosophische Aufsätze, Eduard Zeller zu seinem fünfzigjährigen Doctor-Jubiläum gewidmet* ["Spinoza and the Scholastics," in *Philosophical Essays, dedicated to Eduard Zeller on the fiftieth Jubilee of his doctorate*] (Leipzig 1887), S. 83–138.

leading it to a specific realm of being, the actual being is in the sense of the first rule.

Descartes is connected to our inquiry into the character of being of the thematic field of the discipline that today calls itself "phenomenology." How does this field come to its peculiar primacy? The interpretation has steered us in such a way that it aims at establishing the specific care in which this thematic field is maintained. This was the care about already known knowledge. Fundamental characters of the caring itself confronted us here. The actual factor, from which the thematic field's character of being can be read, has not been established in the consideration up to now and should become transparent by means of the question: In what way is it the *specific care* to which consciousness is able to be disclosed as the thematic field? To what extent is the care about already known knowledge what develops consciousness as a thematic field? For this care, it is necessary to return to Descartes.

*

Supplement 16 (to p. 93)

Seen from this vantage point, Descartes is in fact the founder of modern philosophy, although he founds it in traditional fashion, [and] is in a peculiar sense medieval and Greek.—For its part, consciousness today dominates the actual field of philosophy (person, what pertains to the soul [*Seelisches*], life, etc.). Even where one turns away from a philosophy of consciousness and posits the transcendence of entities compared with the immanence of consciousness, one always sees transcendence compared with consciousness and, hence, does not move beyond the entire sphere of consciousness.

*

Supplement 17 (to p. 98)

See the Fourth Meditation. It is shown in this meditation that what is grasped clearly and distinctly, is true. [At work] here [is] a specific concept of true, a concept oriented to the *esse* perceptum. At the same time what the being of the false consists in is debated. The debate about this—esse verum as the same as perceptum esse—is important in order to nail down the preceding and to understand what follows (Synopsis, p. 5). In the Fourth Meditation, the basis is the certain being of the res cogitans; the issue is to chart the path from this basis—following the lead of the criterion of clara et distincta perceptio, which is itself absolutely justified by being led back to God—to knowledge of what lies extra mentem, the res extensa, that is to say, to knowledge of nature as the object of mathematical natural science.

*

Supplement 18 (to p. 106)

For us that means that Descartes sees in the being of the res cogitans a twofold being: 1. as repraesentans [representing] and 2. as repraesentatum [represented]. De facto, however, both flow together for him into one in the ideas. Thus, cogitatio [thought] serves as well for cogitatum [what is thought] as for cogitare [to think]. So, too, this transposition presents no difficulty for him from the outset since the esse in the sense of realitas objectiva (the *being*-represented of something represented) is contained in the representing of what is represented. The latter is a slighter degree of being, but no *nothing*. Descartes says that what are absolutely given in the clara et distincta perceptio are: 1. the cogitationes [thoughts] and 2. the ideae [ideas].—This is the origin of Husserl's determination that in the sphere of consciousness (conceived as a realm) the following are given in an evident way: 1. *acts*, the noetic, the noesis, and 2. what is meant in the acts themselves, the noemata; they are the ideae in Descartes' sense. The noetic are the cogitationes qua operationes mentis [thoughts as operations of the mind].

*

Supplement 19 (to p. 107)

We now have to ask: 1. How does Descartes explicate the constitution of error? 2. In what does the factor of being [*Seinsmoment*] in the specific being of error lie, the factor that makes it a privatio? 3. From which ontological perspectives does Descartes interpret the falsum and the error? In the course of pursuing the interpretation according to these three points, we must hit upon definite, basic categories of being and, indeed, the sort that stand in some sort of connection with the forenamed categories of res cogitans. That is to say, we will hit upon the remnants of Aristotelian ontology.

*

Supplement 20 (to p. 112)

With these sentences that appear here to be set forth so self-evidently, the entire contemporary background reveals itself, in keeping with the fact that this entire *Fourth Meditation does not have the slightest originality [Originalität]* at all. The rejection of the indifferentia is a blow against the Jesuits, and the positive determination of libertas as propensio takes the side of the Port-Royal and the Oratorians' new opposition [to the Jesuits]; Cardinal Bérulle, whose confidant, Père Gibieuf, wrote *De libertate Dei et creaturae* (1630).—Descartes' *Meditationes* appeared in 1641. From correspondence, it is evident that Descartes received from the author an inscribed copy of the work and studied it himself.—This passage in Descartes points to the fundamental theological context of the question of the relation of God's grace and human freedom. [This is a] problem-context that goes back to Augustine's critical engagement with Pelagius. [See, too,] Luther's main theological writing, *De servo arbitrio* (1525/26): *On the Servile Will.* It is already evident from the title that it is directed *against* the doctrine of genuinely being-free in acting before God. This writing was occasioned by that of Erasmus: *De libero arbitrio diatribe* [Diatribe on Free Will]. Luther's work played a great role in the development of the Reformation, a role that was *even intensified by Calvin.*—At the same time, the Counter-Reformation was systematically set in motion by the Jesuits. Over against the diminution of the human will, they emphasized the positive possibilities of human libertas. The first significant representative is the Spanish monk, Fonseca, then Cardinal Bellarmine. In Molina's *De concordia gratiae et liberi arbitrii* [On the concordance of grace and free will] (1588), he summed up systematically the discord that arises from the gratia Dei and the liberum arbitrium. Henceforth, Molinism was called the doctrine of the essentia of libertas which consists in the indifferentia or, what is the same, scientia media, that became the genuine object of the Oratorians' and later Jansenism's opposition.

*

Supplement 21 (to p. 116)

Hence, a definite idea of the human being and its possibility lies at bottom here, namely, to seize upon the clara et distincta perceptio and to live in it. Here the model for care about already known knowledge shows itself. *The propensio is nothing other than the care about the clara et distincta perceptio.*—

How is a specific not-being, a privatio, possible within this determinate being as simul esse? What factor of being of the simul esse can be violated, is defectus, and how does the falsum determine itself by this means?—So must this explication of error be seen within the horizon of the relation of gratia and libertas, in connection with the ontological determinations on which they rest. They must be held together with the ontological determinations that we have already revealed in the course of the determination of the idea with respect to its twofold reality.

We saw the background against which the Cartesian doctrine of being-free stands in connection with judging. This background is of a purely theological sort, although in Descartes' case it is de-theologized in a peculiar manner and by this means propelled into the sphere of claims of purely rational evidence. What was previously established in the dimension of the believing conscious-ness' understanding is here secularized. Such secularized sentences are at work today everywhere in philosophy and as soon as one examines the claim of the sentences, one sees that the basis on which they alone have evidence has nothing to do with a purely rational knowledge.

*

Supplement 22 (to p. 123)

This question of the resolutio of the conceptiones to the ens contains within itself a further reflection that is grounded in the further construal of ens itself (Aristotle, *Metaphysics*, Gamma).

*

Supplement 23 (to p. 152)

The basic experience in which Descartes determines a human's being is: sum res cogitans. Insofar as I experience myself as this *something* and, in unity with this, experience that I am not nothing (idea negativa), I have at the same time in the horizon of my specific experiences themselves the idea of a being that is perfect, that I am not, however. I am not nothing, but also not God.—It is a *complete misunderstanding* of Cartesian philosophy, if one directs the interpretation in this way as though at first nothing were given but the cogito sum. Co-posited in it are, namely, the entire proof of God's existence and the ontology on which the proof rests. It is an error to think that his entire phi-losophy is built upon the naked sentence about consciousness, a sentence that is itself contrived to a certain extent. From simultaneously grasping the idea of an ens summe perfectum and the nihil, I acquire the impression: I am a midpoint [*Medium*] between God and nothing. This being itself is qua creatum a bonum and, indeed, bonum insofar as it is being as cogitare. The cogitare is a definite accomplishing [*Sich-Vollziehen*], it has in itself an inclinatio that is directed at a bonum. Insofar, then, as it is a matter of determining what it is for a human to be, the question will be: In what does the determination of being that makes up the highest perfection of a human being lie, so that this determination of being brings human beings into the vicinity of God's being? This determination of being expresses itself in libertas.

*

Supplement 24 (to p. 160)

The individual steps, as Descartes retraces them and at the same time places them in continuous connection with the initial tendency of Greek philosophy (Plato), show how each step in the exposition of the fourth rule is guided by the idea of the scientia certa et evidens. They also show that the formal elaboration of the regula is nothing other than the type of grasp of possible objects that is drawn from the sense of the mathesis universalis; more precisely, it is the regimentation of this sort of grasp with reference to these purely object-oriented relations themselves which contain nothing material in themselves.

*

Supplement 25 (to p. 189)

The question now is how what Descartes found is determined; it is now necessary to see what the formulas mean in view of the question: Is what was found a res or a verum? Meditatio II (p. 21): cogitatio est, haec sola a me divelli nequit: the thinking *is*; this alone cannot be taken from my being. Animadvertit [mens] fieri non posse quin ipsa interim existat[3] [The mind notices that it must be the case that it itself exists during this time] (*Synopsis*, p. 2). Non possumus supponere nos nihil esse qui talia cogitamus [Thinking such things, we are unable to suppose ourselves to be nothing] (*Principia philosophiae*, § 7). (*Principia*, § 49: non potest non existere qui cogitat [not to exist is not possible for someone who thinks].)

From these formulations it is clear that 1. what is sought and found is a *state of affairs* [*Sachverhalt*]; and 2. a *sentence*, a verum of a quite distinctive sort.

Ad 1.: Fieri non posse . . . What is found must be a state of affairs. The sentence speaks of the impossibility of the co-existence of my doubting and my not-being or, stated positively, the necessity of my being insofar as I am doubting. He thus speaks of a specific being-impossible as of a state [*Verhalt*],

---

3. [The term *mens* in square brackets is given as such in the original German edition.—D.D.]

as we say. Non posse supponere ... would be an impossible status. Something's being-impossible in the way characterized is a state of affairs.

Ad 2.: "If–then" is equivalent to a condition. If I think, then I am. Ego etiam sum, si me fallam. Distinctive conditional connection between my being and my cogitare. The distinctive formula "Cogito ergo sum" is characteristic. Is it an inference? From Descartes' doctrine it cannot be decided.—What is being looked at? The ergo is in fact not the expression for an inference; but the finding [*Befund*] has a definite articulation, a structure; the finding is not the cogito, not the esse, but instead cogitare ergo esse. *Being's being-co-given with thinking.* This status [*Bestand*] is a primary one. The given [is] a fundamentum certum. No inference, but instead an immediate explication of the given. What Descartes found cannot be an inference because for him it must be a priori insofar as he, indeed, wants an absolutum and each deductio in the sense of an inference would have to presuppose it already. Cogitare me esse has a character equivalent to that of a state (of affairs) [*gleich (Sach)Verhaltscharakter*]. The "ergo" has a definite sense as an articulation. Finally, what Descartes found is of the sort in which a definite plurality of the given presents itself, so that with the one the other obtains. Hence, the one shows itself in a definite co-givenness with the other. (Meditatio IV: ex hoc ipso ... see p. 189 above.) This concluding is evidently meant here, not in the sense of an inference, but instead in the sense that the me existere [that I exist] is co-given with the seeking. Indirectly, then, it is evident that a sentence is sought, even more clearly by the fact, namely, that the test of whether what is found corresponds with what is sought is entrusted to the principle of contradiction: repugnat enim, ut putemus id quod cogitat, eo ipso tempore quo cogitat, non existere [for it is contradictory for us to believe that what thinks does not exist at the very same time in which it thinks] (*Principia*, § 7). The finding is taken in view of this condition—by means of the principle of contradiction. The denial of being is at odds with the being of denying. The finding is of the sort normatively determined by noncontradictoriness. The finding is expressed in a sentence that is, however, a care of the speech, the φάσις. What is sought and found has a sentence's character. The certum is a verum. *Principia*, § 49: Is qui cogitat, non potest non existere dum cogitat [He who thinks is not able not to exist while he thinks]: in the passage from which this sentence has been taken, it stands in a quite characteristic connection: what is in general a possible object of a perceptio. Vel tanquam aeternae veritates [Or as eternal truths]. 1. Ex nihilo nihil fit [Nothing comes to be from nothing]. 2. Impossibile est idem simul esse et non esse [It is impossible for the same thing to be and not to be at the same time]. (A sentence that in this version is directly false.) 3. Quod factum est, infectum esse nequit [What is done, cannot be undone], cannot be made to have not happened. 4. Is qui cogitat, non potest non existere dum cogitat [He who thinks is not able not to exist while he thinks].—These sentences belong among the Veritates ae-ternae [eternal truths], so-called communes notiones or axiomata [common notions or axioms]. For Descartes then the finding of this consideration of doubt pertains to this [sort of] sentence. Universally familiar notions, universal because no specific type of object in regard to the makeup of its content is relevant for its comprehension. So you see that in fact the finding is not a res, but instead a verum and, to be sure, a truth that holds absolutely, that is universally valid. *This state of the matter, that the finding is no res, but instead a verum, is the genuine and final foundation for our discussion* with respect to the question: How is the character of the res cogitans' being itself viewed? Is this being itself expressed on its own terms or is this res conceived from the outset by the type of search, i.e., conceived as a possible component of a completely specific state of affairs, so that this res comes into view from the outset through its aptness to pertain to a state of affairs and is then also taken up into the finding itself?

*

Supplement 26 (to p. 197)

Husserl has also recently come to be convinced of this, which will be of ground-shaking significance for his conception of the doctrine of truth, insofar as he is consistent. The principle of contradiction is then at most justified if it is provided, as in Aristotle's case, with specific qualifications.

*

Supplement 27 (to p. 207)

Only in this way can there be talk of a possibility of constituting new sciences; it presupposes asking about the entities' being, to see worlds of being within the basic experiential contexts of factical life itself.

*

Supplement 28 (to p. 208)

The question of the sense of being prior to its development into a domain of matters [*Sachgebiet*] should only be posed if a basis is reached that lies prior to any distribution of entities into determinate sciences.

*

Supplement 29 (to p. 210)

On the other hand, the foundation of the evidence [is] still conceived once more in connection with the evidence of theoretically comprehending [it], on the basis of the dominant tendency of the attitude. The evidence is the specific evidence of comprehension and determination, hence, evidence of this object-oriented comprehending and determining.

*

Supplement 30 (to p. 221)

This phenomenon of eeriness is the condition of the possibility that something like *uncoveredness* lies in existence [being-here: *Dasein*]. *Visibility* is only a specific interpretation of the *here* [*Da*], is *merely a specific way of dealing with eeriness.*

This being of existence that stands under the attack of its own eeriness makes it intelligible that care also is inherent in the genuine being of being in the world.

Care—being bent on something encountered in the world—is nothing else than the expression of getting away from the eeriness. To be bent on something, by way of taking care of it, is the same as being in flight from the eeriness.

Existence is: being in a world in the manner of caring: taking care of the world itself. What is taken care of, the world, is thus encountered in terms of the basic characters of what can be taken care of.

What we designate as *language* must also be explicated on the basis of this basic phenomenon of eeriness. Language: a specific manner of being on the part of the human being, the being in the world. Primarily seen (in an interpretative way) as speaking in the eeriness, *language* means: announcing oneself [*Sich-Aussprechen*], *making oneself heard in the eeriness.* ([It is] a familiar phenomenon that, in [experiencing] the eerie, one begins to speak loudly.) Announcing oneself in this sense is not a matter of wanting to tell someone else about something or other—it means: addressing the cared-for *world according to the manner in which existence announces itself.* Existence declares itself to a certain extent *from itself outward—away from itself.* All the *primal conditions of language* are, for this reason, *hermeneutical* in their basic character—they are not meanings regarding the matter of a "thing" but instead concern existence itself. Hence, the primarily primordial character of the personal pronouns "I," "you."

I stress that only from the phenomenon of *distortion*, that together with *eeriness* structurally lies at bottom, can *intentionality* be brought back to the ground to which it belongs. If one reviews how the doctrine of intentionality was taken up in contemporary philosophy, then a resistance to the doctrine is evident. To be sure, the arguments [against it] were always taken solely from definite epistemological standpoints. Yet a vague consciousness of this [grounded character of intentionality] lay in the fact that one noticed that a much too explicit and tendentious characterization of being in the world is given with the [construal of] "being-directed [at something or other]" as the basic structure of consciousness. For phenomenology, however, what matters is to bring existence into focus in a positive sense in its averageness, something rendered impossible from the outset by the interpretation of intentionality as the basic structure of consciousness. This point of departure ultimately led to taking up the old set of problems once again and to making possible within phenomenological research discussions such as whether epistemology is legitimate within phenomenological research.

"How does consciousness or the 'I' pass over to the world? How does the world enter into consciousness? How do these two come to one another?" Questions posited in a principally mistaken way, with regard to a phenomenon that one has not by any means looked at beforehand. In question is, indeed, a human's being: being *in* the world pertains to existence's being. From the outset, in regard to existence, the question how it might come to the world or the world to it is utterly senseless. What in general can be clarified is: How does it come about that existence develops for itself a science that leads this basic phenomenon (being in the world) to be concealed in this way, a science that establishes a position that interrogates existence in this forlorn sense?

This question would have to be answered not in the sense of exhaustive reflections but instead by taking a concrete look at the history of existence—at the history of knowledge and science.

With the characterization of *care* as a basic manner of being in the world, it was said: it is a way of being bent on the world in the manner of taking care of it. What is taken care of is also anticipated: in a certain sense existence leapfrogs itself, such that it keeps in view and keeps in its care something *that is not yet here*, something that first has to be taken care of. From the midst of an ongoing existence [from what already is-here: *Da-sein*], from a specific care, something that is not yet here is striven for. The peculiar grounding structure of existence as being in the care shows itself in the *stretch* [*Erstreckung*] of existence from the "already" to the "not yet." This *temporality* [*Zeitlichkeit*] makes for the fact that the existence itself is *historical*. (That does not mean something like the external fact that every human existence stands in history, in the juxtaposition and succession of all sorts of events; it is also not meant that existence has history, in the sense of a consciousness of a having-been, but instead:) Existence is in the time of history insofar as it is itself temporal.

Existence is temporal: here time is no measure (something like numbers in history, dates), but instead *existence has in itself this specific stretch, this temporality*, that on the basis of the *anticipation* [*Vorweg*] of something *futural*, that is placed in [its] care, it also *takes care of its past* [*mitbesorgt seine Vergangenheit*] and thereby *brings* itself *into the present*.

Past—present and future are not dimensions shoved next to one another, but instead determine the how of existence in a unitary way.—If that is the case, and if all philosophy in some sense or other interrogates existence, explicitly or not, then it is possible to read off the extent to which a philosophy sees existence as such from how it stands toward history. We will have to take this as the clue also for a radical deliberation on the possibilities given in the present-day philosophical situation, in order to bring existence itself into view for research.—Next to the tendencies of phenomenological research and in a certain connection with it, Dilthey's investigations obviously move in a direction that is explicitly directed at seeing the lived reality of life in such a way that history is also taken into consideration.—But everything that Dilthey undertakes is still caught up in traditional ways of posing the question and only by instinct is he out to reveal existence in itself. But he has not become free from precisely the history of science, the questions handed down to him by the tradition, so that the instinct is buried under the tradition.

The next publications will make it possible to see what Dilthey's relation was to contemporary philosophy of history. An interesting supplement can be expected; debates with Windelband's 1894 Rectoral Address "History and Natural Science," that is itself determined by Dilthey's *Introduction* [*to the Humanities*].

Here it is apparent how much Dilthey is clear about the task of a special psychology—but the entire question is oriented to the problem of history, is seen as a science of history—(history [as a] region for a science). This science is again set off from natural science.—Compared with Windelband/Rickert, Dilthey's conception of history is progress, to be sure, insofar as in their case historical knowledge is still only questioned with a view to its conceptual character. Dilthey sees that psychology is not natural science and cannot be classified at all as a natural science, as Windelband and Rickert want. Psychology as the basic science of the humanities means a doctrine of life, of a human's being (anthropology)—it is the basic discipline for history. In this regard Dilthey's instinct—his instinct to see life as it is—is simply diverted into the tendency to lay the foundation for the humanities by means of a new sort of psychology. This tendency [is] itself fulfilled and secured in his case through a concrete, intimate familiarity with the history of the [human] spirit [*Geistesgeschichte*]. Proceeding systematically did not lie among Dilthey's possibilities. The basic deficiency [is] that he developed no categories, no uniformly precise inquiry. What he saw, he sought to reproduce through an aesthetic-artistic sort of presentation. Although he saw, in his last years, that an actual basis for all these questions [was] prepared by Husserl's *Logical Investigations*, he did not see that here new sorts . . .[4]

*

4. [The text ends with this incomplete sentence.—D.D.]

Editor's Afterword

The present volume 17 of Heidegger's *Gesamtausgabe* contains the previously unpublished text of the lectures that Heidegger held four hours weekly in the Winter Semester of 1923/24. He held these lectures as full professor *ad personam*, having just been called to the associate chair for philosophy at the University of Marburg [Philips-Universität Marburg]. Heidegger's first Marburg lectures were announced in the catalogue of lectures under the title "The Beginning of Modern Philosophy," but were in fact held under the title "Introduction to Phenomenological Research," as the original document and all the lecture notes of those listening to the lectures unanimously testify.

A typed transcript [*Abschrift*] of the original manuscript was available for editing the text of the lecture. This transcript, presumably prepared soon after the close of the lectures, was revised by Heidegger, in part with pencil, in part with ink from his own hand. On the cover Heidegger noted in green ink: "First Marburg Lectures, Winter Semester, 1923/24." The title page of this transcript bears the following note, made by Heidegger in red pencil: "Introduction to Phenomenological Research. Winter Semester 1923/24. Original manuscript *destroyed*." At the time that Heidegger set up his *Gesamtausgabe* with the help of the editor and handed over to him, among other things, the task of editing this first Marburg lecture, he communicated to the editor in conversation that the call to Marburg and the move there from Freiburg had placed him in such time constraints and distress that he was only able to write the lecture down hurriedly [*mit flüchtiger Hand*]. The hurried character and, as a result, the difficulty in reading the handwritten text are the reason why he had the original manuscript typed up and then destroyed.

Besides the typed and revised "original transcript," as we will call it, two sets of lecture notes [*Nachschriften*] were on hand, one from the surviving papers of Helene Weiß and another from those of Herbert Marcuse. The "Weiß" lecture notes, encompassing 514 handwritten sides, contain the note "transcript of Friedel Landshut" beneath the title of the lecture. The lecture notes of the hourly lectures from February 15 to February 25, 1924 are written in someone else's handwriting. Above the notes to the final hour of the lecture, there is the following reference: "End of the final hour (February 26), lecture notes, Elli Bondi." Dr. Hartmut Tietjen deserves thanks for having made a clear, typed transcript of these lecture notes that on the whole are quite readable and this transcript considerably eased work with the lecture notes during the job of editing. At the time that Heidegger was planning and preparing his *Gesamtausgabe*, he had asked Professor Ernst Tugendhat, the nephew of Helene Weiß, to make available to him from the surviving papers of his aunt copies of all the notes taken in his lectures [*Vorlesungsnachschriften*]. Professor Tugendhat had kindly complied with this wish. Heidegger thereupon commissioned Verlag Klostermann, the publisher, to have the lecture notes copied by a photocopying firm and sent on to him. These copies were arranged chronologically in folders at Freiburg and immediately afterwards were incorporated into the surviving papers of Heidegger, preserved in the Archive of German Literature at Marbach [Deutschen Literaturarchiv Marbach].

The second set of notes taken at the lectures is a copy of the typed exemplar that belongs to the Herbert-Marcuse-Archive preserved in the City and University Library of Frankfurt am Main (see Thomas Regehly, "Overview of the 'Heideggeriana' in the Herbert-Marcuse-Archives of the City and University Library in Frankfurt am Main," *Heidegger Studies*, vol. 7 [1991]). Since Herbert Marcuse first met Heidegger in 1928 and hence did not himself hear the lecture, these lecture notes go back to some other author who cannot be named with any certainty. Quite possibly, Herbert Marcuse also obtained these lecture notes, like many others, from Walter Bröcker. Yet the text of these lecture notes is incomplete; it extends only from November 1, 1923 to January 11, 1924 and comprises 81 typed pages.

Through the kind mediation of Professor Gerhart Baumann (Freiburg), the editor obtained yet another set of notes of this lecture during the editorial process, this time from the surviving papers of Gerhard Nebel who heard Heidegger's lectures and drafted the lecture notes himself. Here it is a matter of a black oilcloth notebook, written in a mixed German-Latin handwriting; on the inner side of the front cover it contains the inscription: "Heidegger, Introduction to Phenomenological Research, III." Hence, it is the third of presumably four notebooks in all. This third notebook begins with the lecture on January 8 and ends with the lecture on February 15.

In the typed, original transcript, Greek words are added afterwards by hand with ink, but not by Heidegger's hand. Heidegger's handwritten revision of the text consists in stylistic reshaping, sharper formulation of a thought, in occasional deletion of sentences or even insertion of newly formulated sentences. On the whole, however, these revisions keep to the level of deliberation of the lectures. Here and there notes [*Notizen*] are to be found to the left of the typed sides, which are on the right side; these notes are accordingly on the reverse side of the foregoing side of the text. The origin of these notes, mostly in shorthand, is uncertain and thus they had to be left out of consideration in the edition. That this original transcript was also in other hands is evidenced by the penciled markings and traces of reading which strongly deviate from those that are typical for Heidegger. In the original transcript, but not in the lecture notes, the text of the lectures is divided into three parts, each numbered independently: the first part encompasses 103 sides, the second part 140 sides, and the third part 49 sides. This major division mirrors the composition of the text of the lectures.

All three sets of lecture notes are furnished with indications of the dates the lectures were held. In the case of these lecture notes, it is consistently a matter of carefully completed, clean writings [*Reinschriften*] that depict the sequence of the hourly lectures practically word for word. Through comparison of them with the original transcript it also becomes apparent that Heidegger repeatedly deviated from the handwritten text and gave this lecture in a more or less modified, occasionally even expanded form.

After this description of the texts on hand for the edition, some explanation should be given of the editorial work done on the text of the lecture [*Vorlesungstext*]. The lecture edited here reproduces the handwritten revision, including the deletions. Only in one case, namely, the sentence that contains Heidegger's critique of Spengler's understanding of history, was the deletion of a sentence not honored so that this critical position would not be lost. A footnote inserted by the editor provides information about this matter.

Even without an exact comparison of the original transcript and the lecture notes, the attentive reader encounters countless mistakes in deciphering by the unknown transcriber that disturb the sense of a passage. Since only a small portion of these mistakes were corrected by Heidegger in the course of his unevenly distributed, handwritten revision, one can conclude that he did not collate the original transcript, like the transcripts later made by his brother Fritz, with the handwritten text. For this reason, the editor had to pay particular attention to the correction of these mistakes of transcription that disturb the sense of a passage in order to secure the standing of the words and text. The mistakes in deciphering that one might have supposed in the course of merely reading were confirmed in each case through comparison with the lecture notes, in particular with the only complete lecture notes, the "Weiß" lecture notes. The original transcript and the lecture notes were compared repeatedly. All words that proved to be false readings were quietly corrected. In the case of the decision about the mistakes in deciphering, the fact that Heidegger deviated from his handwritten text during the oral presentation and chose a variant to his handwritten formulation was taken into account. Such variants were not corrected; only mistakes in transcribing that obviously ran counter to the sense of the passage were corrected.

A further false reading presumably lies behind the name "Hegel" in the remark placed by Heidegger in round brackets on p. 16 [22], a remark that can be found only in the original transcript but in none of the lecture notes. As the remark with the name "Hegel" stands in the text, it hardly yields any sense. Hence, it may be presumed that in the handwritten text, "Hegel" is not there at all but instead either a barely legible jotting or an abbreviation that the transcriber deciphered as "Hegel." If Heidegger's remark were supposed to refer, not to "hermeneutics," the word preceding it, but to the sentence of Aristotle following it, then it might possibly refer to Husserl and his doctrine of nominalization (see *Ideas I*, § 119).

In the course of comparing the lecture notes and the original transcript, it

became evident how rarely the transcribers made a mistake because they did
not hear what was being said. More often, the editor had to connect the
sentence-parts which the transcriber—presumably occasioned by the hurried
character of the writing—had treated as self-standing sentences, but which in
fact belong together. The editor had to reconnect them with one another according to the sense of the passage and oriented by the lecture notes. Occasionally even a word was added that had fallen out in the original transcript
and certainly already in the handwritten text, and it was added, with the help
of the "Weiß" lecture notes, on the grounds of the better readability. In only
one case was use made of the freedom imparted by Heidegger to the editor,
namely, in the case of the paragraph in which Heidegger gives a brief overview
of the use of the word "phenomenology" since Lambert. In the original transcript, this paragraph stands midway in the discussions of seeing and the seen
in Aristotle. In order not to interrupt this flow of thought, the paragraph about
the use of the word "phenomenology" was placed immediately before the
Aristotle-interpretation and now forms the beginning of the first chapter of
the first part of the lecture. The remarks in this paragraph were expanded with
three short additions taken over from the "Weiß" lecture notes, additions that
Heidegger only made in the oral presentation. These three additions read: "in
Lambert's *Neues Organon*," "in connection with analogous developments popular at the time, like dianoiology and alethiology," and "(based upon oral
communication from Husserl)."

Because of the already mentioned circumstances under which Heidegger
wrote down the lectures, he did not include the longer Greek and Latin quotations in the handwritten text. Instead he conveyed them orally from the
editions of the texts. These quotations had to be transferred from the "Weiß"
lecture notes to the text of the lectures. In each instance, comparison of the
original transcript and the lecture notes made it possible to establish with
certainty the place for the insertion of the quotations.

Heidegger's peculiar manners of writing were retained to the extent that
they are recognizable in the original transcript. The punctuation had to be
corrected and supplemented in accordance with the text and its sense.

The entire division of paragraphs was undertaken in accord with the sense
of the passages, in a way that is appropriate to the subject matter, and for the
sake of the orderly form of the text. This division was undertaken by heeding
the paragraphs indicated at least in part by Heidegger in his handwritten revision. The major division of the text of the lecture into three parts formed
the foundation for the general division of the text fashioned by the editor. The
formulation of all headings was likewise part of the editorial process. As in
the case of the edition of all Heidegger's lectures, it was also a matter here
of recognizing the division immanent to the quickly written text of the lectures, to set them off in corresponding sections, and to formulate the headings

with the help of those words and word-combinations that form the center of gravity and that identify the main thought of the respective section.

In the course of his handwritten revision, Heidegger underlined individual words or parts of sentences. These underlinings were taken over and replaced by italics in the typographic stylizing of the text [*Textauszeichnung*] that was otherwise done by the editor. In particular, those words and word-combinations that went into the formulations of the headings were italicized, as were the leading terms respectively introduced by Heidegger for the first time into the flow of thought. As a rule, for the sake of easier overview, all names were also italicized, with the exception respectively of the name of that thinker to whom—as the headings make clear—a chapter or a paragraph is devoted.[1]

Heidegger's sparse quotations and references to literature as well as his altogether abbreviated way of citing them were researched, bibliographically completed, and provided in the text as footnotes. All the footnotes are numbered by section and stem from the editor. To check the quotations and the references made to titles, copies from Heidegger's own library were drawn upon to the extent that they were on hand. Belonging among these copies are Aristotle's *De anima*, *Metaphysics*, and *Physics*; Thomas Aquinas' *De veritate* and *Summa theologica*; Descartes' *Meditationes*, *Regulae ad directionem ingenii*, and *Discourse on Method*; and Husserl's "Philosophy as Rigorous Science," *Logical Investigations*, and *Ideas I*. Also among the publications from Heidegger's own library drawn upon for the edition is Husserl's hand copy of the second part of the *Logical Investigations*, interleaved and furnished with countless annotations, that Husserl had given to Heidegger as a gift. In both volumes that make up this text, the following same handwritten insertion by Heidegger is to be found: "Presented by Edm. Husserl on the occasion of the call to Marburg/L. in the summer of 1923 (from the Winter Semester 1920/21 to the Summer Semester 1923, respectively, private seminars on the Fifth and Sixth Logical Investigations on Saturday morning) Martin Heidegger." The editions of *De veritate* and *Summa theologica* belong to that Complete Edition of the Works of Thomas Aquinas that Heidegger had once left over to Eugen Fink for the library of the Freiburg Seminar for Philosophy and Pedagogy. Descartes' *Meditationes de prima philosophia* and *Regulae ad directionem ingenii* were cited by Heidegger according to the page numbers of the original edition, page numbers which were included in square brackets in the margin of his own copies. These page numbers can also be found in the text-editions provided by Artur Buchenau and accessible today as text-editions of the Philosophical Library of the publishing house of Felix Meiner. In cases

---

1. [The English translation departs from the practice of italicizing all names.—D.D.]

in which Heidegger's own copies were missing, the editions of texts available
in 1923 were drawn upon.

In the *Appendix* thirty shorter or longer text-segments from the "Weiß" and
the "Marcuse" lecture notes were taken up as supplements to the text of the
lectures. These segments concern those elaborations by Heidegger in which
he essentially expands on his handwritten text in this or that respect in the
oral delivery. For the sake of a better overview and differentiation from the
bibliographic footnotes, the footnotes referring to a supplement in the Appendix are marked by a little star.[2] Where there are several supplements within
a paragraph, these footnotes are numbered with two or three such stars. The
texts of the supplements are reproduced in the form in which they are to be
found in the lecture notes, hence, without any particular editorial work done
on them. All the Supplements were taken from the "Weiß" lecture notes,
except for Supplements 7, 8, and 10, which were taken from the "Marcuse"
lecture notes due to their greater incisiveness. Supplement 30, which forms
the conclusion of the "Weiß" lecture notes, breaks off in the form reproduced
here.

                                    *

As an "Introduction to Phenomenological Research," the lectures aim at grasping phenomenological research more originally, i.e., as a phenomenology of
existence. They pursue this aim by way of a critical investigation of the phenomenology of consciousness and under the guidance of phenomenology's
research tendency to be beholden to "the matters themselves." The *first part*
of the lectures accordingly begins with an interpretation of Φαινόμενον and
λόγος in Aristotle in order for it to become clear in this way that the basic
components of philosophical research, elaborated by Aristotle, are the world's
being and life as being in a world. By contrast, later developments in pro-
curing philosophy's basic components, particularly since Descartes, are guided
by the predominance of an idea of certainty and evidence, oriented to the
rigor of mathematics. Guided by what Heidegger is looking ahead to, namely,
the existence that is to be pointed out, he conceives that idea of certainty as
care about known knowledge prior to any question of the matters themselves.
In the place of what is of the first importance, an appropriation of the matters
themselves, an idea of science that has been uncritically set forth guides the
choice of the field of vision for philosophical tasks. That even Husserl's phenomenology stands in this historical tradition, that the predominance of care
about known knowledge is at work in it prior to freeing up the possibility of

2. [Footnote references to a supplement in the Appendix are numbered sequentially along
with other footnotes in the English translation.—D.D.]

encountering fundamental matters of fact, that in the process the matters them-selves are expressed only to the extent that they correspond to the precon-ceived idea of knowledge and science—all this is what the interpretation of Husserl's own rendering of phenomenology in the 1911 programmatic text "Philosophy as Rigorous Science" is meant to demonstrate.

Yet the care about known knowledge, the care at work in Husserl's phe-nomenology of consciousness, only becomes transparent in its historical line-age through a return to this care in its historical concreteness in Descartes and its disclosing of the res cogitans in the *second part* of the lecture. Because the detailed interpretation of Descartes is guided by the question of the sense of the truth of knowledge, the interpretation of the *Meditationes* takes the Fourth Meditation as its point of departure and at the same time ascribes to the *Regulae ad directionem ingenii* a leading function for Descartes' procedure in the *Meditationes*. Insofar as Descartes' determination of the verum as cer-tum is accomplished amidst the retention of Scholastic ontology, an historical return to Thomas Aquinas' *De veritate* and *Summa theologica* also became necessary.

Building on the hermeneutical insights of the second part, the *third part* of the lectures shows how the question of the genuine sense of res cogitans' being is blocked by Descartes' care about certainty, how Husserl contorts the findings of phenomenology and, in the process, neglects existence through the care, derived from Descartes, about known knowledge. As a whole, the lec-tures are guided by the insight that the investigation of the history of the origin of the transmitted categories (phenomenological destruction) is a pre-supposition for seeing and determining existence and that only by proceeding in this way does one correspond to phenomenology's original intention, an intention articulated in the maxim "to the matters themselves."

*

For his attentive accompaniment at all stages of the work of editing, I would like to express my sincere thanks to Dr. Hermann Heidegger, the administrator of the surviving papers.

Special thanks are due from me to Professor Gerhart Baumann (Freiburg) for passing on lecture notes of the first lecture and some lecture notes of the other Marburg lectures of Heidegger. These lecture notes, which stem from the surviving papers of Gerhard Nebel, the later writer who listened to Hei-degger's lectures at the time, are now incorporated among Heidegger's sur-viving papers at the Archive of German Literature in Marbach. I also would like to express my sincere thanks to Professor Hans Hübner (Göttingen) and Professor Otto Pöggeler (Bochum) for the extremely helpful information that they communicated to me.

For the expert assembling of bibliographical documentation of books that were not easily accessible and for the laborious work of searching for sources of uncited quotations, I extend particularly cordial thanks to Ms. Paola-Ludovica Coriando (doctoral candidate in philosophy). Dr. Hartmut Tietjen had taken over the collating of the handwritten parts of the lectures and, together with Mr. Mark Michalski (doctoral candidate in philosophy), also took over the task of making a complete and thorough inspection of the copy-ready text [*Satzvorlage*]—according to particular aspects, respectively; I cordially thank them for that work. Ms. Paola-Ludovica Coriando and Mr. Ivo De Gennaro (doctoral candidate in philosophy) aided me with their wealth of knowledge and with their considerable carefulness in the work of correcting the proofs; for this enormous help I owe them my very heartfelt thanks.

Freiburg i. Br., March, 1994   Friedrich-Wilhelm von Herrmann